PRAISE FOR *HOLLYW̲ ̲ ̲ ̲ ̲ ̲ ̲ ̲ ̲ ̲ ̲ ̲ ̲ ̲*

"Here is the story of one man's testimony in Tinsel Town. Steve viewed Hollywood as his mission field, and Hollywood didn't know what to do with him. Reading Steve's candid and compelling account made me wonder what I would say had I a moment to share Christ with Brad Pitt, Kiefer Sutherland, or Tori Spelling."

—Robert J. Morgan, Author, Speaker, Pastor

"Hollywood continues to set the pace in leading millions in Western culture to think and behave in more godless and self-destructive ways. The brokenness and hopelessness that accompanies Hollywood's philosophy is rarely pondered and less frequently exposed by those within its ranks. I am grateful for Steve Cha's heart, which so passionately desires to see those in today's movie and television industry come to realize their need for the gospel of Jesus Christ. How strategic it is to have those within the industry stand up and unabashedly proclaim the Lordship of Christ in such a needful time."

—Dr. Mike Fabarez, Pastor
Compass Bible Church, Alison Viejo, CA;
Focal Point Ministry

"You may not agree with Steve's methods, but this book will motivate you to be a more passionate evangelist. *Hollywood Mission: Possible* is a fast-moving look at Cha's life, as well as his approach to evangelism, but ultimately it ends up making the reader ask this question: 'Am I doing all I can to reach the lost?'"

—Jesse Johnson, Outreach Pastor
Grace Community Church, Sun Valley, CA;
Professor of Evangelism, The Master's Seminary

HOLLYWOOD

MISSION: IMPOSSIBLE

Great Gift Idea!

To Audrye,

Thanks for the support!
God bless !

Eph 6: 19-20

HOLLYWOOD

MISSION: IMPOSSIBLE

Piercing the Darkness of a Decadent Industry

STEVE CHA

WinePressPublishing

Great Books, Defined.

WinePress Publishing (PO Box 428, Enumclaw, WA 98022) functions only as a book publisher. As such, the ultimate design, content, editorial accuracy, and views expressed or implied in this work are those of the author.

ISBN 13: 978-1-4141-1998-4
ISBN 10: 1-4141-1998-4
Library of Congress Catalog Card Number: 2010942195

To fellow brothers and sisters who work and pray
for spiritual awakening in the world of media.

CONTENTS

ACKNOWLEDGMENTS

A LIFE WHICH began on August 15, 1984, led to a missional journey in February 2008. A missional journey which began in February 2008 led to the writing of a book in September 2009. The writing of a book which began in September 2009 led to the production of the book in November 2010. And now, here I am in the final stages before the publication, adding the final touches to a work that is nearly two years in the making.

First, I would like to thank my Lord and Savior, Jesus Christ, for His mercy over my life. Thank you, my Lord, for Your kindness and Your guiding hand. I am a slave forever indebted to my loving Master.

I would like to thank my mother and father for all their years of endless support. Thank you for your patience and care, and for providing for me in a way that would make any child grateful. I am forever humbled and honored to be your child.

I thank my grandparents for their years of prayers and for being examples of strong, godly people. Your work has paid off, and I am now all the better for it.

I thank my sisters, brother, and entire family for their support and encouragement. You are all continually in my prayers.

I thank Jonathan Khan for his friendship and his major contributions to this project. Without his brilliance, this book would not be as exciting as it turned out to be. Thank you, Jonathan, for your encouragement and wisdom and for challenging me to always be the best ambassador for Christ I can possibly be.

I thank Ray, Kirk, and the rest of the people at Living Waters/Way of the Master for teaching me how to reach the lost. You guys were a phenomenal influence in my Christian life. Take joy in knowing that the stories in this book could not have happened without your resources and teachings.

I thank all my close friends who have supported me throughout this entire book formation process. I'm truly blessed to have you all in my life.

I thank all the pastors and Christian leaders who provided endorsements and positive words for my book. My sincerest gratitude for your priceless time. I hope to someday endorse your projects in return.

I would like to thank Adam, Mike, Josiah, Carla, Janice, Abigail, and everyone at WinePress Publishing who made this final work possible. Thank you all for your diligent effort, creativity, and discernment. This collaboration has been wonderful, and my book is now sharper because of it.

I would like to thank Hollywood for giving me the opportunity to make these evangelistic events happen. Such gratitude may sound strange, considering how much they frowned upon my work and persecuted me. But God is able to take downfalls and turn them into victory, much like He

ACKNOWLEDGMENTS

did in the case of Jesus and Judas Iscariot. May the Lord's good work come to full fruition in Hollywood very soon.

Finally, my deepest gratitude goes out to all who have purchased this book and have been influenced by its contents. May God bless you and your journey in becoming a great missionary for God, whether in Hollywood or not.

FOREWORD

'VE BEEN PURSUING the creative arts (acting and writing) since the last millennium, but it seems like yesterday! When I arrived in Hollywood, I quickly learned that underneath the glitter of Tinsel Town is a dark force, hence the glorification of evil on the big screen, as well as the smaller one. Even my brothers and sisters in Christ said they would pray for me to leave this industry.

I began to ask myself: Lord, are you sure this is where You want me to be? The Lord answered me through the Scriptures: "Delight in the Lord and He will give you the desires of your heart" (Psalm 37:4) and "Trust in the Lord with all your heart and lean not on your own understanding, but in all your ways, acknowledge Him and He will direct your paths" (Proverbs 3:5-6). Jesus (God in human flesh) pierced the darkness of this world with the light of the truth to rescue sinners from hell. I can't think of a better mission field in America than Hollywood! If I didn't make a foray into the darkness, then who was ever going to see the light of Christ?

I'm sure many professing Christians have pursued a career in Hollywood only to be waylaid by the lust of the eyes, the pride of life, and the lust of the flesh. I should know—I was one of them. You can't serve two masters, God and mammon (money). Either you live to please yourself (which is idolatry—the breaking of the first and second commandments) or you live to please the Lord. Those who love the world and its enticements give evidence of being slaves of the master of darkness, to which many in Hollywood are chained.

I am not over the top when I say that Hollywood is a mecca of cults and the occults. Every false teaching, every aberrational doctrine, every heresy is right here in my own backyard! Within a one-mile radius of the famous (or infamous) corner of Hollywood and Vine, the sidewalks are choked with psychics, astrologists, and tarot card readers. Mormons and Jehovah's Witnesses abound. The Scientology Celebrity Center is nearby. Two of its biggest proponents are Hollywood's own Tom Cruise and John Travolta. The spiritual cyanide is ubiquitous.

Despite being outnumbered, my resolve to speak the truth has never been stronger. If God is for us, then who can be against us? Broad is the way that leads to destruction has never been more evident than in Hollywood. My heart goes out to the spiritually deceived, since I too was once an enemy of God and hostile to the gospel until I was saved by God's grace.

I've been on numerous movie sets and TV shows, and never once did I hear a Christian initiate a spiritual conversation. I began to think: *Am I the only Christian in Hollywood who cares about the lost? Am I the only believer who's put on the armor of God and fighting the good fight? Am I in this battle alone?*

Then, lo and behold, I met Steve Cha in September 2007 on the TV show *Life* (how appropriate). He said he was a Christian, so I asked him, "Do you ever come across Christians who never share their faith or rarely share their faith?" From the look in his eyes, I could tell that he was one of them. So I asked, "If you saw a blind man heading toward a cliff, you'd warn him, wouldn't you? He emphatically responded, "Yes." I continued with, "Well, the Bible says that all unbelievers are spiritually blind and they're heading toward a cliff that leads to the lake of fire. How can we not try to warn those whom the Lord puts across our path everyday?"

A spark was lit in Steve! A few months later he called and expressed how much my exhortation had challenged his spiritual walk. He committed to being an ambassador for Christ (no longer a secret agent) and wanted to share the gospel with everyone, not just in Hollywood, but wherever he went! My heart overflowed with ineffable joy!

Steve's resolve would be greater than I imagined. He spent the next few years evangelizing everyone he met in the entertainment industry. He even reached out to big name celebrities, many times at the expense of his reputation and professional wellbeing. Next thing you know, he's writing *Hollywood Mission: Possible*, an autobiography about his evangelistic journey in Hollywood, and asking me to write a foreword to his piece!

Whether you are a Christian who shares his/her faith, a Christian who doesn't, or simply a seeking unbeliever, I highly recommend this book. Never before have we witnessed firsthand the gospel being preached behind the scenes on actual movie sets and TV shows! I'm deeply humbled that Steve also included some of my most memorable evangelistic encounters on set. This book is apocalyptic in that it reveals how spiritually dark Tinsel

Town truly is with its widespread degenerative ways, evidenced by the many blasphemous TV shows and movies spewed forth by Hollywood.

If you are a Christian, ask yourself these questions: Are you more concerned about saving your career or saving a soul? If you were on your way to hell, when would you want someone to warn you? Remember, people are dying every day and most of them are going to the lake of fire forever. What are you doing about it? Luke 9:26 declares, "For whosoever shall be ashamed of me and of my words, of him shall the Son of Man be ashamed."

I pray that *Hollywood Mission: Possible* will encourage Christians to reach out to those in the world who are spiritually deceived and imprisoned in the dungeons of darkness. Broad is the road that leads to destruction—narrow is the road that leads to life. Which path are you on? Read this book. Tomorrow is not promised to any of us!

—Jonathan Khan
Dear Friend and Ambassador for the Master

Chapter 1

FAST PASS TO INFAMY

BRIGHT SUNSHINE AND cool winds exemplify another typical day for Southern Californians. Life is rampant, but perfunctory. Citizens bustle to school and to work in order to serve their mechanical roles in society. It is a cycle of life that characterizes much of the modern world. In Century City, however, there was one particular day that was anything but typical.

Within Stage 8 of the renown 20th Century Fox Studios lot, an adrenaline-filled event was about to begin. A heated debate between Sebastian Stark and his once-trustworthy colleague was about to take center stage in a make-believe, television court of law. It was an intense battle for the fate of one man's future—an ultimate war between righteousness and injustice. I am describing a scene from the television show, *Shark*, starring James Woods.

Woods plays Sebastian Stark, a hotshot prosecuting attorney whose mission is to take down criminals in Los Angeles. He and his team of ambitious new lawyers, which include the supporting crew of Madeleine Poe and Casey

Woodland, stand for authority. They will stop any citizen who spits in the face of justice, righteousness, and truth.

I had an opportunity to see James Woods in action as Sebastian Stark during one of the shoots on April 1, 2008. I was a working background artist (also known as an "extra") and had been booked onto the show to be part of the courtroom gallery. We worked on Stage 8, which housed most of the program's set pieces. Within the maze of this structure was a specific section built to resemble an actual federal courthouse. Although it was by no means a real courthouse, it could have easily passed for the real deal if a person was dragged onto the stage blindfolded and was unaware of its true location. Set structures like these seem so real, vivid, and detailed, yet they are merely shells that appear to be real when viewed from the outside. They are purely illusions for the mind and no more true than something from a magic show. Nonetheless, these sets are works of wonder to behold at most times.

A few hours after the background players checked into work, the staff directed them into the courtroom and positioned them for the scene's shoot. I was placed in a third-row seat with other gallery attendees, while the jury members were seated to the middle left of the courtroom. Within minutes, the sharply-attired Sebastian Stark waltzed into the room to find the judge, jury, and defendant all awaiting his presence in the impending trial. In reality, it was nothing more than James Woods walking onto a set full of camera operators, producers, and the director, who call all the real shots in the scene. As actors, we were just pawns in the eyes of their vision. They were the creators, and we were the created, including Woods himself.

In a couple of minutes, the production was about to start. Fluorescent lamps were positioned for scene lighting, the director of photography took his last looks through the camera lens, and the make-up artist put her final touches on James Woods. The film crew cleared the stage immediately. All actors assumed their first positions as the room went utterly silent. The warehouse bell rang thunderously, signifying to the world outside the sound stage not to walk through the doors while the cameras were rolling. It truly was lights…then camera…and *action*!

The scene slowly unfolded before my eyes. I looked somber to stay in character with the other gallery members and tried to make sense of the "court case" I witnessed before me. The plot began with Sebastian sitting next to Madeleine, his partner in crime. As the trial commenced, Mr. Stark rose from his chair and started to spew out a monologue supporting his case with regard to the defendant's guilt. The judge and the jury steadily soaked up the information as Mr. Stark moved in on the defendant like a rabid dog and interrogated him. Although I don't recall the defendant's name or his particular felony, I do recollect that he was an authority figure, either a cop or a former attorney, who was being tried for professional dishonesty that led to a major scandal in his field of work.

Although the defendant labored in vain to cover his culpability and justify himself, he was no match for Stark. By the end of the day, Sebastian triumphed. Stark had the last word, the last laugh, and the last dance. The judge ruled in Stark's favor and declared the defendant guilty. I guess I now know why this character is revered as the hottest DA in the business. Not only is Stark a doughty winner, he is also the epitome of fairness and truth, an ideal figure that is often missing from the real world in which I live.

Speaking of real-life situations, I must ask, do the high standards of Sebastian's political and civil philosophies also align with those of the actor playing this role? And what about his spiritual values? Just because a television audience knows all about Sebastian Stark, what do they know about the man who shows up to play this character every week? I sought to find out.

ENCOUNTERING SEBASTIAN STARK

Although the courtroom scene itself comprised about only fifty to sixty seconds of the entire episode, it took well over an hour to shoot. It was hardly work to sit there and look the part, but it's natural to become exhausted and even develop hunger after staying in the same room for nearly an hour while the crew shoots countless takes of the same scene. Usually the directors get the desired shot after three or four takes, but this time it required a few more rounds since James Woods botched his lines during a couple of the takes. Woods was gracious enough to admit his fault and apologize to the crew, committing to do better on the following take. I admired the fact that he didn't become excessively sour when he made mistakes, as some actors do. Instead, he reacted in an honest, if not facetious, manner. I guess it's reasonable to cut him some slack, considering these actors have the arduous task of memorizing a truckload of lines for each day's filming!

After the scene was completed, most of the extras scurried over to the craft service station at the opposite end of the building to munch on some snacks. Of course, the word "snacks" is an understatement when describing the available food options on the set. That day they included the likes of steak sandwiches, meatballs, fries, tortillas, rice, and other artery-clogging foods. Although craft services were usually designated for the extras and the technical crew, occasionally the principle actors would make their way over to the station and carve out a piece of the pie for themselves. This turned out to be our lucky day as the lead star, James Woods, came to our station a few minutes after the completion of the courtroom scene.

This is my perfect opportunity, I thought. If there were ever a moment when I could converse with the main actors in the context of an appropriate setting, this was it. I say this because technically, I am not allowed to communicate with the principle actors. This is a big rule imposed on all background artists from day one, but I figured that the production crew would be a little more lenient on this occasion, considering that Mr. Woods was talking up a storm with some of the people around him. He was even courteous with a couple of the extras standing nearby. Most folks casually called the actor by his nickname name, Jim, and from the looks of things, it appeared that Jim had quite a jovial personality. I decided that it might be safe to go up to him after all. I chose to approach him to share some good news.

As Woods finished a conversation with one of the crewmembers, he turned and suddenly walked in my direction, so I took the initiative to step up and garner his attention. James bore a slightly curious expression as I extended my right hand.

As I stood before the man's tall, hulking presence, I quickly said, "Hi, Mr. Woods. I just wanted to introduce myself. My name is Steve, and I'm a big fan of your work. I saw the movie *Once Upon a Time in America* for the first time a few days ago."

Woods shook my hand and asked, "Did you watch the three-and-a-half-hour director's cut or the hour-and-a-half version?"

This was an interesting question because I had just learned about the two different versions a few days prior. I'd watched the 229-minute version of the film on DVD, yet hadn't been aware that it was any different from the theatrical version. Mr. Woods made this distinction clear.

I replied, "The version that I saw ran close to four hours."

He explained, "That's good. The director's cut is the best one. The theatrical release is crap."

I continued by casually asking, "Was there also a five-or six-hour version as well?"

James replied, "No, just those two."

"You sure there wasn't a six-hour-long version?"

"Yes, I'm sure."

As we playfully bantered about the movie, our conversation began to pick up steam. Then, someone motioned for Jim, and he abruptly walked away to attend his call. I was disappointed that our conversation had been cut off. The whole purpose of my chitchat with Mr. Woods hadn't been to ruminate about which film cut was superior. It was supposed to be an icebreaker to jump-start a much more vital agenda. My whole intent was to give Mr. Woods the "good news," and I had to do it before I lost my chance. This news might never come to him again. This could have been my only chance!

Miraculously, the opportunity presented itself again. When Mr. Woods finished his conversation with the other staff members, he again walked in my direction. My heart thumped violently as I mustered up some much-needed courage to accomplish my task. Talking to him the first time was already a risky maneuver on my part, but now I had to find a way to squeeze in another meeting somehow. Reaching into my jacket pocket to grab what I needed, I stepped forward cautiously. At the same time, I swiftly pulled out a Christian gospel tract titled, *Are You a Good Person?*[1]

I said, "Hey, Jim, have you ever taken a Good Person Test?"

Mr. Woods took the tract from my hand. He glanced at it for a second with a slight sense of intrigue and answered, "Why, no, I haven't."

I quickly went on, "Read it when you get a chance. It's awesome stuff."

"I'll definitely take a look at it later. Thanks."

With the tract in hand, Jim marched out the stage door and back to his trailer outside. He probably needed to change into his next costume for the upcoming scene. Although I was apprehensive about what I had just done, I felt a sense of relief and even joy that I had actually placed the gospel message in Jim's hand. Even though I didn't have the opportunity to go into a conversation with him about my faith, I was glad to have at least given him something that could potentially influence him.

It's uncommon, if not rare, for someone to share his religious faith with a movie star on the work set. What I did could be considered fairly groundbreaking, if not dangerous, by some people. In a moment's time, I realized that it was definitely both!

SHARK ATTACK

Although my proselytizing led to a brief feeling of euphoria, it soon thrust me into a deep hole that filled me with fear. As I mentioned earlier, background artists are not allowed to converse with principle actors in any given situation or time. Failure to conform to this rule could lead to disciplinary action and even expulsion from the set.

A few seconds after Mr. Woods departed from the stage, a production assistant (PA) approached and motioned me to follow him into a nearby dark, quiet corner. I don't recall his name, but I remember that he was skinny and sported a gruff expression. He was in his mid-twenties, was fairly new to the job, and had a desire to make a great impression with the big dogs in the game.

I honestly did not know what the PA wanted to talk to me about. I could only start with the predictable question, "Yes. What's up?"

The PA looked serious and almost paranoid. In a frantic manner he asked, "What did you give James?"

I replied, "It's a Good Person Test. Would you like one too?"

The PA's glare further soured as he addressed me in a grave, silent, and condescending tone, "Do you realize that what you did was wrong? You crossed the line, pal, and that's unacceptable. You are *not* allowed to talk to the actors, and you can't give them anything. If James gets upset, then it's my butt! Do you hear me? *I* have to answer to him! Do you understand?"

I was somewhat speechless. I couldn't remember the last time a coworker approached me with such a caustic attitude. At one point, I even felt that it was uncivilized. Nevertheless, I kept my composure intact and politely said, "But he came to me and we started talking."

The PA retorted with the same intensity, "If the actors go around talking to you first, there's not much we can do about it, but you actually *gave* him something. What you did was out of line. You cannot be spreading your religious stuff here on set."

I think it was his attitude that caused me to ask, "How do you know it's religious?"

"Okay then, read it to me. Come on, read it," he snapped and stood smugly, waiting for me to obey.

I opened up the small "Good Person Test" booklet and started to read aloud, sounding like something out of a books-on-tape narrative. It went, "Do you consider yourself to be a good person? Most people do. However, most of us differ as to the definition…"

The PA quickly became impatient. "Just skip to the end! What does it say at the end?"

I casually flipped to the back of the gospel tract and read, "Please forgive me, change my heart, and grant me…"

It was obvious the PA wasn't hearing what he expected. "Forget it! Just tell me if it says God in there?"

For a split-second, my heart caved in with fear. I was tempted to lie just to uphold my professional integrity and lessen my potential punishment, but in a split second, my overwhelming reverence for Christ, His ministry, and the gospel propelled me to speak the truth.

"Yes. It does."

The PA remained silent. Painfully absorbing the news, he breathed in a heavy dose of Stage 8 air as he pondered for a few seconds. I sensed he was debating in the depths of his mind whether to fire me or not. I stood my ground, anxiously awaiting his verdict.

After a few seconds, the PA finally opened his mouth and said, "I'll let it go this time, but I don't ever want to see you doing that again. Don't ever bring crap like that to any of these sets again. You got it?"

I nodded. The PA then turned and stomped away. As I watched him leave, a sense of relief came over me. I was glad to still have my job. Though the conversation was over, the emotional effects rattled me for the next few hours. It disturbed me enough that I couldn't even sit in the extra's holding area anymore, out of trepidation that the PA would walk by and stare a burning hole right through me. I spent the rest of the workday hiding behind the other set complexes adjacent to the extra's holding area. The PA passed by a couple of times as I cowered behind production equipment, removing myself from his view. I felt like a marked man!

INTRODUCING...

You may be wondering: Just who is this religious freak? What did he just say he had done? Why would he do something like that at *work* in the entertainment capital of the world?

Allow me to introduce myself. My name is Steve Cha, and I am an active evangelist in Hollywood. The encounter with James Woods was one of countless witnessing opportunities I have experienced in the last three years. During this time, I have evangelized everyone from celebrities to background artists to crewmembers. As a devoted ambassador for Christ, I have been loved, hated, misunderstood, ignored, questioned, admired, and insulted by the many faces of Hollywood.

I didn't plan my life to be this way. At one time, I was a lover of the world, and the Hollywood dream was my idol. It was what I lived for. I wasn't devoted to serving Christ or any other religion, and certainly never fathomed promoting godly agendas in my line of work. Growing up, I passionately desired becoming a media mogul in Hollywood. I wanted the spotlight. I wanted to be the center of attention. I wanted to break into the business and be a successful, box-office-smashing film director. I wanted to work with the greatest actors and the most beautiful actresses, to produce the best films, and to rake in all the money the world had to offer. I was all set to conquer Hollywood.

Yet here I am, many years later, doing something entirely counteractive to my lifelong passion. I am advancing the gospel cause in Hollywood, and in case you didn't know, that's one of the biggest faux pas in the business. It is career suicide. As you observed from the James Woods' situation, I courageously entered the battle, fighting against the people I once sided with, and took a bullet in the process.

The funny thing is that I didn't really care. My heart is in cooperation with my newfound passion, which is Jesus Christ. I delight in serving Him unto death. I want to fulfill His mission, which is to seek and save those who are lost. This has become more important to me than any wealth or fame that Hollywood has to offer. Yet, this is something I would have been surprised at before Christ took hold of my heart.

To this day, I ask myself how I suddenly got the urge to undertake such a mission in life. How did I get to the point of risking my job by sharing the gospel with people like James Woods? How did I shatter the Goliath that was my dream of self-glory and trade it in for a life of being a humble, destitute, and self-denying servant of Jesus Christ?

This is my story.

Chapter 2

THE WONDER YEARS

I N THE BIBLE, Genesis 1:3 records the Lord's first words as, "'Let there be light,' and there was light." In my case, the Lord said, "Let there be life!" I was born on August 15, 1984, about 5:16 P.M. when I pushed my way out of my mother's womb and into the pearlescent light of the world. The locale was Garfield Medical Center in Monterey Park, California. I weighed in at a respectable seven-pounds-one-ounce and measured twenty-and-a-half inches. I was a newborn baby, a new creation by God.

Reflecting on my early years, I honestly wish I could remember the moment of my birth as well as my life a few months thereafter. It would be spectacular to remember my infant experiences and share those stories with others. Contained within a large, brown cardboard box in my bedroom closet is a photo memorabilia of all my baby pictures. The most interesting part of this album is a section that contains an extensive written record by my mother about my infant years. It is an observation of all my activities and inclinations from the time I was born until I was approximately three years old. Some of the insights include my growth patterns, idiosyncrasies, first words, foods I hated, places I liked to go, and even some psychological notations of my fears and needs.

I commend my mother for taking the time to journalize the many facets of my infancy, yet in no way can it effectively revive the dead memories I once had of that period in my life. Attempting to envision the words of the memorabilia is as foreign to me as someone trying to describe the sights and sounds of a city I've never visited. If I never live in or visit Shanghai, I'll never truly know the feeling of an existence there. I cannot accurately internalize the sights and sounds of the city, whether it is the Chinese billboards, the city's skyscrapers, or the million-plus bicyclists on the streets during rush hour.

Sometimes I wonder what I felt the moment I left my mother's womb. What must it have been like to lie in an incubator at the hospital? How bored was I lying in my crib on most days at home? How curious was I about the state of my own existence? These memories are so distant and unknown to me that I feel as if my old self never existed and that I literally started to live at the point where I can draw on my earliest recollections. Having my infant stories told to me is like hearing a fable about a person who sounds familiar. He may or may not have my current personality, emotions, and preferences. In the end, he is a completely different being. The most I can do is stand back and admire the person I once was.

Although I was technically born on August 15, 1984 (on paper), my inner, present state-of-mind life is indefinite. It has no beginning and it has no end. At times, it's unfathomable for me to imagine that before my conception there was nothing. There was only darkness, and yet, I cannot even describe it as that. Everything was just…blank.

I highlight these thoughts of infancy not to mourn it or criticize any aspects of my past, but to use it as a platform to describe a state of amnesia from which all of us suffer. My infancy stories describe the condition of *physical amnesia* that arises from the loss of early childhood memory. However, I want to use this concept to touch upon another type of memory loss that some of us may not be aware of. Such an issue is so significant that if we fail to give heed to it, it will affect the entire course of our lives. But most importantly, it will affect the welfare of our eternity.

More Than Meets the Eye

I recall one of my earliest meditations on the issue of life and death at age seven. Around this time, my Taiwanese-born father owned a Chinese restaurant named Fortune West. It was a couple miles from my former home in Studio City, California. I used to visit the restaurant every weekend just to be around my dad. It was a time I looked forward to the most after five arduous days of school.

On one particular Saturday, I had a brief discussion with one of my father's close friends who visited the restaurant that day. My brother and I used to call him "Uncle Michael" or "Uncle Mike." Uncle Mike and my father had known each other since their days at Belmont High School in downtown Los Angeles. They were best of friends for many years.

During a lunch-hour conversation with Uncle Mike, the subject of death came up out of nowhere. I told Uncle Mike that I was afraid to die and that I didn't want it to happen. Uncle Mike chuckled at my premature thoughts of death. He answered me with a reassuring smile. "Aw, don't worry about that! That won't happen for a long time from now, a very loooooong time!"

Uncle Mike may have had benevolent intentions, but his response did not alleviate my deep-rooted anxiety about death. Although it did help me forget about the subject matter for a while, in no way did this denial change the fact that I would have to face death someday. Uncle Mike had no solution for my dilemma. He knew it was impossible for anyone to just stroll into a hospital and decide to purchase a cure for death, no matter how much money they had. The only accommodation that Uncle Mike could offer me with his limited, atheistic knowledge was a sense of delayed depression. This meant that I should enjoy life while I was young and worry about the emotional agony of death when I got much older.

I didn't know if it was so much the dying process that frightened me or if I feared the state or condition I would be in afterward. Was death painful? After death, would it be pitch black for all eternity? Was it game over? Was there some place I would go after I died? All I knew was that I didn't want anything to stop me from being able to live forever. I didn't want my years of knowledge, memories, love, happiness, and companionship to be abruptly cut off and driven to waste. There had to be more to life than this.

These issues indicate a real ailment that all people experience. It is the disease of *spiritual amnesia*. "What is spiritual amnesia?" you ask. Simply said, spiritual amnesia is the improper understanding of one's purpose in life as set forth by God, in which people live outside the purpose of the Creator and wander directionless in life.

Unlike physical amnesia, spiritual amnesia does not occur with the passage of time. Rather it is something that mankind is born into and can suffer from the moment of his birth to the moment of his death. Mankind was originally made for the sole purpose of glorifying and loving the Lord. But when the first humans, Adam and Eve, sinned against their Creator, they created an impassable rift that has separated a holy God and unholy men ever since. Because of this development, people have wandered away from the Lord and lost the memory of their life's purpose. The end result is spiritual amnesia.

In other words, man does not know who he is. He does not know why he exists. From the day he is born, man lives his life attempting to fill the void in his soul by indulging in hedonistic pleasures, hoping to find a sense of fulfillment. When that fails, he has no other alternative than to look for scientific answers to satiate his curiosity about life. Science attempts to produce a comprehensible explanation as to how man was formed and came into existence. But even the most advanced level of scientific research can never explain *why* man exists. What is the meaning of man's life? What is the meaning of all life in general?

In the predicament of physical amnesia, there really is no cure. Those memories have long dissolved and will never return. However, hope does exist for the case of spiritual amnesia. The answer is in the gospel of Jesus Christ. Because of Christ's vicarious death on our behalf, we receive the chance to be forgiven of our trespasses and to be brought back into a right standing with God, with no more rifts. The Holy Spirit enters us the moment we repent of our sins and put our faith in Christ's atoning work on the cross. Through God the Spirit's indwelling work, we come to a true spiritual self-awareness for the first time, and we finally gain the power to love God and live out the life He purposed for us.

THE CONNECTIONS OF LIFE

God's Word, the Bible, states that the Lord's will and purpose for man is divided into two parts. The first and foremost part, the *vertical connection*, deals with people's direct relationship to the Lord. In the Old Testament, God ordered Moses to declare His holy law to the people of Israel so that they would worship the Lord in a way that was pleasing in His sight. Inscribing the Decalogue (Ten Commandments) on two stone tablets, God wrote as His first decree, "You shall have no other gods before Me" (Exod. 20:3). The Lord expounded on this commandment further by declaring to the Israelites in the plains of Moab, "You shall love the LORD your God with all your heart and with all your soul and with all your might" (Deut. 6:5). Jesus affirms in Matthew 22 that this is the first and greatest commandment. The purpose of our lives is to love, glorify, and praise the Lord. God the Father created us to have a perfect, eternal union with Him. He loves us as much as He desires us to love Him back with the same fervor.

The secondary purpose of our lives, the *horizontal connection*, deals with our relationship with each other as human beings. Responding to the Pharisees' question about the nature of the greatest commandment in the law, Jesus asserted the first commandment regarding the Holy One—the vertical connection, yet He did not end there. He immediately followed with this statement, "You shall love your neighbor as yourself" (Matt. 22:39). Because it immediately complements the first and greatest commandment, the Lord's second declaration reveals the significance of our obligation to fellow brothers and sisters. It is our mission while here on earth. Without our cooperation in carrying out the second part of the commandment, we can never fully follow the first. If God commands us to love our neighbors, then we are to obey.

As the New Testament indicates, it is not merely enough to respect or socialize with our earthly brethren, but the Lord commands us to be salt and light to their spiritual wellbeing. Since the fall of Adam and Eve, the earth has been filled with unspeakable evil acts that have flourished and have come from the very hands of God's beloved creatures—humans. War, death, murder, hatred, idolatry, blasphemy, self-centeredness, paranoia, and sexual immorality represent only a sampling of the ungodly deeds perpetrated by people throughout history, even more so now in this particular age. Because God is righteous, holy, and just by nature, He will have His day of justice against all lawbreakers. That great and horrifying day will come in the form of the Great White Throne Judgment described in Revelation 20:11-15, when all those who die in their sin will be sentenced to the lake of fire forever.

Though the Lord holds a resolute disdain for evil, He does not wish for any soul to perish, and that is how our earthly mission comes to the foreground. Before Jesus ascended to heaven, He laid down the mission of the church with special words found three times in the New Testament. He commanded the disciples to: "Go therefore and make disciples of all nations" (Matt. 28:19), to "Go into all the world and preach the gospel to all creation" (Mark 16:15), and to be His witnesses "both in Jerusalem, and in all Judea and Samaria, and even to the remotest part of the earth" (Acts 1:8).

This command indicates that followers are called not only to be friends to the lost, but also to be heroes to them. We are to love our neighbors as ourselves by sharing the gospel with them. This opens doors that will allow the Holy Spirit to save them, train them in the knowledge of God's will, and encourage them to go out into the world to be disciple-makers themselves. That is the golden cycle of life. It is what gives our lives meaning and fulfillment because it is God's perfect will.

Anything that deviates from this standard characterizes spiritual amnesia. Symptoms include such prevalent factors as self-centeredness, narcissism, idolatry, sloth, love of earthly possessions, reckless sin, and lack of love for others and/or oneself. For as much as people experience physical amnesia due to loss of early memory, so are the many who are born into spiritual amnesia and are not even aware of their sickness, which is why they do not actively search for treatment to their condition.

As with every person who has ever lived, I too have suffered from my own dosage of spiritual amnesia. It led me on a path of bewilderment, danger, and the expectation of eternal wrath from a holy God. Thankfully, I did not remain so for too long.

Bridging the Vertical Line

Despite filling the earth with an overwhelming population since the beginning of time, the Lord was gracious enough to give me life. It's humbling to acknowledge this reality, considering I did not exist for the past six thousand years. Regardless of the reasons why I was birthed in 1984 or why I was birthed at all, the fact is, the Almighty chose to create *me*. He personally gave me life—the same me causing my hands to write these sentences in this book.

If the miracle of life isn't enough, I am also blessed to be a soul chosen by God for eternal salvation. During my youth, I heard and received the gospel message, and that allowed me the opportunity to be cleansed, eventually, of my unrighteousness and to live eternally with my holy Maker in heaven. Sometimes it boggles my mind that Christ Jesus elected to save me, especially when I could have easily been one of the multitudes to die in sin and fall into eternal damnation. I know that I am truly one blessed soul.

The name of God was first revealed to me at the age of eight. Before that, when I was four years old, my parents divorced. After that, I lived with my father, but I frequented my mother's home for visitation and scholastic tutoring. One day, my mother gave me a children's storybook based on the Bible. I don't remember the name of this book, but I do remember that it contained colored pictures of the main biblical accounts from Genesis to Revelation. However pedestrian it may seem to me now, this children's book played a considerable role in my adherence to the Christian faith even to this day. Whether it was due to a nostalgic feeling or a sheer recognition of a mother's love, it is safe to say that the book was the first seed planted in the development of my faith. As with anything that grows, it must begin with a seed.

I spent the next month perusing the book and delighting in the biblical figures. During this period, I learned more about the reality, truth, and hope that comes from God. Through the picture illustrations and narrative, the book slowly revealed to me who God is. He is the Creator of the universe and has worked in the lives of various people throughout history, especially in guiding those who trust in and obey Him. He has performed miracles of an epic scale to display His majestic glory. He is Yahweh, the God of Abraham, Isaac, and Jacob.

They say that a suspension of disbelief, and a fascination with the miraculous, is more feasible for a child than for an adult. This is especially true with the accounts in the Bible. This was why I fully marveled at the feat of the Lord parting the waters of the Red Sea for Moses. There were other such spectacles, which included the six-day creation, the Noahic flood, the physical enervation of Samson due to his loss of hair, and Jesus walking on water. I can honestly attest that I had never read anything so amazing in my life.

The funny thing is that I believed everything I read as it was revealed to me!

I was quick to accept every happening in the Bible as truth. The reality of a God who formed everything from the birds in the sky to the trees of the Earth made perfect sense to me, since they all indicate an ordered and intelligent design. Though the Bible's miracle accounts may be a bit difficult for some people to believe, they didn't alter my belief in God. I figured that with God, all things are possible. At least, that's what I wanted to believe in order to satisfy my curiosity about the existence of life. I wanted to believe there is a deity who hears me and will be there to comfort me, especially in moments when I feel no one else in the world loves or cares about me. The fact that love even exists showed me that a belief in a higher and personable being is very reasonable.

There was fascination in discovering God for the first time, but the even greater joy arrived in discovering the reality of eternal life. In the summer of that same year, I was further exposed to the Lord and biblical truths when my mother sent me to a summer VBS (Vacation Bible School) retreat. It was a five-day camping excursion hosted by the Los Angeles Young Nak Presbyterian Church (now Young Nak Celebration Church). I was in third grade, and it was my first time attending any sort of recreational program.

The typical five-day VBS schedule encompassed a variety of creative Bible study, discussion times with cabin leaders, worship and praise, games, and arts and crafts. As much as I cherished memories of the games, sports, and even the awesome meals, I took even greater joy in learning the most crucial piece of information that every student needed to learn from the program. It was my newfound knowledge of heaven! I don't recall at what moment during the VBS program that I first came to learn of salvation. I can only assume it was due to the experiences I had with the program, my teacher, group mates, and the lead pastor as they opened doors for the Holy Spirit to work in me.

This particular VBS was the first turning point in my spiritual life. Not only had I come to know more about the nature of the higher, living authority that is God, but I was given hope of an extension for my own life. It was still intimidating to think that I would have to die physically, but death did not have the same level of reigning power over my state of mind as it once had. No longer was death something to be feared. It became an event that I could look forward to! This statement seemed perfectly logical to me as I considered that I would venture to a much better place on the other side shortly after death.

Now that I was exposed to the revelation of God and His eternal kingdom, did this mean that I was saved at this point in my life? Did I officially book my reservation for the kingdom of heaven now that I believed in God, as my counselors encouraged me to do? Considering what I know now about the complex nature of repentance, along with true and false conversion, I have to admit that I was not immediately born again in Christ. There are numerous reasons for this (based on things I'll explore with you later in this book), but the first factor comes to light based on the spiritual/carnal path that I subsequently led in the decade after. It was a period I considered to be, by far, the lowest point of my spiritual life walk.

Turbulence on Flight Jesus 101

Though my integrity with the secular world remained safe for the most part, my stance with God Almighty took a turn into a skewed path during my middle school/high school years. My sense of fascination with the Lord and

His holy commands slowly dissipated when I became a teenager. In retrospect to that particular time in my life, I harbor thoughts of remorse and grief. Some of my attitudes and actions toward the Lord may not seem like a big deal when compared to more reprehensible cases, but it is heartrending to me now because of the immeasurable love that I presently have for the Lord. Today, it especially raises my frustration when I observe children and teens showing disrespect toward God or His Son, Jesus. They remind me of the attitudes I used to display.

I went to VBS camp annually starting in third grade, but I didn't officially start attending church until I reached eighth grade. In the fall of 1997, I attended my first Sunday service at Young Nak, the same church that had hosted my VBS retreats. During the service, I instantly recognized the praise, sermon time, Bible readings, and tithing as familiar practices from the retreats. To see them all come together in an organized structure showed me an actual church service. The experience was somewhat daunting, yet memorable. In my mother's eyes, this day should have been a joyous occasion. It should have marked the start of a better life. Sadly, however, this day steered me toward a different path.

After the service, it was customary for the high school department to hold small group Bible studies for all attendees. I was assigned to a particular class where I was the only newcomer that day. Because of this, I expected to be treated with an extra sense of goodwill and amicability from the other students in the group. What I experienced instead was a rude awakening as I encountered hostility and sarcasm from two of the students in my group. A couple of times during the class, I was called upon to voice my opinion about the scriptural topic of the day. Each time, my two "brothers in Christ" chose to belittle me through prideful criticism of my thoughts. The group leader didn't really take notice of it at the moment, but my group mates' words crushed me that day. It's still a bit difficult to discern whether I was justified in feeling the way I did at the time. Nonetheless, the damage was done, and it didn't take long before I developed a negative impression of the people at church that lasted longer than it should have.

My heart quickly became hardened as I spent the next three years pouring out the symptoms of my rebellious heart onto Sunday folks. These symptoms included pride, self-righteousness, brazenness, disrespect for biblical topics, disregard for my teacher's integrity, and a lack of faith in church camaraderie. My behavior became so disruptive that my instructors had to expel me from the group on three different occasions.

As impudent as my weekly tactics may have seemed, they were greatly overshadowed by an infamous act of defiance I showed against a pastor one particular Sunday. As Pastor Sam, the education department's head pastor, preached from the pulpit, I clandestinely shot a beam of light from a laser pen right into his eyes! The beam was fully visible as I aimed several rounds into Pastor Sam's pupils. It was surely a gutsy maneuver. Even the students gazed around in bewilderment and utter disbelief. I don't know if this had ever been done before, but I have never seen anything like this happen since.

This remained an amusing act until the worship leader sitting nearby caught me. He came over and confiscated my laser pen. That only drove me into a deeper feeling of antipathy toward the program and its people. It was, in essence, an unfortunate display of my pride. My demeanor soured to the point that I refused to hold hands with my left and right partners for the closing love hymn—a tragic sign of hate.

After the service, the rod of discipline wasted no time in knocking on my door. I was ushered by the department's assistant, Pastor David, into one of the Bible study rooms. For the next five minutes, Pastor David lashed out at my conduct in a manner that no pastor had ever done with me in the past. This wasn't merely a pep talk. Rather, he bellowed about what I'd done with real passion. His frustration over my lack of respect for God and love for my fellow neighbors sank deep into my soul.

In no way am I condemning the actions of my former high school pastor. He did what he had to do in defense of the church, the program, and to uphold the integrity of the Lord's name. I give him respect for that. I describe this particular incident to expound further upon the spiritual declivity that I fell prey to during my adolescent years. I was definitely not the same jolly, innocent camper that I once was during my VBS time. No longer was I optimistic and faithful when it came to the things of God. I had become a near spiritual miscreant.

It's unfortunate that my adolescent syndrome carried over into the religious establishment. However, church problems were not the only issues that I dealt with at the time. I also wrestled with some serious personal problems, mostly in the field of emotional conduct. A sporadic sense of selfishness and unjust anger toward others had suddenly burgeoned in my life, causing some to look upon me as uncouth. Lust had consumed my heart so severely that my transgression of the seventh commandment far outweighed my breaking of the other laws. Violent conflicts with my stepmother took an emotional toll on my family life. My relationship with my brother soured to the point where we didn't communicate well for a number of years. The list goes immeasurable.

If I had been more spiritually mature at the time, I would have properly dealt with and even avoided some of the pressing problems that I had to live with for five years. Instead, I made my mistakes and bore the consequences. During this time, a sense of sadness, anger, loneliness, fear, insecurity, and lack of fulfillment characterized a noticeable portion of my life. It caused me to seek something I felt God couldn't provide for me. I looked for new meaning and a new adventure to guide my ways.

I desperately wanted something that would heal my pain. I needed something to make me happy and provide me with unspeakable fulfillment. I searched for something that would allow me to be someone special in the world. I longed for something for which I could live. What I thought I needed is also known as an idol.

It was obvious that Jesus was no longer a priority at this point, so where would I go from here? The answer was in the very city where I lived. Like countless other dreamers in town, I was driven to the one Goliath that enraptured my very soul. It was something that could provide me with the adventure I sought. It was something that could make me feel joyous. It could make me truly prosperous.

The Goliath I speak of is Hollywood.

Chapter 3

THE ROAD TO FAME

I T WAS DURING my first year of high school that I developed an entrancing passion for cinema. It was as if I had discovered films for the first time in my life. Although I had watched a number of movies, until then only a few were as artistic and significant as the ones I inevitably viewed during those high school years. I actually stopped watching mainstream popcorn movies in favor of the more art house, Oscar caliber, and qualitatively more advanced films considered as cinema. I became familiar with all the great artists in the field, from the historic works of Akira Kurosawa and Alfred Hitchcock to the modern projects of Ridley Scott and Ang Lee. I was able to accurately critique films and predict which ones were going to get nominated in every single Oscar category! I developed a love for everything that involved the magical world of cinema: auteur directors, serious actors, independent/foreign films, screenplays, producing, film editing, cinematography, and on and on.

My parents, however, did not share in the same passion of my dreams. In fact, they were somewhat dismayed at my career choice. They had a strong notion that I would not excel in this field, no matter how much I liked film or knew the craft. I grew up in an Asian household, and while it may sound like a cliché, I was expected to follow a professional path of becoming a doctor, lawyer, or an engineer, regardless of whether or not I was interested in those fields. Any vocation involving arts and humanities was considered too risky, and would lead to financial failure. My life had to be built around a prestigious, lucrative profession or else I would bring shame upon my family.

Regardless of my parents' thoughts or social expectations, I had no passion for these conservative, safer jobs. I did not want to study law, medicine, engineering, or even psychology. They just didn't appeal to me. All of my energy and heart's desire was geared toward filmmaking—however risky, dangerous, and romantic the dream may have seemed.

I was highly encouraged to take the appropriate career route, but I was never forced. That's because my parents were a little more liberal and open-minded than those born of the typical, first-generation parents from China or Korea. I was grateful to take advantage of this opportunity, but that didn't mean I was privileged to compromise other obligations in my life. I was still required to complete school up until college, even if my school credentials did not contribute much to my breaking into the entertainment business.

In all humility, I faithfully complied. I labored diligently throughout high school, completed both honors and AP courses, obtained top grades, achieved a decent score on my SAT exams, and actually got accepted into UCLA (University of California Los Angeles)! Amidst all these technicalities and obstacles, I had just one dream, and that was my career as an established Hollywood director. This image was my shining star, my treasure, my ticket out of my dump and into true paradise.

I was ecstatic when UCLA accepted me because it housed one of the nation's most acclaimed film schools. I had long desired to study with the UCLA School of Theater, Film, and Television and use it as my launch pad to enter Hollywood afterward. It was the whole reason I was motivated to do well in high school. The UCLA film program was where I wanted to go since day one, even more than the higher-ranking USC School of Cinematic Arts.

I was sure that God was guiding my life to this perfect point in time. He had answered my prayers to get into UCLA so that I could be associated with the film school. After that, I'd be on my way to Hollywood and become an industry hotshot. With my zeal and knowledge for film, I knew I was ready to conquer the world. I was poised to become one of the greatest film directors of all time!

One day, however, a curve ball suddenly hit my life hard. It turned out to be the first major turning point in my life, one detour in the course of events that would eventually lead me to where I am today spiritually.

FALL OF THE DREAMER

After my second year at UCLA, I applied to the university's film program to pursue a Bachelor of Arts in Film and Television degree. At the time, I was certain that I had turned in an impeccable portfolio to the school committee, but to my shock, the application was turned down! I still remember it well. On May 25, 2004, at 10:40 A.M., I received the news over the phone as I was discussing a class project with my Spanish professor at an outdoor campus commissary.

This failure was life-altering for several reasons. First, it defeated the purpose of why I had chosen to attend UCLA. I had not prepared a portfolio for an alternative field of study. I ended up completing a major that turned out to be useless to this day. Second, it deprived me of the formal education, training, and social networking that I desperately needed to succeed in such a voracious industry. Lastly, it paved a dispiriting road of unemployment and disorientation after graduation day.

I may have stumbled along life's road, but I was determined to rebound from my setback. I couldn't let this disaster stop me from achieving my destiny. After graduating from UCLA with a BA in Asian-American Studies, I immediately enrolled in CSUN (California State University of Northridge) with the intention of finally being accepted into a film program. During my first year there, I produced two short films along with a documentary. It was pleasing to know that I had at least two projects in my resume.

To my horror, however, I did not succeed in my attempt to infiltrate the CSUN Film School! Upon completion of my first year of prerequisite courses, I sent a portfolio to the film directing concentration department, for which my appeal was denied. It was mysterious and ultimately frustrating. Much as with UCLA, CSUN's particular concentration of directing drove me to go to that school. Because of my rejection, my association with CSUN became suddenly futile.

I couldn't help but wonder if it was my portfolio that was really that bad or if it was just a misplaced case of bad luck. Could it have been some sort of divine message? The questions circulated in my mind without end, but in the end, it didn't matter. I could have wallowed in self-pity over the situation, but instead, I chose to let it go and move on with my life. Unlike my predicament at UCLA, I did not continue and complete another major. In a matter of days, I resigned from CSUN.

Though the UCLA and CSUN application debacles served as a possible hindrance to my professional goals, another window of opportunity opened up a few short months after I left school. In late August of 2006, one of my mother's clients from her educational facility offered me a position as an accounting clerk for a television show on the 20th Century Fox Studios lot. This was a great offer because it made my transition from school life to the workforce much smoother than I had originally imagined. The fact that this job was centered directly in the entertainment field was even more incentive for me to be jubilant. I immediately signed on for the job. I figured this would be one of the greatest opportunities for me get my foot in the door of the Hollywood system.

On a slightly comical note, I should also mention that the production that hired me was the TV show, *Shark,* starring James Woods. Yes, it was the same *Shark* that I was nearly terminated from because of my on-set proselytizing of its star! My job as an accounting clerk represented my first stint with the show. I had the job a year and a half before my infamous witnessing encounter with Mr. Woods. In other words, my gig as an extra in April 2008 was not my first time being affiliated with the program or seeing James Woods himself.

During my stint as the accounting clerk for the TV show, I would occasionally see the actor as I ran errands to the sound stage. I did not officially meet him until that fateful 2008 meeting. You may also be surprised to hear that the link between James Woods and me ran even further back than the *Shark* days.

You may be asking, "How is this so?"

It's pretty simple. At the time my father's restaurant, Fortune West, was in business back in the early 90s, it was one of the most popular restaurants in Studio City. It was a celebrity craze and a dining spot for top actors such as Tom Cruise, Drew Barrymore, Kirstie Alley, Jeff Goldblum, Michael J. Fox, and believe or not, James Woods!

Although I fully enjoyed working in the production office of *Shark*, my time there was short-lived. I was originally hired onto the production on a temporal three-month contract. After this period, the executive staff would decide whether I would continue working on the show. Nothing was guaranteed. Unfortunately for me, the pendulum shifted in the wrong direction as the company informed me of their decision to release me about a week before my contract expired in late November. I wasn't entirely shocked by the outcome, but there was a side of me that wished the production would have found a way to keep me on board permanently. It would not only have solved some of my problems in relation to my lack of connections in the film industry, but it would have also helped with my personal financial condition.

Soon I was jobless and remained so for nearly a year. After my release from *Shark*, I returned to the drawing board to devise a few new strategies to penetrate Hollywood once again. The first order of business was to send out resumes to the other productions on the Fox Studios lot, but they bore no harvest whatsoever. I also used the year to write a couple of feature length film scripts, one of which was submitted to the 2007 PAGE International Screenwriting contest, but it lost out in the quarter-final round. There were even times when I attempted producing a feature length film for submission to film festivals, but I never had a chance to move forward with production due to funding deficiencies and a lack of commitment from my amateur actors.

My options seemed to be drying up, and it didn't help that my parents continued to pressure me to provide a standard living for myself. In other words, they wanted me to move on to something different. It was time to set aside my stubborn, romanticized ways and be practical. I had to acknowledge the urgency of my situation and get real.

Was this my reality check? Were my Hollywood dreams, career, and ambitions coming to a screeching halt? I didn't want to think so, but the realization of failure suddenly dawned on me like a black cloud covering the effulgent rays of the sun. My world was starting to look dim—very dim.

When it seemed as if all was lost, hope was rekindled in a manner that I least expected. In the summer of 2007, another path manifested itself to me. It was a way for me to re-enter the world of Hollywood. Unlike my past experience working behind the scenes, this time I would literally be in them, not behind the cameras, but in front of them!

I was going to break into the world of acting.

LIGHTS! ACTION! CAMERA!

I learned about the business of becoming a background artist during a Friday night church fellowship in May 2007. During the socialization segment after dinner, I met with one of my friends, John, who informed me about the nature of the acting business. He was a veteran background artist who worked on numerous films, including *The Island* and *Memoirs of a Geisha*. By the sound of this, I knew I had to get more information from this man. It sounded too exciting to pass up.

As the discourse progressed, I became further intrigued with his involvement in Hollywood. I was curious as to how he established his connections to obtain these film roles. I knew nothing about the business of being an extra and certainly did not know how Hollywood went about casting positions. I was very interested in performing roles similar to those that John had just for the experience, even though being an extra wasn't my primary passion. Filmmaking was still my number-one love, but I was willing to do anything to get back into Hollywood, even if I had to be an actor. I originally assumed that breaking into the field of acting and working on the set was an insurmountable feat for an ordinary guy. I presumed that a person either had to have the right connections or be extraordinarily talented to be in the spotlight.

To my delight, John gave me some welcome advice about entering the business. He said it was a relatively simple process. I was required to register with a casting agency that accepts everyone. After that, the agency would dispatch me to various movies, commercials, and television shows. John referred me to LA's most renowned background artist company, Central Casting Agency.

It was an understatement to say that I looked forward to getting involved in this business. I figured that I would not only be working in the entertainment industry again, but I would also gain firsthand knowledge about the process of on-set filmmaking. I would even get to stand alongside famous actors and actresses!

I joined Central Casting the following month, and by August, I was working my first gig on the hit NBC television series, *Heroes*. Although I was not originally scheduled to work on the production that day, I received the offer because I made myself available as a rush call. Rush calls are last-minute contacts to available extras, who replace those who do not show up to work on a given day. When I got my call, I accepted the job and immediately drove to the location in Thousand Oaks. It was exciting to realize that I would be heading to my first-ever, on-camera job in Hollywood!

My first time on the set was a highly impressionable one. It started by my getting lost while driving to the set location that had no defined address. It was in the middle of farmland deep in the countryside of Thousand Oaks. I eventually found it, but I was fifteen minutes late.

When I arrived on the set, I checked in with the PA and received my first-ever extras voucher. I was excited to receive a timecard after having been out of work for so long. I was surprised to learn that the pay was lower than I anticipated. You would think that even the background artists would benefit from the loose Hollywood change floating around! I originally thought I was going to get paid hundreds of dollars for my acting work, but the salary turned out to be just minimum wage, a rate of $7.50 per hour at that time. This is what they refer to as the non-union pay rate. Since I was in a desperate financial position, I didn't complain.

Immediately after signing in, I received my costume. The crew dressed me in a navy blue kimono, along with period piece sandals and a bandana. It felt peculiar to be in such a garment because I had not worn costumes of any kind since my childhood trick-or-treating days. Nevertheless, I found role-playing to be somewhat amusing. What further heightened the sense of alacrity was the black paint they applied to my face afterward. It was evident that I was going to play the role of an ancient-era Japanese villager!

After suiting up, the other villagers and I were shuttled in a white van to the shooting location a few blocks into a rural woods setting. Upon exiting the van, I saw the village in its entire splendor. Straw huts, haystack provender, rusty wheelbarrows, and fire pits were only a few of the set decorations that formed the fictional community. Add in the horses and peasants, along with some Samurais, and the on-screen magic came to life! Although it was not on the same scale as that of *The Last Samurai*, the Japanese ambience was still absorbing.

My day's work consisted of interacting with the other villagers and peasants. Background artists were not entitled to any dialogue, as that privilege was reserved for principle performers. If the production did invite an extra to speak, it was required to upgrade that extra to a principle player contract. Such an action would automatically entitle the upgraded extra to a hefty pay of $750! This was not the case on the show that day. Nonetheless, I did whatever I could to gain on-screen exposure. During my eight hours on the set, the crew shot me rolling a wheelbarrow, stirring vegetable soup in a large cauldron, playing games with other villagers, and even arguing with one of my peers in silent ad lib.

I finished the day weary, but I had an optimistic impression of the overall process. However easy the task may have seemed initially, it was really quite taxing physically, especially having to stand on my feet the whole day. The one-hundred-five degree August weather didn't help matters, and we filmed outdoors the entire time!

I was delighted to learn that Hollywood productions provide free catering and meals to all the crewmembers, including the non-union extras. As I had not come to work expecting food of any kind, I was surprised when the stipulated lunch break was called. They served everything from steaks to cakes. Atop all this, the crew even had an on-hand catering booth during the work hours!

The food was surely bliss, but by the end of the day, I was most exuberant that the film crew had captured me in five separate scenes. Although other background artists were included in the same shots, the director exclusively featured me in each one with a conspicuous action! *I was going to be famous!* I thought. *This was going to be my big Hollywood break!*

To my dismay, I later learned that these scenes were cut from the episode due to time constraints. They had omitted every single shot, which meant that my scenes were left on the editing room floor. It was if my presence on set had never taken place, and the production had never hired me in the first place. I was disappointed, but soon learned there was no need to be. Even had I gained the exposure, it would not have done much to bolster my chances of breaking into the league of principle performer. So much for my role as an extra turning me into the next Tom Cruise.

BACKGROUND PLAYER ON THE RISE

Two days after my *Heroes* gig, I received my next project on the TV show *Chuck*, in which I played a clubber. The scene took place in a Chinese bar, which was located on one of the indoor sets at the Warner Brothers Studios lot in Burbank. My experience with this show was very similar to that of *Heroes*. The only difference was that *Chuck* was a night call. This meant that the production started shooting in the afternoon and didn't wrap up until the following morning. Not only was this my first night shoot, but it was actually my first all-nighter too. I never even pulled an all-nighter in my college days!

The outcome of *Chuck* turned out to be more personally beneficial than that of *Heroes*. Although I didn't like the night shoot hours, I was glad I was included in a couple of shots that actually made it into the final cut for national broadcast on NBC television.

This particular *Chuck* episode was called "Chuck Versus the Sizzling Shrimp." My scene takes place in a Chinese bar inhabited by Asian mobsters and innocent patrons, of which I am a part. Toward the end of the scene, two cops crash the party and engage in gunfights with the mobsters.

As wheelchair-bound Ben Lo Pan (mafia ringleader played by James Hong) attempts to maneuver his way toward the exit door, one of the cops fires a bullet from the rear into Pan's shoulder. At this moment, a helpless woman and I react in shock to Pan's injury as we are crouched behind an overturned table. My acting opportunity took place at the very end of the scene.

After the thirteen hours of work that day, you might think that the scene would comprise a large portion of the episode. I was surprised to learn that it made up only thirty seconds in the final cut! Most of my scenes disappeared by the time the episode aired on television, and that seems to be normal. In most cases, extras have their scenes severely trimmed during post-production. It's astonishing to observe how much time and effort a production pours into a project, only to have so much of it scrapped in preparation for the final presentation! The realization of this process tremendously lowered my expectations for personal advancement through background acting.

During the next few weeks, I continued the momentum of working show after show in Hollywood. I hit most every production and gig in town, including television programs like *Samantha Who*, *Dirty Sexy Money*, *ER*, *Without a Trace*, *CSI*, *Journeyman*, *House*, *How I Met Your Mother*, and *The Sarah Connor Chronicles*. I saw more celebrities than I had seen before I entered Hollywood, which included big names like Reese Witherspoon, Alicia Keys, and Robert Downey Jr. However, my goals had changed, as I was on a mission more for money and survival than for any celebrity thrills and exposure.

After about two months in the business, I started to feel weary. I was no longer excited as I once had been about being on the set or about the glitz and glamour that surrounded the experience. For anyone inquiring about what it's like to be an actor, I can honestly attest that it is not as fun and dreamy as it appears in the media. It's strikingly more grounded in reality. The supposed glamour of the work environment never overshadows the physical and emotional feelings of fatigue, even if it is Hollywood. Most times, there is absolutely nothing glamorous about the environment. It is really nothing more than a fictional extension of real-life locations.

Even the opportunity to stand beside celebrities quickly wanes and loses those heart-thumping moments I initially desired. Extras do not respond in the same manner as frenzied teenagers encountering their favorite pop star. We quickly discover that the on-set celebrities appear to be normal people, much like everyone else God created. The truth is that some of them are so strange that you would probably not want to chat with them at all!

How exactly do the physical and emotional feelings of burden spring forth as a result of acting? It begins with having to wake up as early as 4:00 A.M. to arrive on the set for a 5:30 A.M. call. The work days span from eight to fourteen hours, and that's excluding the one-hour lunch break. A single shot for a scene can require as many as ten takes. During these intervals, a background player must perform the same routines incessantly until the director is fully satisfied with the overall picture. If an extra is not in a scene, he or she lingers about in the holding facility for hours on end, just waiting their turn. Books and portable music players, if available, work as diversions for only so long. Last, but not least, the commute can be cumbersome, particularly if the shooting location is fifty miles or more from home.

While it may sound peculiar, Hollywood can be a surprisingly lonely place. Although there is a plethora of people in every work environment, the overall mindset of the people involved is capitalistic. Every soul is out for his or her own good. Because self-enhancement leads to promotion in this field, actors must follow their predatory instincts. An aura of materialism, artificiality, and spiritual bankruptcy makes true friendships (especially those that are morally bound) a limited commodity. The sad reality is that life in Hollywood often affects the hearts of professing Christians too. In their zeal and lust for prominence, these believers indulge in dishonest favors, participate in wild orgies, succumb to moral corruption, and most distressingly, fall away from faith altogether.

The question was whether or not I would eventually fall into that category as well.

THE ROAD BACK HOME

Where was God when I was in the midst of my college years, post-college life, and my stint in Hollywood?

I am relieved to say that God was a part of my life, even after high school. While He played only a small role in my immediate affections, His presence never left me. In fact, as I journeyed through the scattered mazes of Hollywood, my heart longed more for Him. I guess this is what anxiety and suffering does to humble a proud soul.

After high school, I stopped attending church for about a year and a half. The transition into UCLA was such a paramount stage that the socialization and studying completely dominated any crumbs of leftover time I would normally have given to church activities. I'm not inferring that I became a rabid sinner and no longer had respect for my faith and God. I just had less priority to maintain any sense of duty to the Lord. Unfortunately, I didn't look for ways to serve His kingdom. It would have meant sacrificing some of my own sense of comfort and reputation. Because of this unfortunate development, I knew I had to get my discipleship life in order.

A specific Bible verse kept me inspired and trusting in the Lord's sovereignty. "'For I know the plans that I have for you,' declares the Lord, 'plans for welfare and not calamity to give you a future and a hope'" (Jer. 29:11). My seventh grade junior high school used this verse as the main theme for a retreat. I remember the verse so vividly because it was the only phrase that inspired hope in me for the years that followed. Although I misconstrued the theological meaning and used the verse as a personal drive for safety, health, and future economic success, Jeremiah 29:11 was one of the few spiritual devices that helped me keep faith in the Lord and His sovereign will. It was the hope that I wanted, especially in a time when I needed such help to succeed in my life.

During my second year in college, I began to frequent church once again. In an era when multitudes leave church at the age of eighteen, never to return, I was one of the few people to come back in good faith. I guess I made this decision because of a sense of guilt of not observing Sundays for so long. I returned to my old church of Young Nak and started attending the adult services. My experience was noticeably different this time in that I was now with a group of grown-ups. Everyone was remarkably more mature. The facility itself was more sophisticated and capacious since they had constructed a brand-new chapel, which is currently the main worship hall for YNCC (Young Nak Celebration Church).

I didn't stay at Young Nak very long. About two years after returning to my childhood church, I made a fairly bold decision to leave it for another. This decision was groundbreaking for me at the time because I had never been to another church in my entire life. I was clueless as to what other congregations offered, what they preached, or how they orchestrated their music. In some ways, relocating to another church almost felt like switching religions.

So why would I abandon my old stomping grounds and relocate to another body? I needed a change. Around the end of college, there grew within me an expanding emptiness that Young Nak could no longer fill. Whether it was spiritual or emotional, I was in need of something that my church could not give me. I sensed that the new church would have to be unfamiliar and possibly even a bit adventurous, but certainly not heretical. Upon leaving Young Nak in late 2006, I spent the next year searching for my new church home. I visited several different churches before I finally settled into Family Chapel Church in September 2007.

BLOSSOMING SOUL

It's interesting to mention that during the time I attended Family Chapel, a marvelous change came about in my personality. I slowly started to gain interest in the Lord and display His characteristics. Feelings of humility and gratitude began to blossom wholeheartedly within me. There were various reasons why this occurred, but ultimately it was due to a combination of my failures, monetary deprivation, and spiritual emptiness mixed with warm-hearted church folks and powerful testimonies that all played key roles in cultivating my heart for godly desires. I no longer took anything in life for granted. There was just too much for which I was thankful. My ego and self-centeredness became less and less important as I started to rejoice more in serving the needs of others.

Was this the time that I became born again? It's difficult to know for sure, since my life had always consisted of scattered prayers and confessions of sin. Regardless of how my fruits of humility and gratitude came about, I do have to acknowledge that it had a tremendous impact on my outlook on life. I had finally softened my formerly hardened heart from my adolescent years. God was indeed working in my life so that I would be ready to become a devoted servant to Him in the fast-approaching future.

Various times in the past, when I looked to church as a means for relational formation or pure escapism, there were those moments when I sincerely wanted to devote my life in full service to the Lord, but nothing ever came of those situations. I was never given inspiring reasons as to why I should be so passionate about my faith or ministry work. Those reasons eventually surfaced in a near future day, but they came in response to a question I posed to the Lord at a particular Friday night Bible program in October 2005.

The program consisted of casual reflections on scriptural themes through musical worship, discussions, and prayer within a small group. Near the end of the night, every person found a secluded place around the worship hall for a solitary activity. The purpose was to delve into a quiet time to pray and reach out to the Lord's presence.

Although I had not done much of this before in a group setting, I complied and sought out the Lord in this quiet moment. I lay on the floor in a dark room, closed my eyes, and reached my hands out to the heavens in earnest, deep prayer, asking the Lord to show me His will. I immediately followed with a bold request—that God would reveal Himself to me. I didn't mean this in a figurative or metaphorical sense. I wanted God to reveal Himself to me literally! I didn't care if it was His face, hand, or even voice. I wanted something concrete from Him. I wanted to see the Holy One for the first time in my life. It even came to the point where I demanded it in slight frustration because of His lack of appearance in my past predicaments.

As you may have guessed, Jesus did not appear to me that night, at least not in the literal fashion that I desired, and to this day, I don't know why I beseeched Him for such a task. The Bible clearly explains that no man has ever seen the Lord eye-to-eye and lived to tell about it. In Exodus, the Lord Himself informed Moses, "You cannot see My face, for no man can see Me and live!" (Ex. 33:20). The power of God's goodness and holiness will destroy sin because the nature of sin resides in the soul of man. This, in turn, is accessed through the eyes.

Looking back, I wonder why I demanded something like this. Was it because I wanted the Lord to affirm His desires for me verbally? Was it so that I wouldn't stumble upon future mistakes? Or did I do it because I was jealous of His revelation to others in history but not to me? They are all reasonable guesses, but in the end, I think the answer may be more disturbing. Perhaps I did it because I wanted to know if God really existed and this was my test to leave the faith.

I yearned for God's voice that night, but I did not find it. I desired meaning for my existence in this world and prayed for the Lord to show me why I wasn't finding it. Unable to discern answers, I left the program that night discouraged, even bewildered.

Where are you Lord? I cried in my heart. *Do you hear me? What do you want of my life? Why am I not growing spiritually, even when I am finally asking for it?*

Little did I know that God would give me the answer to this exact prayer two years later in a time and place I least expected. The Lord would be waiting for me right on the red carpet, ready to hand the solution to me in a sealed Oscar-like envelope, and when I opened it, His answer would shift my life forever.

Chapter 4

ENLIGHTENMENT

ON SEPTEMBER 27, 2007, AT 7:30 A.M. I headed toward my next gig at the NBC television program, *Life*, a detective crime series about a former police officer wrongly imprisoned for years, who had now returned to the police force. It was my first time working on a show of this particular genre, but to me it was just another day on the job, regardless of the topic, territory, or people involved.

The *Life* shoot was one of many productions to take place on the NBC Universal Studios lot that day. The palatial facility is undoubtedly the most renowned studio in all Los Angeles, as evidenced by its tourist attractions such as Universal City Walk and the adjacent theme park. The moment I left the employee's parking structure and entered the studio lots, a sense of wonder came over me. I remembered visiting this very same lot when I was younger. Most natives can relate when I say that I rode through the premise as a passenger on the Universal Theme Park tram ride. At the time, I didn't view the atmosphere as a professional working environment, but as a genuine attraction where King Kong, Jaws, and dilapidated bridges served to thrill patrons.

Arriving on the lot as an employee rather than a tourist provided me with a completely new perspective. The studio back lot didn't seem to be much of a diversion anymore. Instead, it was an industrious work environment where levity and free-spirited will were not as apparent as with passengers and tour guides from the theme park. That's not to say that the back lot was no longer a fun place to be, but for an employee, the priority was to get the job done for the day. I arrived ready to work.

My role on *Life* was as a computer technician. As you can surmise from the description, the crew and I shot our scenes in an indoor environment—more specifically in a police office and in a skyscraper that overlooked downtown Los Angeles. I played the computer whiz whose main task was to assist stationed police officers with their monitor functions. Meanwhile, the show's main character, Charlie Crew (played by Damian Lewis), conducted a conference in a nearby unit. This was the focal point of the shot, while the extras and I filled in as the nondescript ambience in the background.

Although the principle actors were amusing enough to garner everyone's attention, they paled in comparison to what also roamed the set that day. I first discovered this something (or rather someone) around noon, and it made a tremendous impression on me. It was something I had never seen before or even conceived. In fact, it astounded me to the point where his actions will serve as a recurring subject throughout the remainder of this book!

HEAVEN'S OFFICER

During one of the breaks, some other background actors and I stepped outside the stage to eat gelato that was served near the catering station. It was always a pleasure to indulge in specialized desserts, especially since they only came around occasionally. I gleefully ate my Italian ice cream, while the person beside me shared the same pleasure and then started conversing about the joy of eating on the set, as well as the goodness of life in general. I couldn't have agreed more with his statements.

That person was Jonathan Khan. He was a crew-cut-sporting, Chinese-Irish man who had on a police officer's uniform. He evidently played one of the cops in the episode. Although Jonathan was only a background player, he looked apt enough to be a real cop! This was a compliment to how well cast he was, even if only as an extra. He certainly was a cop with a winsome demeanor.

As we began to chat further, I discovered that Jonathan was no ordinary man. At some point in the conversation, I mentioned the word death, similar to the way I discussed it with Uncle Mike as a kid. I don't remember how the subject came up, but Jonathan was eager to grab hold of it.

He smiled at me and asked in a straightforward manner, "So, what do you think is going to happen to you when you die, Steve?"

I thought, *Why would he ask me a question like that?* Still, I wasn't at all offended. It just seemed peculiar that he would pinpoint me on such a morbid topic, especially while eating ice cream on a pleasant day. I thought about how to respond for a beat, keeping in mind that if I answered him honestly, others would see me as a "religious freak." Not very skilled in evangelism at the time, I was apprehensive about sharing my faith or mentioning anything about Christianity amid a group of my secular peers. Nonetheless, I remained truthful to my beliefs.

I said, "I believe I'll go to heaven."

Jonathan then asked, "Do you think you're good enough to go to heaven?"

"I hope so."

"Have you ever told a lie?"

"Yes."

"Then what would that make you?"

"A liar?"

"Have you ever stolen anything?"

"Yes."

"Then what would that make you?"

I was unsure of this one, so I answered, "A stealer?"

Jonathan gently corrected me, "It starts with a T. It's thief. Have you ever used God's name in vain?"

I answered, "Yes."

"That's called blasphemy. God lavished His goodness and blessings upon you and yet you've used His holy name to express disgust. That's a very serious offense in His sight. Years ago, people were stoned for using the Lord's name in vain. Jesus said if you look at a woman to lust after her, you've committed adultery with her in your heart. Have you ever looked at a woman with lust, Steve?"

I had no choice but to affirm my failure to uphold that divine law as well. That was the last of the Ten Commandments against which Jonathan measured me. He then gave me a succinct summation of the state of my morality. I was a self-admitted liar, thief, blasphemer, and adulterer-at-heart, and that was only four of God's Ten Commandments. *Wow, I never knew I sounded so corrupt!* I thought.

If this interrogation wasn't direct enough, Mr. Khan followed up with a grave question, "So, Steve, if God were to judge you by this standard on Judgment Day, would you be innocent or guilty?"

What was Judgment Day? I wondered, having no clue at the time. It sounded terrifying! I never learned about it in my church, and none of my Christian friends ever came close to mentioning such a biblical concept. I thought that once a decedent passed into eternity, they would go to heaven or hell and that was it. Did Judgment Day signify a separate judgment for Christians who are unfaithful, and thus disqualify them to inherit eternal life? Did this mean that I was in deep trouble? Based on my guilty nature, it seemed that I was in a theoretically bad position.

I replied, "Probably guilty."

He asked, "Then would you go to heaven or hell?"

It seemed only logical for me to answer, "I guess hell."

"Does that concern you, Steve?"

"I guess."

I was slightly disturbed as I thought about the logic of his argument. It did make a great deal of sense to me, which resulted in my thinking that I was headed for hell. I was totally guilty. Jonathan asserted that guilty lawbreakers would indeed be on the road to eternal damnation, because God is righteous and just. The Lord will bring every deed to account on the Day of Judgment (Matt. 12:36),[2] and the extent of our criminal activities would determine the severity of our punishment in hell.

This fact was portending in a fearful way, but Jonathan used it as a backdrop to bring forth the good news in a sublime fashion. He asked me, "Do you know what God did so you didn't have to end up in Judgment Day?"

I wasn't quite sure. Maybe it was because I had never had the gospel message presented to me in such a manner. I couldn't immediately connect the dots between the Ten Commandments, divine judgment, and the purpose of grace.

Jonathan asked, "Do you know about Jesus and His sacrifice?"

At that moment, I breathed a sigh of relief in my mind and answered, "Oh yes, yes."

Jonathan proceeded to explain the gospel to me nevertheless. He delineated how Jesus died on the cross as a substitute for the punishment I should receive. In doing so, the Son of Man took my sins upon Himself so that I can be set free from God's wrath and be declared eternally innocent. Christ lived a sinless, perfect life so that, in exchange for my sins, He will give me His righteousness. Only then can I be holy enough to enter heaven. Only then will I be without guilt, and the Judge will dismiss my case due to lack of evidence. That meant I could have everlasting life and be with my loving Lord for all eternity. In closing his brief presentation, Mr. Khan urged me to get my life right with the Lord if I hadn't already done so, by repenting of my sins and trusting in Jesus Christ alone for my salvation.

I sensed that I was already saved, and I didn't feel the urgency to pray the sinner's prayer again. I agreed with Jonathan's statements and shared briefly about my recent spiritual walk with the Lord, which included my prayer life and service to church. Pleased to hear about my spiritual condition, Jonathan encouraged me to keep my faith strong and to continue fighting the good fight against the dark forces of this world. I fully complied with his advice, delighting every bit in the man's passion and knowledge of the Christian faith. I was just glad that I had a fellow brother to work and associate with on set. I rarely encountered such things at work, so it was truly refreshing. The two of us would have probably chatted more, but we received a call back into the soundstage to resume work within a matter of seconds.

On Fire for God

I don't lie when I say this, but Jonathan was the only Christian who had ever witnessed to me one-on-one. Nobody had ever tried personally to evangelize me during my twenty-three years of life, not even my pastors! I find this reality to be somewhat disturbing because it shows how unmotivated most Christians are to share their faith. They know that anyone who dies without the salvation of Christ will end up in the eternal lake of fire, yet most don't seem to be alarmed or feel an urgency to act. The prophecy of ultimate damnation should give Christians all the incentive they need to carry out the sobering yet God-glorifying task of reaching out to the lost, no matter how far or close the prospect may be. To do otherwise would be to exercise a tragic display of brotherly hate.

I have to admit that I was also among the negligent. I did not seek opportunities to share my faith with lost sinners. I knew that multitudes of blind men and women were headed toward a cliff that led to eternal suffering, yet I wasn't even compassionate enough to at least warn these people about their eternal fate. Though I may have made mistakes in the past, I knew it was not too late to change my ways. Jonathan Khan proved to be the catalyst that sparked my curiosity in evangelism.

I was fascinated to observe that Jonathan did not cease his gospel proclamation with me. During the rest of the fourteen-and-a-half-hour day, Jonathan engaged in friendly conversations with the other background players solely to get Jesus' message across. Whether it was in the background holding area or even on set between takes, there was no stopping Mr. Khan. Anybody who came within ten feet of Jonathan was setting himself or herself up to be a potential target!

It was fascinating to observe the different reactions of the prospects. The extreme ranged from one African American gentleman acquiescing to Jonathan's every word to another Jewish fellow debating with Mr. Khan about the truth of soteriology (the study of salvation). In any case, watching Jonathan Khan dive fearlessly into action for God's kingdom was mind blowing! It actually inspired me to want to make a difference as well, even if it meant having to lower my standard of complacency to do so.

Regardless of people's impressions and opinions of Jonathan that day, it's undeniable that the man was passionate about God. He loved the Lord and His people enough to follow every command from the Bible and to carry it out faithfully. He was willing to tell everyone about the gospel message much as Jesus and the disciples had in their days. He was fully prepared to take the insults and become a martyr for his actions if necessary.

Even when he was not evangelizing, Jonathan was surprisingly vigilant in edifying on-set Christians in the knowledge of spiritual growth, concentrating heavily on the issue of the Great Commission (see Matt. 28:19-20). He sat next to seeking prospects, read Bible passages with them, and gave them resources for them to be effective witnesses of Christ in this world. His actions truly exemplified the model Christian servant in my eyes.

I benefited from this edification process as well. At the end of the day, Mr. Khan gave me some gospel tracts, which were resources that he claimed to have used frequently for his witnessing opportunities. They were composed of three small brochures and a DVD in a sealed case.

Jonathan bestowed these resources on me with the hope of widening my eyes to the important truths of the gospel and practical evangelism. I gratefully accepted Jonathan's gifts before we parted ways that night. I wholeheartedly thanked him and gave him my best blessing before leaving the Universal Studios lot.

You may think that my passion as a Christian would have immediately surged from this point forth. However, it didn't turn out that way. As stimulating as the day was with Jonathan's hallowing presence, my spiritual vigor mysteriously leveled off when I left work. It was as if I had experienced a temporary high in those few magical hours.

When I got home, I threw the resources into one of my desk drawers. I didn't glance at them again for several months. This shows how unenthusiastic I was toward Christian material. I hardly ever looked at my Bible outside of Sundays. Instead, my concerns turned once again toward the things of this world. I had worries about money, procuring my next acting gig, secular entertainment, food, and so on. That's what my mind immediately focused on as I slept that night. As far as I was concerned, tomorrow would be another worldly day until the weekly Sabbath rolled around.

In the next several months, I continued to work show after show in Hollywood. During this time, my spiritual perception hadn't changed much. I was still careless in my evangelizing the lost on set. I was not seeking measures to elevate my servitude to the Lord in any groundbreaking way. It seemed as if I had almost forgotten about Jonathan Khan, along with his words of wisdom.

In truth, I was in need of someone or something to rock my world to the core. I really needed a forceful light to blind my eyes and awake me to my calling. Interestingly, that is exactly what happened in January 2008.

THE ROAD TO DAMASCUS

In January 2008, I experienced a rude awakening that had a similar impact on me as the one the Apostle Paul experienced in Acts 9:1-19. In this chapter, Paul (or Saul of Tarsus at the time) encounters the Lord Jesus on the road to Damascus, where he is blinded by the light of the Savior's presence. Such a stunning act rocks Saul to the core, and this incident convinces him of the truth of Christ's deity. The event was, in essence, the starting point in Paul's ministry of service to the Lord.

It wasn't a cosmic scale incident that physically blinded and then miraculously healed me, but I did have a humble discovery that caused me to undergo the same presto transformation that Paul experienced. It wasn't so much an issue of my discovering salvation for the first time and being born again like Paul. Instead, I obtained a newfound conviction of God's purpose for Christians here on earth.

On a casual weekday in late January, I finally retrieved the materials Jonathan had given me and that I had tossed into my desk drawer after my gig on *Life*. I scrutinized each one carefully. Something in my soul beckoned me to look at them. Maybe it was a meager sense of guilt for ignoring the Christian material freely given to me as an aid to help others, or perhaps I thought my actions might have constituted blasphemy. It could very well have been the Spirit of God speaking to my conscience. Whatever the case, I finally fulfilled Jonathan's request.

During the next hour, a flash of light surrounded my mind. It was so forceful that it blinded both my soul and conscience. I first read the tract titled "Are You a Good Person? Try the Ultimate Test." After completing it, I suddenly remembered everything Jonathan had preached to me on that fateful day at Universal Studios. I recalled the manner in which he structured the use of God's Law, Judgment Day, hell, grace, heaven, and repentance as part of the gospel presentation.

Inasmuch as I found the *Good Person Test* to be a helpful memento, what I encountered next took everything to the next level. I watched the DVD Jonathan gave me called "The Greatest Gamble." It is one of the episodes from a reality television show starring Kirk Cameron and Ray Comfort titled *The Way of the Master.*

This particular episode from season two focuses on the intriguing question surrounding the ultimate gamble in life. The show's two hosts roam the streets of Las Vegas asking pedestrians if they are willing to play Russian roulette for ten million dollars. They have a revolver and cash in their possession. It is a legitimate offer. One gun, one bullet, and ten million dollars. Would *you* bet your life? I knew my answer. Who in their right mind would do something that insane?

Watching the episode provided me with my first introduction to Kirk and Ray. I vaguely recalled Kirk Cameron's name. It sounded familiar, yet the face didn't register until I learned later that he had been a part of the popular *Growing Pains* television series back in the late 80s. I didn't recognize Mr. Comfort at all. He appeared to be an Albert Einstein-looking figure who might have been a university professor for all I knew. His New Zealand accent was a distinguishable trait and gave him a somewhat comical Steve Irwin-like presence and an aura of dignified intelligence. Ray and Kirk were both evocative, entertaining personas, and it delighted me to see that they were both Christian, especially when their sophisticated facade could have easily categorized them as evolutionists or even Scientologists.

"The Greatest Gamble" ran a concise twenty-eight minutes, but the message delivered by the two hosts packed a wealth of life-changing information that showed me the gospel in its greatest glory! The episode was eye opening, not so much because of Kirk and Ray's deal with the gun and money, but because it explored an even graver reality—the true nature of God. I'm not talking just about the God of love that we have typically grown up learning about since grade school. The episode explored the God of holiness, righteousness, and justice to its fullest depth.

Why was this study so enlightening to me? Because I had never really known or been exposed to this kind of God before in full depth. Throughout my life, I'd been taught that the Lord was an all-loving, merciful, and forgiving God. I agree that Jehovah is very merciful, but that is not *all* He is. The picture painted by some churches can easily portray a false notion that God's bar of justice and wrath is set on a pathetically low level and can be compromised without a price (this price, of course, is the blood of Jesus Christ). I had never before learned about a God who fully exercised other divine attributes, ones that were not as easy to internalize as some of His more felicitous traits preached every Sunday from the pulpit.

This parochial view caused me to fall into three unfortunate missteps in my early spiritual life. First, I stumbled into sin much easier because of my lack of fear. Second, I did not esteem the sacrifice of Jesus as much as I should have. Last, I did not have much reason to care about ministry work or evangelism.

"The Greatest Gamble" revealed the answer to life's greatest question a few minutes into the episode. The answer was that *there is no hell.* Kirk and Ray argue for the existence of this eternal location by making two key points. The first is the reasoning for God's goodness. The second is the manifestation of the conscience in every human mind.

In presenting the first point, Kirk and Ray show the existence of hell to be reasonable because of God's infinite righteousness. Most of the world believes that God is good. If that were indeed true, it would be sensible to believe that God would have to be angry with all the evildoers in the world. If God turned a blind eye to their crimes, then instead of being good, He would be corrupt by nature (Job 37:23).[3] The Bible declares that God is infinitely good (Ps. 7:9)[4] and His justice is equally proportionate (Deut. 32:4).[5] He will punish murderers and rapists, but He won't stop there. God is so good, He will also deal with liars, thieves, fornicators, idolaters, blasphemers, adulterers, coveters, haters, and those filled with deceit, pride, and so on. (1 Cor. 6:9-10).[6] Pleading for pardon or apologizing to the Lord is futile, because the Holy One is a God of justice who will by no means clear the guilty (Ex. 34:7).[7] God's just place of punishment for transgressors is therefore a place called hell, where all who are not acquitted of their wrongdoings are delivered after death (Rev. 21:8).[8]

Finally, the reality of hell is testified through the existence of the human conscience. The conscience is the inveterate mechanism within a human brain that communicates to a person about right and wrong conduct. It speaks purely on moral agendas. Scientists cannot satisfactorily describe the biological formation of the conscience, but the Word of God provides the most likely explanation. The Bible declares that the Lord has placed his holy laws in the minds and hearts of His children. Therefore, humans recognize innately that it is wrong to lie, cheat, steal, murder, covet, and blaspheme. We cannot plead ignorance at the Great White Throne Judgment because of the inner light that God has given to every person (Rom. 2:14-16).[9] The conscience testifies to the reality of an objective truth that is governing the world in the moral sense. This same standard will hold humanity accountable to God in His appointed time.

"The Greatest Gamble" utilizes these two arguments to prove the existence of God's eternal judgment and ultimately extend a salvation that can only come through grace. This lesson forever changed my perspective on Christianity. Before this day, I didn't fully comprehend the theological meaning behind Jesus' death or why He was the only way to heaven. I didn't know the relationship between sin and hell. I didn't even know that repentance was part of the salvation process! I did practice repentance toward the Lord in the past, but my former offerings were a means to make peace with God so that He would not hinder any blessings on me. I didn't know that it was actually the means by which I would escape eternal death!

It seemed all the more logical to learn that people are punished in hell not purely because of their disbelief in Jesus, but because of their endless, premeditated crimes against God in thought, word, and deed. Jesus died not in vain, but to satisfy the real demands of eternal justice and to pay the price for my freedom from the wrath of God on Judgment Day.

Everything suddenly made sense to me after twenty-three years!

A CALL TO BE A WITNESS

Although my soul had been blinded, I immediately sought the Lord to open my eyes to a new vision and purpose in life. After much thinking, I decided to call Jonathan Khan for his advice. This would be my first opportunity to speak with him since our *Life* shoot. I was able to reach him through the contact information he had stamped on the back of my *Good Person* tract, which fully indicated Jonathan's openness to his prospects.

Jonathan was pleasantly surprised to hear from me, and in many ways, the feeling was mutual, even though I was the initiator of the conversation. We spent the first few minutes conversing about our respective lives. During this time, I expressed my gratitude and joy in my new perception of the gospel. Jonathan immediately entreated me to visit the Living Waters (ministry sponsor of *The Way of the Master*) website[10] to become acquainted with the resources. This included doctrinal statements, articles, gospel tracts, and free audio and video sermons.

At the close of our discourse, Jonathan instructed me to watch one of the videos titled "Hell's Best Kept Secret." Because I was so enraptured by the other features on this website, I didn't immediately view this episode. When I did eventually watch that particular video later in the year, the personal effect of the experience was so confounding that I will discuss it in a later chapter.

I wasted no time in browsing the Living Waters website. I primarily focused on the gospel tracts in the store section. I may be one of many to testify that these tracts are truly a novelty. They aren't the typical insipid brochures that people glance at, recognize immediately as religious material, and quickly discard. The Living Waters tracts are creative, relative, and even enticing. A good example is their popular *Million Dollar Bill*, which is a tract that resembles an American reserve note but with a one-million-dollar logo printed on the front. On the back, the gospel message is laid out in its unadulterated form. These tracts are so engaging that many people actually request them, rather than the witness assertively placing them into their hands as an evangelistic gesture.

However useful the tract descriptions were in providing me with deeper insights into Christian theology, the most pertinent effect they produced in me was the conviction to take evangelism more seriously. Every tract was equipped with information on a particular subject, and it was easy to use them as impetus to share the gospel message. One tract presented a case for anti-evolution. Another explored different religions in contrast to Christianity. Every tract aimed to educate infidels and Christians on the truth of the gospel message, regardless of its topic or audience.

The pamphlet that finally did it for me was called the *101 Last Days Prophecies*. It's an Eternal Productions resource[11] dedicated to exploring innumerable Bible prophecies that have been fulfilled through this century. I won't take the time to explore them here, but suffice it to say that they caused me immediate concern after reading through them. The information was so convicting that my selfish priorities didn't seem so significant anymore. These prophecies enlightened me to the apocalyptic reality that the rapture of the church was going to occur soon. The Antichrist was waiting to fulfill his destiny as the most powerful demagogue ever, and Jesus was going to descend to earth as the King of Israel and rule the world in righteousness.

I suddenly felt a new calling in my life, and that was to convince the world of this truth. Time was running out and people were perishing at a rapid rate. Before this day, I feared being an open witness for Christ due to lack of confidence in myself and an unstable trust in the veracity of the Bible. That's because I didn't know if the Word of God was true and worthy of defending.

The biblical prophecies, along with scientific and archaeological data from other sources, proved to me that Jesus' words about life and death were in fact the ultimate truths governing this world. God is real, and so are heaven, hell, and the coming Tribulation! People must be warned before it is too late! I decided that I had to be resourceful with my time from now on. My labor was definitely going to be worth it. I would not waste it in vain, but use it to my eternal benefit and God's glory.

In the book of Acts, the apostle Paul's journey to Damascus resulted in two fruitful outcomes. The first was his rebirth in the water and in the Spirit of the true, living God (see Acts 9:18). Not only were Paul's damaged eyes healed by the grace of God, but the eyes of his heart were also opened to finally see the Lord and the true path to salvation. With the aid of the disciple Ananias, Paul became a born-again Christian after repenting and being baptized in the Holy Spirit.

The second outcome was the apostle Paul's newfound passion for the lost (see Acts 26:16-18). As he stood before King Agrippa to plead his case against the charges of condemnation from the religious leaders, Paul fully advocated the truth and supremacy of Christ. The apostle further stated that the Lord chose him to fulfill a specific agenda in life—that of an effective witness to both Jews and Gentiles for as long as he lived. Jesus declared to Paul, "For this purpose I have appeared to you, to appoint you a minister and a witness…rescuing you from the Jewish people and the Gentiles, to whom I am sending you, to open their eyes so that they may turn from darkness to light and from the dominion of Satan to God, that they may receive forgiveness of sins and an inheritance among those who have been sanctified by faith in Me" (Acts 26:16-20).

Jonathan Khan appeared to be the Ananias in my life in that he steered me to a specific course where God ultimately met me with His will. When Jonathan led me to the Living Waters website to learn imperative theology from Ray Comfort, my stunted eyes suddenly healed. They opened to a dazzling new world where evangelism stood in the vanguard of my priorities. I heard the Holy Spirit speak the same words to my heart that Paul spoke in Acts 26:16.

The Holy Spirit definitely worked through Jonathan Khan and the Living Waters resources to lead me to serve the Lord. Because of Living Water's bold and unrestrained presentation of the gospel, I came to fully understand and appreciate God's grace in richer resonance. Jesus was now truly worth loving and serving, something I never really felt in the past! It was certainly something that other gospel presentations had never moved me toward in the same degree. I now wanted to share this same philosophy with the whole world. I wanted to proclaim the gospel to my friends, family, and strangers the same way Ray and Kirk taught it to me.

Like the apostle Paul, I was now on my way to the world to share God's message. I knew it was going to be a tough fight, but as Paul declared in his solemn yet joyful state, "I can do all things through Him who strengthens me" (Phil. 4:13).

It didn't matter if I encountered Jews, Gentiles, rich, poor, healthy, lame, smart, or uneducated. I was ready and equipped!

Chapter 5

MASTER AND APPRENTICE

O NE OF THE recurring questions people ask me about my line of work is whether I have been in any famous movies. Regrettably, my resume in that department is underwhelming since most of the projects I get booked on are television productions. However, there are sporadic occasions during the year when feature film jobs unexpectedly cruise into my life. One of the prominent ones to have come racing through was *Fast and Furious*, the fourth entry to the popular Universal Pictures franchise.

Until that time, I had only worked on three other theatrical releases: *The House Bunny*, *College Road Trip*, and *Four Christmases*. *Fast and Furious* is undoubtedly the most reputable, if not the most bankable film of them all. It may not be a revered achievement in terms of storytelling or cinematic art, but it passes as a grand piece of entertainment, and that's probably all that matters to the mindless masses. It was a high-budget, summer blockbuster at its loudest, most mind-numbing, and most death-defying period in time!

I arrived to work at 6:00 A.M., punctual as always. The set was situated in the rear parking lot of an outdoor shopping center on 8th Street in Korea Town. I parked in the crew lot as directed and was led to the background holding area in the conterminous building. To my surprise, the holding area turned out to be an arcade room, and that put a smile on nearly everyone's face.

There was, however, another reason to be even more excited on this day. Movie fans and most of my friends may not have agreed, but my elation stemmed from a different cause. I was still reeling from the effects from my discovery of *The Way of the Master* a few weeks prior. The Living Waters ministry had changed my spiritual perspective in a colossal fashion. That's not to say that I became the apostle Paul overnight, but my personal will to gear more effort in that direction had finally been piqued by the work of the Holy Spirit. I was now committed to saving the lost.

I had become so convicted that I must participate in outreach that I placed a bulk order for Living Waters gospel tracts the same day I visited the website. They all arrived at my home a week later. The titles included everything from the basic *Good Person Tests* to the ominous *101 Last Days Prophecies* booklets. I couldn't wait to share these convincingly outlined truths with non-Christians. Just like Jonathan, I even had my contact information stamped on the back cover of each resource.

Although I had the inclination and materials to start sharing these life-changing messages on the set, I admit I was still somewhat apprehensive. I understood *The Way of the Master* gospel outline, yet I did not know how to explain it to a prospect. I hadn't listened to the presentation fully enough to memorize it and then withstand objections. At this point, the most I could do in my disadvantaged state was simply to hand out my tracts and pray for the Spirit of God to move the hearts of the infidels to salvation.

Just when I thought my handicap would de-escalate the power of God's agenda, help came in an unexpected and even hilarious manner. A few minutes after settling into my chair on the set, I turned around and saw Jonathan Khan march into the room.

I couldn't believe my eyes! It was too good to be true. It didn't take me long to figure out that Jonathan was one of the background artists scheduled for the day. It was quite a coincidence that I had spoken to him just a few weeks prior. Now here he was, at work with me once again!

Upon seeing Jonathan, the first thought that popped into my mind was, *I wonder if he's going to be hardcore with his preaching again.*

I reasoned that Christian matters couldn't possibly consume his mind all the time. That would seem almost inhuman in some ways, since most of us naturally gravitate toward sin and the world. He was probably going to display some spiritual levity this time around and discuss other subjects like sports, politics, and maybe even automobiles, since this movie was about cars.

As Jonathan dropped his duffel bag onto a seat, a woman nearby asked him a question in a lighthearted, jesting manner. I have only a vague recollection of what she asked, but I do know that it pertained to my initial thought after seeing Jonathan enter.

Jonathan replied to the woman in a pert, salesman-like manner with arms raised high, "Everyone is going to hell! I've got to save them!"

Oh boy, I thought with a chuckle. *This is surely going to be one interesting day.*

The Cat and Mouse Game

The scene we worked on comprised the medial segment of a long-winded chase between Brian O' Connor (played by Paul Walker) and a skin-headed, Hispanic juvenile (Cesar Garcia). The scene occurs toward the end of Act I, during the introduction of Paul Walker's character. Undercover agent O'Connor chases the juvenile through streets, corridors, and across apartment rooftops. The thug then ravages his way through an outdoor swap meet before scurrying into the last building and being taken down by the pursuing FBI agent.

The marketplace scene was ours for the day. Two hours after checking in, they led the extras to the set and positioned us all around the swap meet. By this time, I had already greeted Jonathan and chitchatted with him about life and work. He was very glad that I had gained interest in evangelism and showed progress in other areas of my spiritual walk as well. I informed him that I had even purchased some of the Living Waters tracts a week earlier. I suppose I confessed this in some way to make myself look more like a faithful participant in God's ministry.

Despite my outward appearance of readiness, Jonathan knew I was a novice, so he took me under his wing that day to show me how to use the resources effectively. The plan was for him to engage in conversations with people while I stood nearby like a pupil and observed the encounters. This turned out to be extremely helpful not only in learning the structured gospel presentation, but also in knowing how to counteract some prevalent objections to Christianity.

To my befuddlement, our first prospect happened to be one of the principle actors. Jonathan and I met Cesar Garcia (a.k.a. the juvenile) at the craft service station shortly before we started shooting. Contrary to his outward appearance, Cesar was a courteous and well-bred gentleman. I wasn't too familiar with Cesar at the time because of his low-profile credentials. I didn't even know he was one of the principles until he happened to mention it.

Moments before, a bald-headed, thug-like man had performed repeated stunts of falling onto a pile of cardboard from an elevated steel fence. I figured he was definitely one of the principles for the production. When Jonathan and I encountered Cesar, we noticed that he bore a striking resemblance to the principle thug in complexion and apparel, so we figured he was probably the stunt double.

Cesar corrected our misconception when he said in a cool yet modest tone, "No, I'm the principle. The other guy is my stunt double."

What a slick declaration, I thought. I figured Cesar's statement was valid, considering he was a slightly better-looking man than the one who performed all the stunts. As sad as it is to say, Hollywood is all about appearances.

After Cesar shared a bit more about his involvement with the film, Jonathan nimbly shifted the conversation to the spiritual realm by making a casual reference to Mr. Garcia's costume prop. Around Cesar's neck was a large silver chain with a bulky, glittering cross hanging from it. Jonathan asked Cesar if he was really a Christian or had any related background. Unfortunately, Cesar claimed to be agnostic, although he had been raised Roman Catholic in the early years of his life.

Jonathan knew the time was right to share the Word. He began his gospel presentation by taking Cesar through the law. That meant he asked Cesar if he had kept any number of the Ten Commandments. He inquired if Cesar had ever lied or stolen, along with other questions similar to those Jonathan had asked me in our first encounter. This method reveals sin effectively and shows that no one can merit salvation by his or her own works, since every person must be held accountable for his/her crimes before a perfect Judge. The law shows the reality of a perfectly righteous God and why sinners desperately need a Savior. It's the law that illustrates how the good news (the gospel) makes sense and it explains why Jesus is the only way to heaven.

Predictably, Cesar admitted to breaking all of God's laws, yet this reality did not rock his sense of security. Each time Jonathan mentioned heaven and hell, Cesar sanguinely brushed off the idea and asserted that heaven and hell are here on earth as an intimate state of mind. He further described hell as a haunting vision he used to observe of himself when he led a former lifestyle of engaging in drugs, theft, criminality, and other insidious practices. Cesar's past life somewhat resembled the character he played!

Jonathan attempted to persuade Cesar in acknowledging how much more terrifying the literal hell could be compared to his figurative hell and past problems. Then Jonathan posed a thought-provoking analogy by asking Cesar, "Would you sell one of your eyes for a million dollars?"

Mr. Garcia chuckled and replied, "Oh no."

"How about selling both of them for fifty million dollars?"

"Definitely not."

"That's because your eyes are so precious and priceless to you. No person in his or her right mind would sell them, yet your eyes are merely the windows into your soul. If your eyes are worth that much to you, then how much more must your soul be worth? Jesus said in Mark 8:36, 'What does it profit a man to gain the whole world, and forfeit his soul?' You're saying you don't care if you take a gamble and end up in hell?"

Cesar chuckled a bit. He was steadfast in his undaunted perception as he replied, "I appreciate what you're trying to do, but like I said, I know what hell is like. I used to see hell every day in the mirror when my life was messed up. Now that I've cleaned myself up, I make my own way through life, and I live for my children. I've changed my ways."

In one final attempt to help his prospect see the depths of his grave predicament, Jonathan brought up the law once again by asking, "Well, do you still lie?"

Cesar resolutely replied, "Oh no, I don't lie anymore. At least I try not to."

"Do you still steal?"

"No, I don't steal anymore."

There was nothing much more Jonathan could do. He thanked Cesar for his time and encouraged him to think about his salvation since tomorrow was never a guarantee for anyone. It was a relief to see that Cesar maintained a positive attitude the entire time. This subject matter could have easily stirred pandemonium, especially when the prospect is more prominent in the production team. Cesar, however, was gracious to us.

After Cesar shook hands with us and walked away, a sudden query popped into my head. I quickly called out to Cesar, who was still only a short distance away. As the principle actor turned to me, I asked, "I was just wondering, you said you were messed up before but now you've gotten your life back together. What caused you to change?"

Cesar replied with an optimistic smile, "It was my kids." Cesar left it at that as he turned and walked on.

The purpose of my question to Mr. Garcia was to see if there was a possible correlation between religion and morality. Most of the stories I've heard in the past regarding behavioral reformation attributed the cause to Christianity or finding the love of Jesus Christ. In Cesar's case, it wasn't God who caused the revolution, but his children. His kids apparently acted as his savior—at least for today.

I find it amazing how love can transform the heart of even the vilest soul on the planet to become the greatest of saints. I was dismayed that Cesar didn't experience this love in the context of both his children and God's grace. I say this not so much to boost Mr. Garcia's happiness, but for his eternal condition. For indeed, what shall it profit a man if he (Cesar) gains the whole world (children and fame) yet forfeits his soul? It's especially disheartening to imagine that his children may go to heaven without their father, or perhaps his children will be deprived of going to heaven too. Eternal separation between family members is a monumental tragedy.

Like the criminal he portrayed in the film, Cesar was currently on the run, much like the rest of the unredeemed sinners in the world. He may be a fast mouse, but the cat will eventually catch him. The pursuer isn't a mere FBI agent, but God Almighty Himself, the divine law enforcer of the eternal realm, and His justice will be hard.

I pray that Mr. Garcia will take up Jesus' offer of mercy before it is too late.

Hanging with the Big Boys

Back at the holding facility, I took a little time to reflect on the incident that had transpired earlier. Jonathan informed me that Cesar wasn't the first principle actor to whom he had witnessed. In fact, Mr. Khan had proselytized some other prominent celebrities in the past, some of whom are highly influential figures in global media. My curiosity was piqued as I asked Jonathan to elaborate on some of his stories.

One of Jonathan's most considerable anecdotes was his past encounter with director Steven Spielberg! Yes, the same Spielberg who is known for producing such worldwide hits as *Raiders of the Lost Ark*, *E.T.*, *Schindler's List*, and *Saving*

Private Ryan! However, it was on a lower profile Spielberg project, *The Terminal*, that Jonathan received his moment of glory with the media mogul.

Jonathan worked *The Terminal* on the very last day of filming, which shot at the Universal Studios lot (the same place I first met him). When the production officially wrapped up at the end of the day, Spielberg bade farewell to some of his colleagues and walked alone to the stage exit. It was there that Jonathan quickly intercepted Mr. Spielberg, jogging up to the famed director before he got to the stage door. Jonathan actually had the opportunity to stand alone with the director at that moment.

Jonathan started by verbally introducing himself to Steven. Then, in a slightly hasty manner, Jonathan reached into his sport coat for something. At this peculiar action, Steven's face froze in terror, as if this unknown man were reaching into his jacket to pull out a concealed firearm. Jonathan's hand heaved back into view to reveal a little pamphlet, or gospel tract, which eased Mr. Spielberg's tension a bit.

Jonathan spent a short time elaborating on the tract and sharing the gospel with the director, then closed by saying, "Steven, I wrote down a scripture verse from the Old Testament: Zechariah 12:10.[12] Read it when you get a chance."

Spielberg reacted with amusement, "Ah, Old Testament. I love this stuff." The two soon ended the conversation by shaking hands. Steven then proceeded out the stage door as intended.

Some can probably attest to Jonathan's Spielberg encounter as a surreal experience. I don't think anyone can disagree with this being the consummate opportunity for an aspiring actor or director to get his resume across, especially to the one who can make fairy tales come true for any commoner. But in Jonathan's case, there was nothing being sought or desired from Spielberg. He wanted no favors, no recognition, and no money. It was just Jonathan looking out for a fellow brother's eternal welfare.

Jonathan's experience with Spielberg displayed a remarkably selfless act in which Khan wanted no remunerative gain in the worldly sense. Jonathan chose to serve the kingdom of God rather than the kingdom of self. Though he may have missed out on any earthly opportunities, Jonathan benefited tremendously in the eternal realm. That is a guarantee from God's Word (Matt. 6:21).[13]

Another one of Jonathan's incredible witnessing opportunities was with actor Dan Aykroyd on the late 1990s TV series, *Soul Man*. Jonathan worked on an episode that shot in Walt Disney Studios in Burbank. Aykroyd played the show's lead character, Mike Weber, and Jonathan was one of the background artists for the day. During the lunch break, Jonathan approached Dan near the set bleachers and started to openly converse with him about casual subjects. Dan was quite friendly and open to dialoguing with Jonathan. Jonathan used such a prime opportunity to eventually bring up Christianity, candidly asking Dan about his religious upbringing.

Since the show centered on the subject of religion, the dialogue seemed pretty fitting for Aykroyd to want to participate in. Aykroyd mentioned that he had been to both Catholic and Presbyterian churches in the past. Dan wasn't too sure what he believed, as he claimed to be open to many theories. Along with belief in God, the actor mentioned that he also believed in the paranormal, such as UFOs and reincarnation. Jonathan immediately sought to parry off all falsehood by sharing the absolute truth of the gospel message with Dan. Jonathan explained that Christ claimed to be the true God and that He never taught reincarnation, but resurrection. Jonathan punched the point of the resurrection, that the future rising of the dead to eternal life was the thing to be watchful for. Aykroyd listened with genuine attentiveness. During this entire conversation, Dan was humble and gracious towards Jonathan, which was surprising, considering principle actors are not obligated to speak with extras to begin with.

I thought the story sounded good up to this point, but it turned out to be even better after Jonathan explained the last half of it. Following the lunch break, the cast and crew returned to the stage set to resume shooting. Aykroyd got on his first position mark, while Jonathan stood across the other side of the room. Aykroyd psyched himself into his character as the film crew raced to finish up last touches on the camera.

Right before the director yelled action, Aykroyd suddenly broke out of character, walked across the room to Jonathan, and asked him in straightforward curiosity, "Tell me more about this resurrection thing."

Jonathan was a bit speechless, but he responded confidently to the actor. It seemed as if Dan was so convicted by Jonathan's words during the lunch break that he wanted to satisfy his newfound curiosity right in the middle of the shoot! The cast, crew, and extras stood in silence and awe as Jonathan and Dan talked openly about spiritual things. It didn't last for merely a few seconds, but for several minutes! Jonathan once again elaborated on the concept of Jesus' divinity and His resurrection as Dan absorbed the revelation with intrigue. Everyone around was truly amazed, even to the point where one background actor, who was Jewish, came up to Jonathan after the scene and wanted to know more about Jesus!

I don't know if Dan ever became a true believer on or after this day, but I do know that he experienced a positive first step in his journey toward salvation. Situations like this show how important it is to boldly proclaim the Word of God and not remain silent about it. Spoken words truly have impact. Romans 10:17 says, "So faith comes from hearing, and hearing by the word of Christ." A clear understanding of the gospel message is what ultimately leads an unbeliever to come to saving faith. Therefore, a Christian is to faithfully do His part in the gospel proclamation and leave the rest up to God in terms of the sinner coming to belief. I sincerely pray that is in God's will for Dan to come to the Savior. Dan would truly be a wonderful addition to the kingdom.

Jonathan finished off his list by naming some of the other mainstream performers he evangelized, including Jackie Chan, Ted Danson, Michael Douglas, Ron Howard, Sylvester Stallone, Orlando Bloom, Jerry Springer, Will Smith, and Robert Downey Jr. He claimed that they were all highly appreciative. While some of them may have already been Christian, it's better to be safe than to be sorry, as the old saying goes.

As I finished digesting these stories, I saw the endless adventures that could possibly come into the world of my personal evangelism. I wondered whether I would have the opportunity to witness to big-name celebrities myself. Would I ever get past the hurdle of my fears and evangelize those with whom I worked? The truth was that I hadn't even given out a gospel tract to any non-Christian yet.

I knew that it would take time for me to comfortably approach actors with the gospel message and hold my ground. Notwithstanding, there was still a half-day left on *Fast and Furious*. As it turned out, more was in store for us.

The Parable of the Angry Atheist

As previously mentioned, the majority of the day's shoot involved the sequence of the thug running raucously through the outdoor swap meet while being chased by the FBI agent, O'Connor. Before the scenario was officially captured on celluloid, a couple of rehearsal sessions were carried out. During this time, Cesar halfheartedly jogged through the vicinity and leaped over merchant stands while causing minimal damage to the accessories. The scene's design was composed of meticulously laid out toys, clothes, and plastic jewelry. The overall picture had been so well arranged that I cringed at the sight of its ultimate destruction.

As the cameras finally rolled for the first take, Cesar quickly metamorphosed into his character. With a beastly attitude, he sprinted through the marketplace and annihilated everything in sight. He knocked down stands, scattered boxes on the floor, and disarranged station tables as the customers gazed on in terror.

At the conclusion of the shot, the crewmembers stepped onto the set to refurbish the environment in preparation for subsequent takes. It only took about a minute to reposition everything. I was surprised because I imagined that it would take much longer than that. The reorganization was not one-hundred-percent perfect, but it seemed good enough to pass off as tidy for the camera.

Some things in life take little time to be restored to their exact or nearly original state, but it is not easy to recover from the after-effect of being proselytized. The gospel message is so piercing that it can break a person to the point where it may take a few hours for him/her to recompose his state of mind. In some instances, the gospel may leave the person forever convicted and embracing Christianity or defaming it for as long as he/she lives.

During the lunch break, I had an opportunity to watch Jonathan witness to a prospect who was indeed rattled by the good news. This was the first time I saw Jonathan's evangelism result in a heated argument. As I ate lunch beside him, the person facing us from across the table (who introduced himself to us as Sam) started conversing with Jonathan in an upbeat manner, even cracking a few coarse jokes. Jonathan responded with his own humorous remark, which Sam laughed at and slapped Jonathan a high five.

I initially thought that Jonathan would keep the discourse grounded in secular topics for once, but I was dead wrong. Within a minute, Jonathan inquired about Sam's religious upbringing. Sam revealed that he was a former Catholic turned atheist. Jonathan wasted no time in taking the man through the law. Sam cooperated and admitted, somewhat shamelessly, to breaking all of the named commandments.

Jonathan's goal was to conjure up a sense of remorse and humility within Sam by reaffirming his guilt through the law so that he, in turn, saw the need for grace. Tragically, the result backfired. Sam became agitated at the thought of Jonathan's help, because the confrontation appeared as an affront to his sense of pride and self-righteousness.

Sam attempted to debunk Christianity and religion by delineating the truth in evolutionary theory, as well as highlighting the hypocrisy that exists within the religious body. Jonathan rebounded by arguing for the case of creationism, pointing to the beauty, design, and complexity of earthly elements as reasonable proof of an intelligent creator. Consequently, Jonathan advocated the futility of any objective truths apart from the nature, will, glory, and character of God. It was apparent that Jonathan had trained himself painstakingly in the art of apologetics (the study of defending one's faith).

Sam's irritation escalated with Jonathan's every word, and he was no longer as blithe as he had been a few minutes before. He was now convicted to a near state of wanting to stone Jonathan had he been living in the apostolic age. For the next five minutes, Jonathan continued to reason with him as Sam became more ardent in anger and self-justification. It seemed like the conversation (or argument) was about to get out of hand.

A production assistant suddenly intervened, called for the remaining extras to board the white van and be shuttled back to the set. Jonathan had no choice but to close the debate. He bowed out by compassionately offering Sam a *Good Person Test* tract, exhorting him to consider the reality of heaven and hell.

Sam flashed a smirk and sarcastically remarked, "That's okay. I'm fine." He refused to take the tract, arose from his seat, and marched to the shuttle van.

I was surprised to have witnessed such an intense moment. With Sam gone, Jonathan and I briefly discussed the experience before riding back to the set.

Jonathan exclaimed, "Did you see how I brought up the law, but he didn't want to humble himself before God? He just walked away. He's just like the rich young ruler, Steve. The ruler walked away before Jesus could tell him the good news, because he wasn't willing to have a humble and repentant heart."

At the time, I wasn't entirely familiar with the story of the rich young ruler,[14] but Jonathan's statement struck me deeply. Perhaps it was because of how he could relate to modern living situations in connection with ancient Scripture; or maybe it was the illusion that Jonathan resembled the way Christ dealt with infidels. Needless to say, I was impressed. A disciple's life suddenly seemed very cool!

Million Dollar Payday

The remaining five hours of the day were devoted to capturing the final end of the swap meet sequence. According to the plot, the thug knocks a security guard down to the concrete floor in the heat of his sprinting. He then swipes the prostrated guard's gun and fires at Detective O'Connor in the cluttered marketplace. O'Connor retreats beneath the tables as the criminal resumes his escape by scurrying into an enclosed alleyway.

Since my presence wasn't required for the shot, I casually observed it from behind the cameraman as the action unfolded several times for different takes and angles. It was exciting to see the thug unload rounds from his handgun because the sound effects were thunderous. The gunfire probably caused the crowd to panic genuinely or at least it instilled a proper stimulation to react in such a manner.

At some point during these takes, I turned around with the intention of seeing what Jonathan was doing. He was caught up in yet another religious debate, this time with two well-groomed men on the set. I soon realized that these two white-shirted, black-tied men were Jehovah's Witnesses, who had stumbled upon the set during their habitual scout for co-opts. As composed as each side tried to be, Jonathan and the Jehovah's Witnesses were engaged in a proselytizing war. It was a competitive match of ideologies!

Considering that he held the keys to the truth of God's Word, it appeared that Jonathan had the upper hand. Still, the Jehovah's Witnesses repeatedly countervailed while bearing optimistic grins on their faces, as if hinting that Jonathan was a sick patient living in an illusory world. The verbal bout stretched on like a ping-pong game. Jonathan's passion glowed more fervently with every passing second as he continued to argue for the inerrancy of God's Word and faith (not works) as the only way to justification.

This incident was just too fascinating not to mention, as it fully demonstrates Jonathan's unending devotion to such evangelism. The guy never stops evangelizing, no matter what the situation may be! I hardly ever see Christians proselytize Jehovah's Witnesses, Mormons, or any other heretical "Christians." But now I had seen it in all its brazen glory. What an inspiring moment!

A few hours later, I got an unexpected chance to stand in the evangelistic spotlight as well. It wasn't as formidable as the undertakings of Jonathan, yet it was probably the most conspicuous in terms of opportunity. When the production officially wrapped up at 5:48 P.M., Jonathan and I lingered on the set because of my sudden whim to greet the director, Justin Lin. I figured that since I was already close to the director's presence, I should meet him before I leave.

As I ruminated on ideas for how to approach the director, an epiphany suddenly came to Jonathan. He suggested, "Hey, why don't you hand the director your *Million Dollar Bill*? Come on, give it a shot!"

Jonathan had given me a *Million Dollar Bill* tract earlier in the day to keep as a gift. I had it in my pocket the entire time, yet I hadn't anticipated handing it to the director. I felt a slight degree of hesitation and fear at such a thought.

I asked Jonathan, "Are we allowed to do that?"

Jonathan replied, "Why not? The day is over, right? We'll meet him together!"

The plan was set. We both progressed deliberately toward the film director in the near distance. I wasn't fearful because of the situation's suitability. I was fearful because of fear itself! I had never witnessed to anyone in my life, let alone a well-known figure in the entertainment industry. What I was about to do was comparable to being implored to enter an ominously dark tunnel. I wanted to begin with the game plan, but I recoiled slightly in my physical emotions. As Matthew appropriately states, "The spirit is willing, but the flesh is weak" (Matt. 26:41).

Before approaching the director, I placed the *Million Dollar Bill* tract in my right jeans pocket. I didn't want to have it in sight as if to ambush Mr. Lin with an immediate solicitation. Jonathan and I started by introducing ourselves to Justin. He graciously returned our greeting as we commended him for his diligent work on the project. Justin responded with a predictable sense of gratitude.

My right hand was in my right pocket the whole time, tightly clutching the *Million Dollar Bill*. As Mr. Lin extended his right arm for the closing adieu, I swiftly pulled my right hand out of my pocket, but by some mishap I hauled out the *Million Dollar Bill* as well and when I shook Justin's hand, it was with the paper between our flesh! He looked down on the tract with utter curiosity.

What an embarrassing moment it was for me. I think it's obvious that I should have shaken his hand first and then handed over the tract afterwards. Justin probably felt the awkwardness of the situation as well. He gazed down on it curiously. Attempting to diffuse the feeling, I explained to the director that the tract was a *Million Dollar Bill*. I even joked that I was giving it to him as a gratuity for his diligent work on set. Justin's solemn bewilderment turned into festivity as he uttered a sharp chuckle. Then Jonathan stepped into the conversation and encouraged Justin to read the content on the back of the tract when he had an available moment. The director nodded as he walked away with the bill.

Did I just relay the gospel message to an established film director? I asked myself, coming to terms with reality shortly afterward.

Giving the gospel message to someone was an indescribable feeling. It was intimidating, nerve racking, but ultimately, it was enthralling. One thing I knew for certain was that my action gave glory to God. His will was being done whether the prospect accepted or rejected the message on the tract.

This occasion was my defining moment in evangelism because I had given out a gospel tract for the very first time. It also happened that my very first prospect was a major Hollywood figure, director Justin Lin!

Chapter 6

THE FIRE BURNS

THE LORD'S SUMMONING of His disciples significant-
ly characterized His early ministry. All of His chosen
candidates responded without hesitation or concern for
their immediate circumstances. One such account attests to
this as described when Jesus "went out and noticed a tax
collector named Levi sitting in the tax booth, and He said
to him, 'Follow Me.' And he left everything behind, and got
up and began to follow Him" (Luke 5:27-28).

Levi, also known as the apostle Matthew, disowned his
worldly profession on the spot, and in a sense, forfeited his
reputation and potential for accrued wealth. Why did Levi
respond in such a reckless manner? It was because Levi
knew that Christ held the keys to life abundant. The Master
summoned his services, and the servant responded with
obedience. It is this childlike faith that drove financially
prosperous, yet spiritually impoverished, publicans like
Matthew to relinquish everything for the sake of pursuing
God's kingdom.

My newfound desire to follow my Lord can be somewhat likened to that of Matthew, Simon Peter and his brother Andrew, James and John, sons of Zebedee, and the other apostles who boarded the Jesus bandwagon. Before my evangelistic on-fire mode started in 2008, the Lord continually prompted my heart with the words, "Follow Me," but I failed to comply wholeheartedly. In the early half of 2008, I rose up out of my comfort and security space (as did Matthew from his tax booth in Matthew 9:9), and abruptly left everything behind to follow Yeshua. My instincts kicked into gear and I suddenly became guided by the same childlike faith that led the apostles and other faithful Christians to a life of devotion, adoration, and servitude.

My spiritual perception drastically changed because of my newfound comprehension of the gospel. *Living Waters Ministry* was a pivotal vessel that the Lord used to help me understand His holy nature, and why His Son is the only means to enter the kingdom of heaven. I understood the reason I had to undertake evangelism with more fervor. As encouraging as *The Way of the Master* program is in equipping and inspiring the children of God to share their faith, there is no amount of televised messages that can ever match the inspiration of a friend's personal testimony. As you can probably surmise, it was this living testimony that I have been highlighting in the last couple of chapters.

I am blessed to give Jonathan Khan due credit for his practical influence in my newfound passion for the Lord Jesus Christ. If there were ever a prime example of a Christian's actions changing an observer's spiritual path for the better, then Jonathan would be it. It is because of Jonathan that I learned the value of modeling the Christian faith to others in the hope that they will prosper as well.

Dances with Wolves

There are sporadic occasions when I call on Jonathan for his discernment on certain Christian topics or to keep apprised of his missionary agendas. On one casual day a couple weeks after the *Fast and Furious* shoot, Jonathan and I had a phone conversation in which we discussed biblical passages, apologetics, and the duty of Christians to bear a life of fruitful servitude. I praised Jonathan once again for his determination to share the gospel with high-profile celebrities, referring to our experience on *Fast and Furious*.

During the conversation, Jonathan informed me about another celebrity witnessing experience. It was with the actor Harrison Ford. Unlike the other encounters in which the principle actors received the gospel message with graciousness or indifference, the interaction with Mr. Ford ended on a rather distasteful note. I pressed my cell phone tightly to my ear and eagerly waited for Jonathan's intriguing anecdote.

Jonathan's encounter with superstar Harrison Ford occurred on the 2009 independent drama, *Crossing Over*. The production called for Jonathan to work as a nondescript extra. He arrived for his early morning call time and checked in with the crew. Two hours after settling in, he saw Harrison Ford grab breakfast from the catering truck and then make his way back to his trailer with his meal in hand.

Guided by the prompting of the Holy Ghost, Jonathan marched up to Mr. Ford's trailer and knocked on the door. The voice from inside thundered, "Yes, come in!"

Complying with the order, Jonathan ascended the staircase, heaved open the trailer door, and walked right into Harrison's station!

I don't think I am alone when I say that it is absurd, possibly even career suicide for a background artist to do something like this. It may even be unprecedented! Whether you believe it or not, Jonathan stood in the unit alone with the film legend, Harrison Ford—Han Solo—Indiana Jones—himself.

Jonathan and Harrison started the conversation by greeting each other in a somewhat conventional sense. Harrison probably thought Jonathan was a PA or some other crewmember, which explains why Jonathan's access was so mysteriously fluid. In any case, this situation worked to Jonathan's advantage.

As Harrison returned to his table to eat his breakfast, Jonathan switched gears and asked Mr. Ford, "Hey, Harrison, I saw a recent interview where a news reporter asked if you were missing something in life, even though you have fame, money, and such. You said you didn't have peace."

Jonathan pulled out a *Good Person Test* tract and handed it to Mr. Ford. He said, "Take the Good Person Test. This may be the peace you're looking for."

Harrison projected a blank stare at Jonathan while egg scraps dangled from the side of his mouth. With nothing further to supplement his case, Jonathan bade Mr. Ford farewell and walked out of the trailer.

When Jonathan descended the steps, a female production assistant approached him. The PA had a bewildered expression as she inquired, "What were you doing in Harrison's trailer?"

Jonathan replied in a jauntily naïve sense, "He invited me in."

The PA was speechless, presumably because principle actors rarely give such intimate attention to extras. Jonathan then walked back to the background holding station.

About a half-hour later, the extras were summoned for the day's first shot on the streets of metropolitan Los Angeles. As the background players were being disseminated to their respective posts, a female assistant director suddenly pulled Jonathan aside, guiding him into an open alley. Jonathan and the AD stood out of public view as the AD proceeded to explain the situation to him.

The supervisor said, "We don't appreciate your giving Harrison that little booklet. I'm going to have to ask you to leave set."

She fired Jonathan on the spot. It's uncertain whether it was Harrison who got flustered or if the film crew over-reacted. Either way, Jonathan was sent home without pay that day. After the termination sentence, Jonathan returned his wardrobe to the staff at the costume trailer, packed up his possessions, and left the set.

It's not every day I hear a story like this. As I took time to digest the impact of it, I asked, "Were you upset or scared—being fired like that?"

Jonathan replied, "Hey, at least I got to eat my breakfast!"

We both burst out laughing. As tragically funny as this tale might seem, it ultimately showed me the depth of Jonathan's heart and how much the salvation of the lost meant to him, even if such prospects are famous people. The mood of the discourse gradually shifted to a more meaningful tone as Jonathan illustrated the motives behind undertaking such a career-threatening mission.

Jonathan explained, "I have every reason to refuse reaching out to others in God's name. I could just serve myself and the world instead. While I may be acting now, I also write screenplays, and someday I hope to play a lead role in them—under God's perfect timing. Yes, it's great fun to act and write, and I sincerely hope to make it big in Hollywood for God's glory, but you know what, Steve? I'm not prepared to hold onto it at the expense of service to my Lord."

Jonathan concluded his account with a remark that knocked me flat on the ground. He stated, "It's more important for me to save one man's soul than to save my own career."

A New Beginning

Jonathan's quote echoes in my mind even to this day. It teaches me to always value the importance of a single soul, no matter how insignificant the person may appear. It prompts me to always sacrifice my own desires and interests to help others see the truth of the gospel. In essence, it inspires me to always regard the will of God higher than that of my own.

I found Jonathan's devotion to the Lord to be overwhelmingly original, inspiring, and peerless. For him to advocate that a single soul was more significant than the highest accolades in the world was groundbreaking for me to hear at the time. I haven't met anyone in my life who acted on, said, or even believed in what Jonathan held dear to his heart. Who would be ludicrous enough to give up an extravagant career for the sake of helping to save just one person? I'm certain that this form of philanthropy is a hard pill even for Christians to swallow.

Jonathan was truly the embodiment of a selfless man. His life transcended everything that I've ever seen or experienced in a Christian. I felt as if one of the apostles or even John the Baptist had sprung to life right before my very eyes! I always pray earnestly that the Lord will bring forth more laborers like Jonathan Khan. Jonathan's humanitarian lifestyle and his love for Father God moved me to such an extent that I wanted to be everything he represented, and so I started my quest.

After March 2008, the one and only thing I obsessed over was my Messiah. I started reading my Bible again—a glorious recrudescence after more than ten years. I read through the Bible for the first time in my life. I also began listening to Christian music, which was something I had never done in the past. I delighted in the tunes of such contemporary artists as Casting Crowns, Chris Tomlin, Mercy Me, and Aaron Shust to the point where I practically ceased listening to any other music genres. Christian music became too spellbinding and emotionally uplifting for me to want to go back to anything else. It kept my disposition from faltering, especially in the many days that required a clear focus to evangelize and live righteously in the face of opposing darkness.

If this weren't enough spiritual progress, my involvement with church also took on a new platform. I began to serve in departments such as the welcoming committee, the outreach ministry, and the elementary school service as a Sunday school teacher. I even was officially baptized on April 20 of that year. It was truly joyful for me to have undertaken baptism in that particular time. If I had pledged to the ritual before that, my covenant with the Lord would have been in vain. My heart was not yet as prepared to commit itself to His will as it became in April 2008.

Out of all the spiritual fruits that burgeoned during this special year, the one that I was most fond of was the fruit of witnessing. I can confidently say that it was the evangelist mentality that initially caused me to seek spiritual growth. It is what inspired me to participate in daily Bible devotionals, serve in ministry, and consciously veer away from as many sins as possible.

As an ambassador for Christ—one who figuratively wears an emblem on his chest—I had a duty to exemplify the essence of that gospel message to the people I was trying to win over. I needed to "walk the walk" and add legs to my words. Slowly, but surely, I became a new creation every day. Just hearing myself preach the great gospel involving God's law, His righteousness, Jesus' vicarious death for sinners, salvation by grace, turning from lawlessness, and becoming a new, fruitful creation always motivated me to be the best Christian I could possibly be. My missionary focus, as well as my zeal to attain apologetic and theological knowledge for the purpose of helping the spiritually blind, caused me to delve into Christianity in a way I could have never imagined. Choosing evangelism as my starting point for serving the Lord was a superb blessing, and I praise the Lord every day for it.

People usually tell me that practical evangelism is one of the most difficult steps on the discipleship ladder, and that it usually serves as the last practice for new Christians to master. How ironic that this step represented the first stage in my spiritual growth. Everything else seemed relatively easy thereafter. That is why I believe it's important for Christians to build a solid foundation in the evangelism lifestyle. You would be surprised to see how much impetus it will give you to undertake all other areas of service to the Lord and to His band of believers. It will definitely foster a mindset that surpasses anything that international, short-term mission programs can temporarily provide you. It is a joy and a will that transcends all human understanding.

I started sharing my faith in every walk of my life in early 2008. I proselytized my family and friends. I evangelized people at work, restaurants, banks, markets, beaches, and theme parks. I even brought my evangelistic zeal to my vacations and witnessed to the hotel staff, city vendors, and tour guides. My excursions to such destinations as Maui, Cancun, and San Francisco had somehow become unofficial mission trips, where I took God's good message all around the globe!

Reflecting on this particular year, I knew that I was never going to be the same person again. I had changed. I thought about the Lord all the time. I praised His name in my dreams. I looked for new ways to serve Him. I had literally become on fire for God in ways that bewitched the minds of my Christian comrades. The old me had unpredictably vaporized into oblivion, and I had replaced it with an apostle-like alter ego.

For once in my life, I genuinely felt that my existence had some real meaning. In providing wholehearted charity to the Lord as well as to my neighbors, I finally discovered who I was. I understood why I existed. I am not simply promoting another subjective, meaning-of-life principle based on relativistic notions. I am stating a fact that goes far beyond my personal and intimate state of being.

We all search for the ultimate, objective answer to the big "why" of life, and my testimony constitutes one example. God created us to love and serve Him in addition to loving and serving our brethren. This is the meaning of life. I don't say this merely out of my personal feelings. I can concretely declare it because Scripture supports it as well. This affirmation pertains to every person living on earth. The only way anyone can ever acknowledge the truth of this claim is by allowing the Holy Spirit to work through his or her heart. Only then will the truth set them free from ignorance and guide them into the light of life.

The newfound passion in my life has provided me with unending satisfaction that no other earthly element can. No longer do I have any reason to feel fearful, disoriented, angry, or hopeless in such an insane world. There is more to this life than just mammon, fame, jobs, disease, and death. There is an answer. That answer is Christ Jesus, the higher Person who loves me with an infinite love and gives me the hope of residing in His presence for all eternity. He gives me a reason to wake up every day. He also gave me a passion to love and serve Him day and night by following His command to seek and save the lost.

I vowed to not waste time in living out God's command. As my first mission assignment, I chose to take on Hollywood, however bold it may seem to a beginning evangelist. Piercing the darkness of a decadent industry with the light of reformative truth was surely ambitious and challenging. I didn't know how much the spiritual culture of Hollywood would be transformed by my actions, but I had faith in God's power. With the Lord's help, no mission is impossible.

Jesus Who?

It was just a little over a week after my *Fast and Furious* gig when I was assigned my next job and was ready to rock n' roll. This occasion differed from my previous engagements in that I was no longer lukewarm in reaching out to the lost. My motivation for action didn't come and go at will. I now began keeping an eye out for evangelistic opportunities and was determined to carry out my plans with or without Jonathan Khan's help.

As anticipated, my newfound awareness to my outreach responsibility caused the world around me to expand to dauntingly great proportions. Now, I felt alone and timid. There seemed to be monsters everywhere willing to devour me if I tried to invade their territory with such a blinding light, but I had to swallow my fears. I needed to propel myself to action. I knew that Jonathan would not always be there to hold my hand. Therefore, it was mandatory to learn how to start witnessing on my own.

My first day out on the missionary field was on the set of *Samantha Who?* I looked at the experience as an experimental and even rehearsal moment as I anticipated that I would make mistakes. But as a mentor once advised me, "It's okay, Steve. Go out! Make mistakes! Fail! That's the only way you're ever going to get better at your craft."

The *Samantha Who?* production took place at the Los Angeles Center Studios in downtown Los Angeles. It wasn't long after my 8:30 A.M. registration that I had my first spiritual conversation with a prospect. Elaine was a married woman in her mid-thirties, sported glasses, and worked as a schoolteacher. What concerned me most was the fact that she was an atheist—someone who does not believe in God's existence. That was a very challenging prospect for a first-time evangelist!

I proceeded with care and patience, attempting to explain the reason for God by pointing to the universe itself. I asked Elaine how everything in the world could be so thoroughly ordered, perfect, well-designed, and meaningful. Could it have all happened by random chance? As Ray Comfort would say, "If there is a painting, then at some point, there must have been a painter. If a building exists, then there surely must have been a builder." They cannot both manifest on their own. The two scenarios represent an intelligent force behind the works.

I asked Elaine, "If creation exists, don't you think there must have been a creator or a designer?"

She replied, "Nope."

Elaine's response took me by surprise. I was just a bit dumbfounded that she couldn't see a concept that seemed so apparent to me and to many other people. If Elaine couldn't even get past the blinder of God's nonexistence, then it would be almost meaningless for me to begin talking about His redemptive plan for humanity. I didn't know what else to say at this point, since I was still young in my knowledge of apologetics. My first instinct was to provide some resources for Elaine to absorb in her spare time. I reached into my bag and pulled out some tracts, which included a couple of brochures and a sermon CD that covered the topics of atheism and disbelief. To my surprise, she accepted them willingly. Usually, I find that non-religious people, especially atheists, reject offers of this nature with a pessimistic attitude, but it appeared that Elaine was a little more magnanimous. It gave me encouragement to continue my missionary agenda.

Our dialogue ended because we were immediately ushered to set. I don't know what became of Elaine, but I pray that the information enlightened her to the truth of the gospel. As long as she can acknowledge that there is a God, everything else about the truth of Christianity should gracefully fall into place.

Show Time

For the first scene that day, Samantha (played by Christina Applegate) exited a building and marched down the sidewalk as taxis and other vehicles cruised by in the background. I was one of the lucky ones to have been booked with my car. I say this only because a fifteen-dollar bonus was added to my wage when my car was used in the shot.

During the intermissions between takes, I had an opportunity to speak with another atheist named Roger. Roger hailed from Tennessee and was another one of the multitudes to arrive in Southern California with intentions of striking Hollywood gold. In his case, however, it wasn't going to be in acting, but with producing films. He appeared to be doing acting as a part-time gig.

I spent the first few minutes getting to know Roger, his upbringing, and his future goals in the business. Then I brought up the topic of God by asking Roger if there were many churchgoers in Tennessee. He answered with an exaggerated affirmation, as if to indicate that he was pestered by the reality of Christendom in his former hometown. Roger's response was humorous in the sense that it supported the claim that this region in America was indeed the Bible Belt.

Roger and I continued to converse about Christianity. As we talked, I listened intently, trying to understand why Roger didn't believe in God and was disinterested in religion. He didn't appear to be antagonistic toward the system, he was just indifferent. As I strove to learn more about his thoughts, the PA suddenly called for us to reposition for the continuation of the shot, thus our conversation was cut off.

Although my momentum was abruptly halted, I didn't let that stop me from finishing my deal with Roger. I was able to reconnect with my prospect after the scene was completed. I handed him a couple of tracts regarding the scientific and prophetic accuracies of the Holy Bible. These two pamphlets were the *Scientific Facts in the Bible* and *101 Last Days Prophecies* from Living Waters. They represent some of the costlier tracts within the selection pool, but I was more than willing to invest the money if the material was potent enough to transform lives. I just needed to be sagacious in who received them. I didn't really want these materials to end up as dumpster food.

I thought that Tennessee man may have been my last prospect for the day, but it turned out that there was one more soul in store for me much later that afternoon. Near the end of the workday, the drivers were ordered to remain in their cars until their services were rendered for the last scene. Since I was a driver, I immediately hopped into my vehicle.

As I sat in my Honda Accord, with my palms on the steering wheel, I glanced to the left to observe the actions of the adjacent female driver. I immediately noticed that she had a cross pendant dangling from her vehicle's rearview mirror. With great curiosity and courage, I stepped out of my car, hovered over the passenger's side of her vehicle, and inquired about the pendent. She responded peaceably, explaining that the pendent was not actually hers but an adornment that was left in the vehicle when she purchased the secondhand car.

I casually asked, "Do you believe in God?"

She said, "Yes." Then I asked her if she was a Christian. She replied, "No," but claimed to have followed her god through the practice of Kabbalah. I didn't know too much about that religion, only that it was a mystical thought of Judaism made popular by the songstress, Madonna.

I candidly asked her whether she was going to heaven or not. She said that she believed so because she prayed to her god somewhat habitually and in some sense had a relationship with him. Knowing that she prayed to a god that was not the God of Scripture, I asked whether she was familiar with Jesus Christ. Astonishingly, she wasn't! I had assumed that most citizens in America knew or at least had heard of Jesus' death and resurrection, yet this woman knew nothing about Jesus Christ.

I was now obliged to explain the gospel to her. It was actually my first oral presentation of the message that day. I gave her a brief synopsis of Jesus' deity, death, resurrection, and offer of grace for her sins. She listened intently, all the while nodding with sustainable interest. I detected that she was intrigued, but definitely not convicted of her sinful nature or need for a Savior. I should have taken her through the Law of God, much like Jonathan did with sinners, yet I was afraid to do so. It seemed too touchy and personal, but this turned out to be a faulty decision, as I will discuss in Chapter 10.

Detecting that the film crew was about to roll camera, I left this woman with one final message, "Please think about what I just said. You may not know it, but the cross that hangs in your car has the most beautiful meaning. It represents life."

The woman nodded kindly. I thought it was a good idea to leave a couple of tracts with her before departing, and I did. She turned out to be my last prospect of the day. My spiritual labor was complete, as was my physical work an hour later with the conclusion of the final scene.

It was ironic that the physical condition of the show's principle character—amnesia—symbolized the spiritual condition of all my prospects. These background artists were as clueless to the knowledge of God as Samantha was to memories of her past. Talk about the coexistence and cooperation of physical and spiritual amnesia.

It was somewhat baffling the way in which I was able to manage three encounters in one day, when up to that point, it was the most evangelizing I had done in my entire life, all on the first day of my spiritual job! I knew that it might well be the start of something big. I was anxious to learn what might be next on my agenda.

THE INSIDER'S SCOOP

A FAMOUS QUOTE DERIVED from a mid-90s film, *Forrest Gump*, continues to beguile the world even to this day. It goes something like this: "Life is like a box of chocolates. You never know what you're gonna get."

Life is truly as unpredictable as the assortment of confections found concealed in a box of chocolates. Each new day brings about its blessings, its vices, its conundrums, and even its voids. The day could offer unilateral extremes or even a combination of everything. Sometimes it is impossible to find meaning in the scattered details until one ultimately examines the big picture at the end of life.

The career of a background artist also captures the essence of Forrest Gump's proverb in numerous ways. An extra's schedule is unpredictable. Every day he gets booked onto a different production about which he knows nothing. He may work with a brand-new set of people or with a familiar pack of wolves. He does not know where he will go, what he will eat, or whom he will influence. Life is ultimately in the sovereign palm of Jehovah God.

(**Note**: The story I'm about to tell contains pseudonyms for the actors, location, and production title involved. One of the actors involved preferred to remain anonymous, so I honored his wishes. Whether it is Vin Diesel, Mel Gibson, or James Franco, I leave the imagination of these actors' identity and popularity up to the readers. However, I will say that they are pretty renowned figures in the acting business).

On March 2008, I obtained an odd job for the television phenomenon, Smash World, in which I worked in an AFTRA (American Federation of Television and Radio Artists) position for the first time. AFTRA is a union association (much like Screen Actors Guild) for principle talents, extras, and musicians. It was exciting for me to acquire a union job, because the pay was much higher than the standard non-union rate. On this day, my wage was an astounding one hundred and fifty dollars for eight hours.

Another unique, if not abashing, element of the Smash World gig was my categorization as an Asian ping-pong player. I only declare this as embarrassing because I previously had harbored a slight aversion to playing stereotypical characters. I would much rather be grouped in an undistinguished, ethnically neutral category than play a standout Asian. In this case, however, I didn't really mind as much because the pay was vastly superior to that of my everyday wages.

Regardless of the quirks and job description, I want to illustrate this particular account with Smash World to highlight a rare spiritual encounter involving one of the principle performers. It was unusual in that I had an unhindered opportunity to converse with this gentleman about God on a Hollywood set—an incident somewhat similar to what happened between Jonathan Khan and Dan Aykroyd. To top it off, my dialogue with this person actually built a bridge that led him closer to Jesus Christ within a year's time!

This extraordinary outcome confirms a spiritual axiom. The missionary life, especially in tinsel town, is a box of chocolates in and of itself. You never know what prospects God will place in your life. One day it may be an extra and the next day it could be an A-list actor.

Whatever the circumstance, God is on target with His people, and I am more than willing to delve into every one of His selections.

Gearing Up for the Play

After checking into the production studios in Hollywood at 8 A.M., I was immediately ushered into a waiting room with the rest of the background artists, all anticipating they would be garbed in "appropriate attire." It would be sarcastic for me to say that I looked forward to it. Most extras do not like wearing set wardrobe because they have to borrow it in exchange for their vouchers, and those vouchers cannot be reclaimed until after returning the costumes at the end of the day. In addition, the costumes can be fairly disgusting, and sometimes uncomfortable to wear.

This was definitely the case on this specific day. After thirty minutes of waiting, the PA finally entered the room and led us to the wardrobe department. As the staff handed me my garb, I cringed in horror as I gazed at a set of tacky purple tank tops and short shorts—or in modern American vernacular, "booty shorts."

After we finished suiting up, we were immediately shuttled to location. It was a thirty-minute drive to the park location in Pasadena. This was by far the longest shuttle ride I had ever taken to any set. Upon arriving at the commodious region on the hills, I noticed that there was only one prop on the grass field—a ping-pong table. Overall, the day's crew size was small. I liked that. This made the relationships among the extras and more prominent staff more pliable than if they had staffed the production more exorbitantly.

One of the things I enjoyed most about this day was the fact that most of the background players appeared to be Christian. One of them by the name of Paul Kwak introduced himself to me after overhearing one of my evangelism encounters with a background artist during the pre-wardrobe down time. I briefly acquainted myself with Paul and learned that he was a faithful man of God. He appeared to be very active at his church and he too was interested in evangelism. In fact, we connected to the point where we became friends and have stayed in touch to this day.

The Smash World episode consisted of three main performers: Jimmy D, Rex Logan, and Xavier Tash. The park scene was part of a drama-like satire in which two men waged war for the love of a woman. The show's regular, Jimmy D, portrayed the humble, warmhearted good guy, while Xavier personified the confident villain, King Nebo. After the maelstrom, the two men decide on the fate of the woman by engaging in a final showdown—a ping-pong match officiated by the referee played by Rex Logan.

The match was our shooting agenda for the day. The extras watched from the side of the field as spectators while Xavier and Jimmy D rocked the ball to and fro in their intense bout. The scene was hilarious in that there appeared to be so much at stake, and all of it hung on the outcome of this trifling game. The hero and villain played as if their lives depended on it. Talk about a serious drama!

It was a good thing we all got a much-needed break shortly after the match.

THE KINGLY WELCOME

What occurred next was unanticipated and had not happened to me before. As I was grazing at the food table under a tree during our brief recess, the actor who portrayed King Nebo, Xavier Tash, walked up and started conversing with me. I declare this act as unprecedented because it is not the usual practice for a primary actor to speak with background players on their own initiative. The opposite is far more likely to happen should a background artist be brazen enough to make the first move and risk trouble, as Jonathan Khan did with Harrison Ford.

What an astounding position the Lord had placed me in. Not only did Xavier greet me, but he also asked about my life. One word accurately describes this feeling: Wow!

Xavier and I talked about random topics, which included my life, his life, family, movies, hobbies, and so on. We even discussed the subject of food after I informed the actor that one of my hobbies was reviewing restaurants. He was so impressed with my resume and knowledge of the restaurants in Los Angeles that he requested permission to use one of my reviews for his personal website. Naturally, I obliged. Two months later, one of my Internet restaurant reviews appeared on his website!

Xavier was immersed in culinary arts because he was an impassioned chef himself. In fact, he operated his own bar and grill in Los Angeles named Ranger Grill (another pseudonym), a contemporary fusion eatery that served some great drinks and delicious cuisine. Mr. Tash said he personally designed every selection on the menu, which is why he took great pride in his establishment. He gave such meticulous attention to the quality of the food that he committed himself to attending the restaurant almost every weekend. That certainly was devotion, especially for a busy actor.

The culinary conversation with Xavier intensified as we shifted into discussing Korean BBQ. I started to name some of the elite Korean BBQ establishments in Los Angeles as Xavier listened intently. At that moment, the other principle actor, Jimmy D, who had been sitting at a peripheral distance, unashamedly leaped into our conversation.

Jimmy D asked me, "What's your favorite Korean BBQ restaurant?"

It was amusing that another principle performer was now also conversing with me. I quickly brainstormed a few selections, uncertain how to answer, as I did not want to promote a distasteful joint. I ultimately chose a restaurant that I had enjoyed since childhood.

I replied, "I guess Soot Bull Jeep."

It turned out that I answered Jimmy D's million-dollar question correctly. He replied, "Soot Bull Jeep is my place. That's where I always hang."

That was all Jimmy D needed to hear, and he left me alone with Xavier once again and returned to the ping-pong area. I missed the opportunity to evangelize Jimmy D, but it may have spared me a pink slip. A few days after this happened, I spoke with Jonathan Khan about my Smash World experience and mentioned my succinct discourse with Jimmy D. Jonathan said he had witnessed to Jimmy D when he worked on the show a few years prior.

In the beginning of that particular encounter, Jimmy D told Jonathan that he believed in reincarnation. This indicated that Jimmy D might have had a Buddhist background. Knowing that he couldn't leave the actor in spiritual ignorance, Jonathan proceeded to explain the gospel message to Mr. D. He didn't hold back on any of the controversial points, illustrating even the hard truths of sin, repentance, and hell. This only made Jimmy D uneasy and possibly angry.

After that day, Smash World never called Jonathan to work again. The incident appeared as a blemish on Jonathan's record at the Central Casting Agency. Apparently, Jimmy D reported Jonathan's conduct to the producers, who in turn notified the background artist agency. Mr. D apparently didn't appreciate Jonathan's act of charity, which led to yet another afflicting act on Jonathan's reputation.

As Xavier and I continued to stand on the field during our down time, I asked him about his religious background. It was a bold question, but Xavier was courteous enough to respond. He mentioned that he had a Christian upbringing because his father was a devout minister. Despite his background, however, Xavier admitted that he did not attend church at the time. He implied that his lack of commitment to a congregation was due to his conflicting schedule, both in the film industry and at his restaurant. I supposed that was better than not attending purely out of indolence or defiance. Yet, dishonoring the Sabbath Day isn't good for the soul.

I couldn't predict how pious Xavier was outside of church perimeters, so I bestowed upon him a token of encouragement for him to continue a healthy bond with the Lord. I gave Mr. Tash a comic strip version of the *Good Person Test* tract and stressed the gospel message contained within its pages. Taking the brochure, Xavier gazed down at it in a reserved manner. It wasn't easy to decipher what he was thinking at the moment, but later in the year, I discovered the precise answer to that question.

Attempting to break the silence, I informed Xavier that I wanted him to have the resource so that he could remember the importance of salvation. Mentioning the reality of the entertainment industry's degenerative influences, I encouraged him to stay in faith and always remember the Lord's gift of salvation in the midst of temptations from the negative forces in Hollywood.

Xavier reached out his hand to shake mine and said, "Why, thank you. Thank you so much for your help. I know it's by divine appointment that we met today."

Our conversation ended as we returned to the sports drama. I certainly knew that it was by divine appointment that we drifted into each other's path. The only question was how much spiritual fruit would blossom because of this incident?

The Final Touch

The day turned out to be a very concise one. We wrapped our one and only scene in three hours. Short days are always sweet, especially if you're receiving a substantial wage for them. Such are ideal work outcomes for background artists.

Marching back to the van with the other extras, I noticed Rex Logan walking parallel to me on my right. Mr. Logan played the referee during the melee between the two competing studs. I decided I should share some of my Christian charity one last time.

As Rex and I walked toward the white shuttle van, I casually turned to him and asked, "Hey, Rex, have you taken your *Good Person Test* yet? Check it out."

Rex took the tract and looked at it with a wide grin, seemingly fascinated by the cover page. I can only hope that it spelled good news for his salvation. We both hopped into the vehicle that transported us back to the production studios in Hollywood.

This was quite a memorable occasion for me as a training evangelist. It was even a blessing to converse and work with Paul Kwak, the other dedicated disciple on the set. Out of all the believers I met that day, he was the one who made the most notable impression on me. I knew there was something unique about him, and that he had great potential to change the community for Jesus Christ. Before we parted ways, I gave Paul some of my tracts as a sample collection in the event he might want to purchase them for his own witnessing opportunities. He accepted them with piqued interest.

My conversation with Xavier Tash represented the last time I had such a long and intimate moment with a principle actor about spiritual things, or even about life in a broader sense. I pray that situations like that can happen more often, because we really need to reach out to celebrities with the gospel message. Not only are spiritual dialogues with celebrities a satisfying experience, but the payoff can be unexpectedly grand if the actors/actresses become receptive to God's grace.

I wondered how many other celebrities would treat the Holy Spirit and me with this kind of respect. Little did I know that I would find my next big adventure on the red carpet.

Chapter 8

FACING THE GIANTS

J EREMIAH, THE SON of Hilkiah, was often characterized as the weeping prophet. He once spoke of the
Lord's revelation to him before the start of his ministry
in Judah. From Jeremiah's standpoint, the Word of God came
to him like this: "'Before I formed you in the womb I knew
you, and before you were born I consecrated you; I have
appointed you a prophet to the nations.' Then I said, 'Alas,
Lord GOD! Behold, I do not know how to speak, because I
am a youth.' But the LORD said to me, 'Do not say, "I am a
youth," because everywhere I send you, you shall go, and
all that I command you, you shall speak. Do not be afraid of
them, for I am with you to deliver you,' declares the LORD"
(Jer. 1:5-8).

Fear is an obstacle that soldiers of God constantly face
when confronting ignoble sinners with the truth. Jeremiah
the prophet was one of countless figures to admit this
desolate feeling. In trying to justify his pathos, Jeremiah
exclaimed that he was not qualified to undertake the

Lord's mission for two chief reasons. Jeremiah was without knowledge and he was only a child.

As much as I possess a commonplace zeal to reach out to the ungodly, there are moments when I falter miserably because of an ever-present threat that lingers in my mind. It begins as a microbe that swiftly morphs into a menacing monster—one that is determined to pulverize me if I attempt to circumnavigate it.

I can fully sympathize with Jeremiah's disposition because it reminds me of my former self. Like Jeremiah, I didn't know how to speak either. I was a child. I was inexperienced in my abilities of evangelistic warfare, occasionally succumbing to fear and insecurity. The fact that my proselytizing ended so negatively at times didn't help boost my passion either.

A prime example of my doubts carrying over into the wrong situation was an unflinching opportunity to witness to actor Woody Harrelson. The feature production was *Seven Pounds*, starring Will Smith. The day I was involved, they shot in the city of Pasadena. Woody and I were part of the film's concluding scene, when Emily Posa (played by Rosario Dawson) meets Ezra Turner (Harrelson) at an outdoor recital. It is the emotionally rendered close to the movie.

Before shooting the first take in which Emily walks up to greet Turner in her empathetic state, the crew positioned Woody and me in front of the scene's catering tables. I stood next to Mr. Harrelson for nearly an entire minute. We both remained silent, although I knew I wanted to converse with him about his spiritual status. He seemed accessible based on my observation of his greeting some of the nearby extras a few seconds beforehand.

In his situation with me, however, Harrelson seemed rather shy. I desperately searched for something to break the ice. As I casually glanced at Woody's gray slacks, I noticed some creases near the knee. It seemed ridiculous, but I decided to use that as my reference point. It was better than having nothing.

I asked Mr. Harrelson, "Are those wrinkles part of your wardrobe look?"

Woody glanced down casually and replied, "Not really. I'm not too sure."

Harrelson went silent again. I don't know if Woody is a naturally reserved man or if he simply wished not to converse with me. The conversation never gained momentum, yet I needed to find a way to evangelize him. I thought perhaps I should just hand a tract to Woody as a kind gesture, but a great cloud of caution hovered over me. I was well aware that my job could be on the line if Woody overreacted to the situation.

A few short seconds later, the director, Gabriele Muccino, called for Woody, and Mr. Harrelson marched away at the director's call. Filming was about to begin.

I lost my opportunity with Woody, I thought, disappointed.

As it turned out, the door of opportunity never opened again. I forfeited my right to share the gospel with the Oscar-nominated actor that day. My chance had probably faded forever and all because of the monster—the same monster that had caused me to be fearful in the past. It was what caused the disciples to abandon their Lord at Calvary despite their strong pledges to die for Christ if necessary.

This monster, as you know, is the monster of fear.

REKINDLED COURAGE

Though trepidation thwarted my agenda from time to time, I vowed I would never let it reign in my life. I couldn't afford to. People were dying every day and going to hell in droves. There was just too much at stake. God blessed me with the zeal to evangelize and even do it in a knowledgeable manner. According to the late evangelist Bill Bright's survey from the 1990s, over ninety-eight percent of Christians don't evangelize on a daily basis when the opportunity presents itself. That is why there is even more pressure on me to make up for the deficiencies of others. Nobody was going to reach out to the lost except people like me.

As I reminisce on the years before my spiritual renaissance, I have deep remorse with regard to every person I had a chance to witness to, but failed to take initiative. I think back to the unbelievers from Grant High School, UCLA, the campus clubs, the camaraderie outings, work places, and even some family members with whom I've now lost contact. My list easily accounts for more than a hundred people, all of whom I knew very intimately at one time. There were numerous opportunities when I could have shared the gospel with my friends, but I neglected to keep my Lord's commands. I did not love these people enough to want to tell them the truth.

It is somewhat discouraging to note that Woody Harrelson was not the only celebrity that I missed a chance to influence. In the couple of years that followed, I also failed to step up to the plate and evangelize stars like Chevy Chase, Drew Barrymore, Adam Sandler, and Paul Walker. I've met and worked with many more prominent names, but these were the people I actually had opportunities to connect with in a situation that was fairly accommodating. The door was open, yet I failed to conquer my fears for the greater good.

With this in mind, I was inspired to lift myself higher than I originally dreamed I could. Not only did I make a rebound, but I also made a resolute commitment. Through the prompting of my conscience, the Bible, and friends like Jonathan Khan, I was better able to defeat my monsters. I conquered them through my love and trust in God. At times, when Goliath confronted me, I depended on the slingshot of the Holy Spirit to defeat the giant. As David lauds in his psalm, "The LORD is my light and my salvation; whom shall I fear? The LORD is the defense of my life; whom shall I dread? When evildoers came upon me to devour my flesh, my adversaries and my enemies, they stumbled and fell.... My heart will not fear" (Ps. 27:1-3).

A TWENTY-FOUR HOUR OPERATION

One of my fondest memories of conquering fear for the greater glory of God's kingdom was with Kiefer Sutherland and Freddie Prince Jr. on the hit television show, 24. Unlike my encounter with Mr. Harrelson, my brief association with the two renowned stars of 24 ended in success. By success, I mean that I was able to get the gospel message across to both of these actors—not just one, but to both of them!

The 24 gig was a unique experience for several reasons. It was my first time as a photo double for one of the show's principle performers, which means that I portrayed the character on camera, although my face did not appear in the shot. It was also the smallest call to which I'd ever been assigned. In fact, I was the only extra on the production set that day. Last, it was the closest in proximity that I'd ever been to the principle actors during an entire scene.

To elaborate, the scene involved Kiefer, Freddie, and two SWAT members riding in a black SUV. Kiefer was the designated driver, while they stationed Freddie in the front passenger's chair. The remaining two passengers—the SWAT officers—sat in the back seat. I was one of the SWAT officers, my body filling in for the character, Agent King.

The scene premise was simple. Jack Bauer (Sutherland), Cole Ortiz (Prince Jr.), King (whom I played), and the subsidiary officer are on a frenetic race to obstruct a terrorist bombing conspiracy. They must get to the scene of the crime before it is too late. It was an intense sequence in what was another intense episode of the crime series.

For the entire ride, I was in sheer awe that both Kiefer and Freddie were sitting right in front of me. As I said, this was an unprecedented experience that very few background artists can claim. Freddie was even kind enough to turn around and greet me with a handshake before the start of the scene, saying, "Hey there, I'm Freddie."

I immediately responded by introducing myself as well. I asked the actor, "Do you go by Freddie or by Fred?"

Freddie replied with indifference, "Fred, Freddie, whatever is fine."

"I only ask because some people get kind of touchy on the subject of names."

"It's cool. I'm not like that."

Not too long after, Mr. Sutherland entered the vehicle, and he was also courteous enough to shake my hand before readying his state of mind for the impending bedlam. Within a couple of minutes, the two actors got the show underway. I watched as Kiefer and Freddie performed their scene in five takes. It was fun to watch this scene play out because of its dramatic and intense feel.

As intriguing as this moment was, I was more concerned about how I was going to evangelize these two actors. Could I get the message across to both of them? At what moment should I approach them? What time of the day?

As it turned out, this car ride happened to be my only scene. After the director approved the final take, I was done and ready to sign out. Elated to clock out early on one hand, I wasn't so quick to run right out of the studio just yet. I still needed to accomplish my mission for God! This was a brief operation to rescue my unwitting colleagues from the grips of another terrorist—Satan. He is undoubtedly the world's most dangerous terrorist, and he was leading my two colleagues toward the wide gate of eternal destruction. At minimum, I had to warn them not to drive down that path.

I stood in peripheral distance to Freddie Prince Jr. as I quickly stripped myself of my props, which included my SWAT helmet, gloves, and M-16 machine gun. Then, in a generous turn of events, Freddie came up to me first.

Freddie extended his hand and said, "Take it easy, Steve."

I worked fast to remove my right leather glove in order to shake the actor's hand. Freddie responded to my action with slight consolation, "Oh, you don't have to do that."

I replied, "That's okay. I want to give you my real hand."

The glove finally slid off and I firmly gripped Freddie's hand. Then I pulled out a *Good Person Test* and said, "Oh, here. This is for you. Check it out."

Freddie looked down on the tract with a slight smile and said, "Great. I'll take a look at it."

Mr. Prince Jr. walked away, undoubtedly back to his dressing room. I was nervous, but nonetheless excited in spirit. Never in my life did I think I would meet Freddie, let alone relay the gospel message to him!

I didn't bask long in my accomplishment. I immediately turned my attention to Kiefer, who was conversing with some of the producers and assistant directors. *I might as well get him too*, I thought. I prudently accosted Mr. Sutherland from behind, speaking his name.

When I got the actor's attention, I said, "Hey, Kiefer. I enjoyed working with you. This was a cool scene. I've never done anything like this before."

I couldn't foretell how the actor would respond me, a mere extra. Based on Kiefer's austere look, I initially imagined him to be a surly or crass person, but I was wrong. To my relief, Kiefer replied in an upbeat, down-to-earth manner, "Oh yeah? Cool. That's great."

I breathed a short sigh of relief deep in my soul. Then we chatted a little while longer until I finally advanced my spiritual agenda. I pulled out another *Good Person Test* and handed it to Kiefer, stating once again, "Before you go, I'd like to give this to you. It has a great message."

With receptive deportment, Kiefer responded, "Okay. I'll take a look at it."

Kiefer nodded and marched away from me. The gospel tract was all that I could give him at that point since he was on the go. I was grateful to have had an opportunity at least to greet the actor and not get lectured by the PA for it. The film crew was surprisingly tolerant on this day, and that worked favorably to my advantage.

To this day I wonder what Sutherland's stance is with the Lord. From what Jonathan Khan informed me regarding a recent story he overheard, Kiefer attended a funeral service (a few months before my 24 shoot) for one of his deceased friends or relatives. It was supposedly a heartrending day for the actor. His contrite spirit was further ameliorated by the pastor's powerful presiding over the ceremony. The message may have actually softened his heart.

If this account is true, then I hope Mr. Sutherland became humbled to the point where the gospel in the booklet I gave him would effectively speak to his life. It's ultimately up to God to bring Kiefer to saving faith. Only time will tell if that funeral had any divine purpose in Kiefer's life, and if the Holy Ghost courted his heart mightily through the *Good Person Test*.

I pray that both Kiefer Sutherland and Freddie Prince Jr. will prepare as if today could be their last day. The next twenty-four hours are never a promise for any of us.

The Nazarene Connection

My spiritual interactions with the industry socialites did not stop with my two friends on 24. I continued to step up when it came to sharing my faith with both extras and principle actors. Fear crept in from time to time, but I was able to overcome and break out of my comfort shell through the Lord's help.

Many people, even Christians, may view me as being tactless or even insane for approaching celebrities in this manner. Of course, they apparently have not seen Jonathan in action. However risky and strange my strategy may seem compared to standard practices, it may be the most rewarding, if not necessary, approach. The most preponderate artists, philanthropists, and business people in history were responsible for accomplishing major goals because of their inordinate approaches to their craft. The case with evangelistic zeal is no different.

In such cases as mine, I really have no choice. People's eternities are on the line. As much as it grieves me to bend worldly rules and expectations, such as on the production sets, I will do it if it means saving someone's soul. Authority figures may scold and manhandle me, but I must take that risk. In my case, the worst thing I can lose is my sense of pride. On the other hand, these celebrities will lose their souls if they die without our Savior. It is an urgent race to save lives from eternal torment. Based on my observations of the industry's philosophy, it is evident that the gospel doesn't land on too many ears around town.

In February of 2009, I was able to witness to a high profile person who was unquestionably familiar with walks on the red carpet. The man was William Friedkin, the Academy award-winning director responsible for such film classics as *The French Connection* and *The Exorcist*. I worked with him on one of the episodes of the long-running television series, *CSI: Crime Scene Investigation*, which was shot on the Universal Studios lot. The episode, called "Mascara," featured the famed actor Laurence Fishburne, who played Dr. Raymond Langston.

I was surprised when I learned that William (or Bill) Friedkin captained the episode. I didn't think a man of such an extraordinary cinematic resume would ever direct a television show, which was an entirely different medium. I was quite happy with this realization. All of us anticipated the legendary Friedkin gracing this episode with his experienced touches.

The man not only gave his vision to the production, but also extended his kindness to the people on the set. He was nice to everyone, even the background artists. When he stepped onto the casino set, Bill shook hands with many of the extras stationed at the blackjack tables and slot machines, displaying a great sense of altruism. Although I wouldn't call him a saint, Mr. Friedkin was one of the most convivial directors with whom I have had a chance to work. This gave me more confidence in sharing the gospel with him.

Luckily, the background artists had a very short day. The casino scene turned out to be our only one for the whole program. When the scene wrapped, the background actors filed out of the set in a single line procession as Bill shook hands with every one of us. When my turn came around, I gripped Mr. Friedkin's hand with gladness.

I said, "It was great working with you, Mr. Friedkin. I want to tell you that I really loved the *French Connection*."

He replied, "Oh, thank you. Thank you very much. I appreciate it."

I had my *Good Person Test* ready in my other hand. After releasing my grip on the director's hand, I gave him the tract and said, "This is for you."

William took it without hesitation and replied in a gratified manner, "Thank you very much, sir." I nodded and continued down the stage ramp as Mr. Friedkin continued to extend his gratitude to the other background players behind me.

That day, I prayed fervently for Bill. I prayed that his humility would be enough to make him receptive to the message of salvation in Christ. Much as Father Merrin proved instrumental in driving out the demons that inhabited the helpless child, Regan, in *The Exorcist*, I exhorted the Holy Spirit to work in Mr. Friedkin so that he would expel the power of sin from his life. I knew that only then could God heal him from the grip of Satan and allow him to wake up to a new world of everlasting light.

To this day, I am still greatly rooting for William Friedkin when it comes to salvation. His generous professional conduct made me more hopeful for his chances of coming to Christ and gave me more desire to pray for his eternal welfare. If only I could have gotten to Laurence Fishburne on that day as well, I would have completed my day satisfactorily. Thankfully, Jonathan Khan took care of Laurence some time later!

The Glamorous Life

Speaking of red carpets, I had a chance to stand beside the red carpet a week later on the television show, *90210*. It was for a movie premiere scene filmed in West Hollywood, across the street from the Los Angeles County Museum of Art. You may think this premiere is unworthy of accolades, considering the *90210* cast members are not as popular as some other more eminent names in the business. Surprisingly, the show delivered, and two guest stars captured everyone's attention on this night. One was media sensation, Tori Spelling, and the other was *Juno* screenwriter, Diablo Cody. I had the opportunity to get the gospel across to both of them, and it happened only a week after my encounter with William Friedkin. I was on a majestic streak!

The red carpet extravaganza was the final scene of the day's shoot. I stood among the boisterous fans, watching news reporters interview both Tori and Diablo before the two starlets ascended the steps into the venue. The sequence was exciting, but I spent the time concentrating more on how I was going to approach these two actresses later that night.

I had more incentive to go through with my agenda because Paul Kwak, the Christian background artist I had worked with on Smash World, was with me on this day. It had been almost a year since I had last worked with Paul, but his faith was as sturdy as ever. Paul, however, was still a bit timid when it came to cold-turkey witnessing, even after I had supplied him with *The Way of the Master* resources. Since Paul was still a novice in the art of practical evangelism, I wanted my actions to inspire him in much the same way Jonathan's had inspired me. There couldn't be a better way to display this act than to apply it to high-profile celebrities!

After the AD officially called a wrap for the night, I wasted no time in making my move. Luckily, there was no guardrail thwarting my path on the red carpet. I marched straight up to Tori Spelling as Paul followed closely, still hesitant at my plan. I figured Paul was hinting at the possibility of trouble, but as I explained earlier, the worst thing that could be lost was our sense of integrity, and in this case, maybe our jobs. I was prepared to glide on thin ice for this cause. I hoped Paul felt the same way.

I stood behind Tori as she conducted a real-life interview with one of the set reporters. After she finished, I called her name. She immediately turned around and faced Paul and me. We were both nervous to be in her presence, but we faithfully moved forward with the plan. We started by doing the only thing we knew how to do in the beginning of a conversation with an actress like Tori. We introduced ourselves. Tori was kind enough to reciprocate our greetings.

I looked for a casual icebreaker to maintain the life of the conversation. I brought up a subject that Paul and I had discussed earlier in the day regarding Tori's background. I asked, "I heard that you studied to be an ordained minister or something. Is that true?"

Ms. Spelling replied breezily, "Oh yeah. Some fun thing that I did in the past."

I guess that answered the question. However, her reply didn't give me any confidence in her spiritual security. It seemed as if she undertook her religious activities more as a hobby or as a means to an end than as a longing for spiritual transformation. I decided it would definitely be wise to get the gospel message to her.

Suddenly, a reporter abruptly summoned Tori for another interview. Acknowledging the interview's priority, Tori asked, "Can you excuse me for just a sec?"

I had a visceral feeling that Tori would not return to us, so I immediately got to the point. I handed her a *Good Person Test* and said, "Before you go, I just want to give you this. It has a great message."

She looked down on it with slight curiosity, replying, "Oh, thank you."

Then, without delay, Tori shifted her attention to the reporters. As it turned out, everyone in the near region garnered her attention to the point where she surely had no reason to come back to Paul and me. Fortunately, I'd gotten the job done. It was amusing to see the actress hold the *Good Person Test* in her hand the entire time as she took center stage in front of the cameras!

With Tori Spelling checked off my list, I peered about for the remaining target. She seemed to be nowhere in sight. Then I caught a glimpse of her fiery orange dress in the far distance. Diablo Cody was about to board a white van and catch her ride back to base camp. With no time to lose, I sprinted after her. Paul lingered behind on this occasion, watching from a distance.

I caught up to Ms. Cody, exclaiming, "Diablo!"

The *90210*'s guest star turned her attention to me. I now stood in the presence of the Academy Award-winning screenwriter—the same woman who grabbed the golden Oscar statue out of the hands of Harrison Ford and delivered her ecstatic speech for her Best Original Screenplay triumph in 2008. I was quick to acknowledge her past achievement, saying, "I just wanted to meet you and say that I loved *Juno*. It was a great film."

Diablo responded with joy. She literally welcomed me with open arms as she embraced me after my statement. It was surely big enough for the principle actors to be talking to extras, but for them to make such physical contact was quite surprising!

She replied to my statement, "Why, thank you! Nobody really said that to me."

Did I hear her correctly?

I asked, "Really? Are you serious?"

She replied, "Yeah."

Wow, I thought. I still can't believe it to this day. You would think that with all the accolades *Juno* received from both critics and award associations, Ms. Cody would have received her share of praise from all sectors in life. I would think she had it practically stamped on her forehead by now.

If Diablo wasn't lying, then the only other explanation was that people either hated her film or admired it but chose not to give her commendation. It was sad to think that maybe she just didn't have nice friends.

I continued, "Interesting, but I liked it. It was a great film."

Diablo thanked me once again for my kind words. I sensed the conversation was coming to a dead end, so I bowed out by delivering the final, more significant message. I handed her the *Good Person Test* and said, "Before you leave, this is for you."

Diablo gazed upon it, enthusiastic as ever. She replied to the question on the cover page by exclaiming, "Why, thank you! I *am* a good person!" Then Diablo turned and hopped into the shuttle van.

I was somewhat flabbergasted by her confident declaration of her moral state. Then again, her views are similar to many others in our current age. Most everyone thinks they are truly a good person, as the Word of God proclaims in Proverbs 20:6.[15] I guess modern civilization's acceptable standard of goodness is simply upholding civil laws, not murdering anyone, and showing respect for others. Men and women rarely measure themselves against God's universal and timeless standard, which is divine perfection in thought, word, and deed. Sadly, even most Christians don't.

I will probably never know Diablo Cody's response to the gospel message, at least not on this side of life. I pray that she will experience the Savior's grace much in the way Mary Magdalene and the Samaritan woman did in Jesus' time. However, there are apparent obstacles that must be overcome before Diablo can meet that desired end.

The major difference between Diablo and the New Testament women is that the females in the Bible were outcasts, scorned by society, and downtrodden in life. They had nothing in the world. They were emptied of their pride and thirsted for righteousness, which Jesus of Nazareth provided as living water. In contrast, Diablo sits atop the world, exalted nationally for her professional talent, having no need for the righteousness that leads to everlasting life. Her life is here and now in this world with the perishing forces of wealth and prosperity.

Situations like these prompt me to pray ever more for people like Diablo Cody and Tori Spelling. I hope the Lord will break their souls and cause them to famish for the Lord's righteousness. Otherwise, the god of wealth will inevitably consume them and forever steer them away from the Holy Spirit, the only One who can save their souls from the Great White Throne Judgment.

It is no wonder that Jesus declares it is difficult for a rich man to enter the kingdom of heaven. These people do not desire or see their need for the God of Scripture because they already serve a god who is powerful, hypnotic, and fulfilling in its own right. This false god promises happiness. It provides people with the desires of their sinful hearts. It grants them unlimited earthly resources, which over time allow them to exalt themselves as gods of their own. The god of wealth is the same god that drove my life's philosophy before the Lord stepped in and steered me onto the right path.

The Holy Spirit must work even harder for the kings, rulers, and rich men of this world. The truth is, they probably need it the most.

Chapter 9

DAZED AND CONFUSED

DO YOU EVER wish that while striving to advance a cause in the world, you didn't have to deal with a certain group of people? Yet, you feel obligated because they have the same dire predicaments as every other group of people? This theme is common in just about every practice in life. Whether it is religious, business, or environmental, there are always nuisances that raise your anxiety in the labor field. It may involve different ethnic groups, particular neighborhoods, the mentally challenged, those who are stubborn and garrulous, religious freaks, and on and on.

In my predicament, I can concretely categorize two groups. The first is the group of hardened unbelievers. These people have never heard the gospel or learned the message, but they have completely pushed it away. The second group is the more disheartening one. It is the demographic of the questionable believers. These are the ones who live carnal lives, but who hang on to faith by a thread because of their unending trials or because they adhere to a false doctrine.

Why is the second group more difficult for me to face? Because I have to take on the burden of questioning the state of their eternal security when in reality I want to believe they are saved. This exposes me to further risk of conflict, and it would be embarrassing if my analysis ended up being wrong.

When these professing followers question their Christian belief or entirely backslide from it, I feel immense sorrow. I feel grief for the fact that they believe the Christian faith has let them down, and that they may possibly never know true saving faith. This puts a great deal of pressure on me to work with them, whether these people have fallen away from Christ or have chosen to follow a false image of God created from their own beliefs. In either case, I must remember that despite my attempts to change destinies, it is the Spirit of God who draws sinners to the Son for salvation and sanctification.

Evangelizing Christians adds another task to my already overfilled plate, but I must be faithful to minister to them as well. As Paul declares to the people in Corinth, "Blessed be the God and Father of our Lord Jesus Christ, the Father of mercies and God of all comfort, who comforts us in all our affliction so that we will be able to comfort those who are in any affliction with the comfort with which we ourselves are comforted by God" (2 Cor. 1:3-4). The message in this verse is that it is a privilege to help confused Christians and apostates in the industry. As much as the ungodly need truth, these struggling believers need it as well. They need guidance, they need support, and most importantly, they need love.

PAINS OF THE ORDERLIES

On April 16, 2008, I worked on the television series *Without a Trace*, where I played an FBI orderly along with fifteen other background artists. This day happened to be an anomaly because it was one of the rare work dates where none of the people I witnessed to were lifelong atheists. Instead, they were mostly false converts and apostates of Christianity.

My day started when I had my first conversation with a fellow named Brad. Brad sat right in front of me in the holding area, so it was easy to start a chat with him. He immediately introduced himself, and we started to talk casually for about a minute, mostly regarding Brad's past time spent as a background artist and part-time production assistant. Brad surely had an interesting social and professional upbringing, yet I was more curious as to the nature of his spiritual position.

I candidly asked Brad if he was a Christian. At that moment, something interesting happened. He gently tapped my arm. After gazing around briefly, he leaned in close and whispered humorously, "You better watch that kind of talk around here. People in the industry can get pretty touchy if you bring religion up."

As true as that statement may have been, I stood firm. I told Brad that I was well aware of the consequences of my actions. I further explained that I was a devoted witness for Jesus Christ and proselytized everyone I met, regardless of the situation or outcome. Brad seemed impressed by my valor. He slowly opened up to me, admitting that he had faith in Jesus Christ as his Lord and Savior. Yet, in his next breath, he told me casually that he was part of the Masons organization.

What is a Mason? I wondered. It sounded like something I read out of a Chick comic book. I knew that it could have been a heretical Christian organization, so I decided to give something to Brad just to play it safe.

I presented him with a *Good Person Test* and said, "Here, take this. This is the gospel message presented in its truest form. Just remember this message regardless of what other people say that might conflict with it." Brad received the tract with gratitude, remarking that he would definitely take heed to the message.

Just then, a girl who sat to the right of Brad made her way into the discourse. She introduced herself as Courtney and said, "I believe in a god or some sort of higher power, but I just don't know who or what exactly he is. But I pray."

Courtney's sudden involvement took me a little off guard, but I was always ready in such cases. I figured this was the best time to explain the message to her as well. I was glad that she was searching, or at least open, to the idea of God. She just needed restoration to the true God so as not to be culpable of idolatry. I took the time to explain the gospel message to her, explaining everything from sin to grace. I was even adamant to stress the exclusivity of Christ as the only way to heaven. I finished by exhorting her to take a leap of faith immediately, since she didn't know when she was going to die.

Courtney responded, "I don't really believe in a particular person or way. How can you ever really know that? I just pray to god or whatever is in control. I even pray to people who may be up there with him as well, whether it is Buddha or whoever."

I replied, "The Bible says that you must pray through Christ alone to get to God. He is the only way you'll be heard and answered. Every other god is just an idol."

Courtney asked, "Well, why can't I pray to someone else? I'm sure everyone else up there hears me. I just pray to whoever is up there and willing to listen. I don't think there's anything wrong with that."

I continued to emphasize the fact that Jesus is the only way to the Father, referencing John 14:6.[16] Although Courtney rejected the idea of becoming a Christian or pledging her allegiance to any one philosophy, I gently accentuated that Christ was the only way for her to be saved. It was the only way that God would hear her prayers, forgive her sins, and guide her life to anything meaningful.

What happened next was a gospel reaction that I saw for the first time in my life. Courtney started to recount the story of her life, in which she discussed her adoption as a child and her Catholic upbringing. The story became grim as she mentioned the deaths of close family members, including her mother. The sad thing was that they all had supposed faith in Christ, but died tragically. Courtney had experienced countless trials and tragedies in her life ever since.

Tears started to flow out of her eyes. She asked pessimistically, "Why would He do this to me if I was following Him? Why would He do that to my family? I don't know what to believe anymore."

Courtney began to sob, and a sense of awkwardness swept across the entire waiting area. Since the room was so small and compact, even whispers could be detected from across the room. Some turned their heads halfway, while others looked down in bewildered silence as Courtney continued to cry, attempting to regain her composure. This scene confounded Brad as well.

I didn't really know how to respond to this act of God's sovereignty. I offered my condolences for her predicament and exhorted her to come to faith in the Lord Jesus Christ. I said this not only for the state of her emotional welfare, but also for that of her spiritual wellbeing. What does it profit a person to be dejected now, only to be more devastated when she finds herself in hell after death?

There is really no alternative other than to come to the Savior, regardless of one's emotional problems. It may be bold, but valid, to claim that God probably put Courtney through all those trials in order to expose her false faith. It would be a tragedy for her to believe that she was saved, only to die and wake up in hell! At least now she had an opportunity to hear the real gospel and come to salvation for certain.

I attempted to give Courtney some hope by saying, "Please put your faith in Christ. We're talking about your salvation. I know that you've experienced a lot of pain and confusion in your life, but I guarantee that if you trust in God, He will use all your downfalls for good someday."

Courtney pointed at me and exclaimed, "Don't guarantee anything. People have been saying that to me all my life. Don't guarantee anything."

Maybe guarantee was too strong a word to put into my sentence, but I believe there is some biblical support for such a statement, as evidenced in passages like James 1:12 and Jeremiah 29:11. I can't say that painful experiences will always lead to happiness, but one thing is for sure, they will be used to magnify God's glory in heaven and on earth. The person involved will also benefit for all eternity. If anything, I have faith in that guarantee.

DOUBT

When we arrived on the set (which was an FBI office constructed inside one of the Warner Bros Studios lots), I decided that I should share the good news of Christ with a few more people. I talked with one gentleman, although it was very brief because he had to depart to the restroom for an emergency. I turned my attention to another brown-haired man who played an orderly and sat to my right at the table.

His name was Matt. During our down time, I talked with my new prospect briefly about his life. He assured me that his day had been treating him well. This was just what I needed to hear for me to start my spiritual conversation.

I remarked, "It seems as if God has been blessing you recently."

This turned out to be a red-light moment. Matt suddenly raised his index finger and said, "Don't start with me now."

Matt apparently knew about my faith because he had eavesdropped on my other conversations. I should have zipped my mouth after his gesture, but I proceeded with a final attempt by asking, "Did you have a Christian upbringing?"

Matt replied affirmatively. I then asked, "Did you have a bad experience?"

He smirked and said, "Yes."

"Well, what do you think will happen to you when you die?"

Matt warned with a caustic smile, "I'm warning you, man. Drop it."

This was my final cue to let the case go. I never knew what Matt's problem was and I will probably never know. I always find it discouraging when I hear about people falling away from Christ because of negative impressions brought on by churches and flawed people. Unfortunately, it was now out of my hands to help correct those misconceptions.

After Matt was repositioned to another mark, a middle-aged woman sitting to my right asked me, "Are you a priest or something?"

No one had ever asked me this question before. In some ways, I took her inquiry to be a compliment because it showed that I was truly doing God's work in the public world, but on second thought, it reminded me of the sad reality that a question like this only comes about because Christians don't really share their faith, except for spiritual leaders. To be honest, even half the pastors don't evangelize either.

The woman stated, "I'm a Christian, but I don't think that all non-Christians will be condemned. I don't believe that God would send good people like the Dalai Lama to hell."

I was somewhat surprised to hear such a compromising statement, but I should have anticipated it since most believers and unbelievers probe into that very same theme. I stood my ground and did not allow her to leave with that question unanswered. This ideology of universal salvation is one of the largest taboos a Christian can advocate. It can even expose a Christian as a false disciple. I wondered if this woman really was a Christian or if she was more of a Universalist. Either way, I could immediately tell that her faith wasn't as rock solid as it should be.

I referred her to Acts 4:12,[17] which states that the only way to heaven is through Christ. Only His grace saves, not men's works. I emphasized the authority of Scripture in highlighting this truth, although this woman probably didn't comprehend my explanation. She obviously didn't have a foundational knowledge of God's law, God's justice, and the extent of man's depravity in understanding why Jesus is the only way to heaven. I would have explained these principles to her more in depth, but we separated to work. This woman turned out to be my last prospect for the day.

Within a four-hour time gap, I had two struggling Christians and two apostates thrown right at me. What a filled day. I don't know how much of an impact I made on Courtney, Matt, and the last lady, but I was fortunate enough to have kept in touch with Brad. He seemed to be the only redeeming factor to my missionary work that day. In fact,

Brad even came to my baptism ceremony at Family Chapel four days later!

ONE PATH MULTIPLIED

Although the last woman's statement on the *Without a Trace* set was the least memorable moment I had that day, it represented one of the recurring problems I most often encountered among professing believers thereafter. While working in Hollywood on the Nickelodeon television show, *Victorious*, I met a young Christian who had similar thoughts on the concept of universal salvation. He sat at the same table as me during an outdoor studio scene. I remained silent as I listened to his conversation with two female background players sitting next to me. For the most part, it was centered on the subject of actors. One of the girls entertained us by recounting a bizarre encounter she had with actor Jack Nicholson at a movie theater. She claimed not to have known who the actor was until he randomly approached her and started to spill out his entire life story and random views on life. She felt more uneasy than star-struck because of Nicholson's quirky actions.

Most of the dialogues I overhear remain within the boundaries of non-religious topics, but this time things turned out different. Interestingly, the conversation shifted into the realm of Christianity as Taylor and one of the girls started to discuss their church lives.

Wow, they are both Christians, I thought. Not too long after, I took part in the discourse myself, as it always gave me comfort to speak with fellow believers regarding Christian matters. Since I am a naturally shy person, it is not easy for me to get involved with new people unless I can comfortably connect with them on a particular topic. That is why anything related to Christianity serves as a great way for me to break out of my shell and start connecting with strangers.

During a recess, I had a private discussion in the studio lobby with this gentleman who introduced himself as Taylor. I asked Taylor to elaborate a bit more on his Christian upbringing. He began to talk about his home church and his father being a pastor. I found Taylor's testimony pleasant and even encouraging. But a few minutes later, Taylor mentioned something that immediately caused a red flag to go up. He informed me about his brief departure from church a year prior because he "…got sick of the religious lifestyle and wanted a short break."

This can't be normal for a Christian, I thought. Because of this, I asked Taylor a solemn question. I inquired, "This may sound a bit awkward to ask, but do you have any assurance that you're saved?"

Taylor asked skeptically, "What do you mean by that?"

"Let me rephrase it. If you were to stand before God when you die and He were to ask, 'Why should I let you into Heaven?' What would you say to Him? What must you do to inherit eternal life?"

Taylor replied, "Accept Jesus Christ."

I asked, "Why do I have to accept Christ? Why is He the only way for me to be saved? Why is there no other way that I can be saved? Can you explain it to me?"

What I heard next affirmed the validity of the red-flag warning. Taylor asserted, "Well, I believe that you can get to heaven even if you haven't heard the name of Christ. I believe that Jesus displays His face as God through many different ways and philosophies."

This is exactly the sort of declaration that a healthy Christian can never conclude. It goes completely against everything Jesus taught about Himself, about God, and salvation. I don't know if Taylor said this out of theological ignorance or if he truly believed it in light of a thorough Christian education. Whatever the predicament, this man needed to be set straight or he would give false hope to other seekers. More tragically, he may even be on the road to eternal damnation himself. Believing in a false Christ is as dangerous as believing in a wrong deity altogether. It is a transgression of the first and second Commandments. Both Galatians 5:19-21[18] and 1 Corinthians 6:9[19] declare that idolaters will not inherit the kingdom of heaven; so this certainly was not a light issue.

I am not advocating an exclusive Jesus VIP club to be intentionally narrow, condemning, or prideful. I truly wish that everyone in the world could be saved through his or her own way. If there were more than one path to salvation, then I would gladly accommodate more needs, but if the words of Christ are true, then no such opportunities exist. There is one and only one way to eternal life and that is through Jesus Christ. He is the only one who paid our eternal debt so that our case will be dismissed on Judgment Day. The resurrection supplied proof to the world that God accepted the payment as sufficient. Whereas Buddha, Muhammad, Krishna, and many other religious and philosophical teachers remain in the grave, Christ rose from the dead and proved to the world that His words were true—that He alone conquered death and gives eternal life.

I immediately asked my prospect, "What do you think about verses like John 14:6 where Jesus says, 'I am the way, and the truth, and the life; no one comes to the Father but through Me.' Christ is saying that His name is the only way to be saved."

The impact of this verse took Taylor by force, but he tried to remain lighthearted. He replied, "I understand your concern, but that's a pretty heavy subject to get into, and now is not the time or the place to talk about such things, but I will say that religious hypocrisy has been the cause of some of the worst wars in history. I don't like the way men divide over these issues that cause needless suffering."

This was a common, yet challenging, thesis that I carefully needed to deconstruct. I would not argue with the man. I do admit that people have been divided throughout the centuries because of religious issues that I consider peripheral, but the topic of salvation is not one of them. It is vital and I had to defend it, even if conflict lurked around the corner. My overall incentive was for Taylor not to harbor the wrong impression of Jesus' words, or even mine for that matter.

As I was in the early process of elaborating on my answer, a throng of extras rushed through the doors into the lobby. Apparently, they had been released for a short break at that exact moment. Amidst the rush, one of Taylor's friends pulled the young man away from me. Taylor didn't even bother to look back as he frolicked with his pal back to the holding area in a giddy mode.

I stood still for about a minute, dumbfounded at what had just occurred. It seemed as if Satan had just pulled a prospect away from me. If Taylor's spiritual condition was so imperative that the devil had to work in this situation, it may have actually been a sign that Taylor was not saved. Worse yet, Taylor may have providentially been left in blindness so he could be exposed with the other false disciples on the Day of Judgment.

This was a scary and sad realization to me, but I could not do anything more in this situation. I never saw the man again after this day. I can only pray that if Taylor is not saved, he will come to true saving faith before it is too late.

Unresponsive Child

If the thought of a misguided follower of Christ worries me, how much more should I be concerned about a professor of faith who doesn't follow God? There are those who claim to be saved by making their peace with God, yet refuse to obey His commands and grow in discipleship. They latch onto God as an insurance policy in the event that there is such a thing as the afterlife, yet they harbor no concern or desire to obey their Lord's commands and grow in faith. These people live out the pleasures of the carnal life before it is all over.

I met one such case when I worked on an episode of *90210*. Her name was Denise, a woman with whom I'd worked on one other occasion thirteen months prior. I was glad to see Denise again. She was one of the people to whom I wanted to witness but hadn't gotten a chance because I wasn't an on-fire evangelist on the previous occasion. I didn't know if she was a Christian or was open to receiving the Word, but as the old saying goes, you never know until you give it a try.

Midway into the day, I casually approached Denise before the shooting of a scene. We had already been positioned for the shot and were waiting patiently while the crew completed the final few touches. I decided to use this time to proselytize Denise and offer her one of my customary *Good Person Tests*.

Denise looked down on the tract without taking it. Smiling sarcastically, she asked, "What is that, one of those chain letters?"

I replied, "No. It's not."

"Does this have to do with church stuff?"

"It's the Ten Commandments."

Denise waved her left arm as she confidently replied, "Oh, no. I already made my peace with the man above. We're all good."

Such a statement gave me an indication of her pride and disrespect for spiritual matters. I knew this couldn't have been good, so I asked her, "Do you go to church?"

"No."

"When was the last time you went?"

"I don't know. I guess when I was eight years old."

In other words, Denise hadn't attended church in more than seventeen years! This was definitely a reason to be skeptical. Church attendance is not a mandate for salvation, but the fact that she strongly implied that she doesn't maintain relationships with God's people shows that she may not have maintained a relationship with the Lord through His Word either. These are definitely not fruits of the Holy Spirit. Denise even mentioned to me during our previous gig that she was living with her boyfriend, not to mention the non-believing friends and social environments in which she participated. There was good reason for me to question her faith.

I told Denise, "I think you should definitely read this. It will be helpful."

She sneered, responding, "You can give it to me, but I'm not going to read that thing." A few seconds later, the scene got underway and Denise walked on to prepare for her action.

How can a follower of God, who says she is in accord with the Almighty, scorn His holy words? That's like a child who claims to be in good standing with her father, yet disobeys and shows him ingratitude every time he offers guidance. It almost sounded like there was no relationship to begin with. At least in Taylor's predicament, he made an attempt to maintain fellowship with his Lord, although his understanding of God's nature was a bit skewed. Taylor was a much better bet for salvation than was Denise.

The Word of God pretty much nails the obvious truth of true and false disciples when it says, "A good tree cannot produce bad fruit, nor can a bad tree produce good fruit. So then, you will know them by their fruits" (Matt. 7:18 and 20).

BACK TO THE DRAWING BOARD

After multiple instances of such cases with unbelievers, false converts, and apostates (whether in Hollywood or out), I came to a crossroad in my evangelistic life. In other words, I began to question the effectiveness of my personal ministry.

Were my oral presentations as convincing as they should be? Was I missing something crucial? Why wasn't I feeling the strength and power behind my evangelistic words? How could I break through to these people?

This concern boggled me for quite a while, but the Lord had not left me in the dark. As quick as my concerns came to me, a divine answer arrived even faster. My spiritual life soon experienced another milestone earthquake, which rocked me in the same manner as when I watched "The Greatest Gamble" in February of 2008.

As it turned out, my life was never going to be the same, yet again.

Chapter 10

TO LAW OR NOT TO LAW

I F YOU ARE familiar with the art of screenplay writing, you know that a script must follow a composed framework in order to be considered sturdy and marketable. The foremost principle is the foundational three-act structure. Without it, your script has no backbone to survive. Even within these three acts themselves, there are points and devices that the writer cannot ignore, or the integrity of the story will be uncertain. The Big Event is one of the first points, which occurs at the end of Act I. This is the plot twist that sets the story into motion. Without it, there is no excitement. There is no main conflict. In essence, there is no story.

The second plot twist, labeled as the Pinch, arrives somewhere in the middle of the movie. Though it may not have as much of the original shock value as the Big Event, the pinch is nevertheless a crucial device because it is responsible for raising the tension of the story to new heights. The film achieves this in one of two possible ways:

1. The central character is strengthened or fully commits toward achieving his or her goal.
2. The character comes to a point of no return. His or her life will never be the same again.

I can definitely liken my spiritual life in part to this screenplay structure. The Big Event happened on the day I reviewed *The Way of the Master* material given to me by my good friend Jonathan Khan. It was the defining plot twist in my Christian walk because it was the moment I became an on-fire, fully committed follower of Christ. I experienced a spiritual revival that started with evangelism. This, then, led to my passion for many other things relating to my faith and God.

Until now, however, I had never really explored the idea of a Pinch affecting my spiritual life, but it happened exactly one year after the Big Event struck my life. I consider it to be a life-changing event because it accomplished both purposes of the Pinch. It prompted me to be fully committed to a particular ideal and it set me on a new path with no points of return to the old ways.

It's interesting to say that this Pinch was initiated by the very same ministry that influenced me to begin. Yes, Living Waters struck again one year later.

A RENEWED PERSPECTIVE

Jonathan instructed me to watch *The Way of the Master* teaching called "Hell's Best Kept Secret." However, as previously mentioned, I did not have the opportunity to view it until much later. I finally got myself to watch this instructional DVD on one casual Sunday night in January 2009. This night turned out to be one of the most life-changing evenings in my spiritual walk, and it was purely because of this DVD's message!

To describe this teaching briefly, "Hell's Best Kept Secret" explores the issue of why so many professing believers fall away from the faith and the biblical principle Christians must utilize to reach the lost and to make sure they are saved. This principle is what Kirk and Ray deem as something the devil has misused and hidden so that much of the church doesn't even know it exists. It is what Jesus, the apostles, and the early church used to reach the lost effectively. This principle is the use of the Law of God (the Ten Commandments) in evangelism.

You may be thinking, "Wait a minute. The law doesn't save people. We are saved by grace." Yes, that's absolutely true. God's grace by faith is what saves us and nothing else. Now go back and ask yourself, from what exactly are we being saved? The Bible mentions that we are saved from our sins, because it is our sin that leads us to face God's judgment and eternal damnation. How do we know the sin from which we are being saved? What will sin do to us? The only way to solve this dilemma is to have a thorough understanding of God's Law. Only then does the gospel (the good news of the cross) actually make sense. Only then do we see what the purpose of the Great White Throne Judgment is, why we need a Savior, and how God's love is truly breathtaking.

In fact, the use of God's Law in evangelism is also the key in reaching false converts, or Christians who are not really saved. Regardless of what they believe the gospel message to be, false converts are exposed to the depth of their sinful natures for the first time after the law is applied to them. It is the law that humbles a person to become ready for true repentance that leads to saving faith.

I knew about the law before this day, since Jonathan himself took me through God's holy standard on the set of *Life*. I just didn't realize how necessary it was to incorporate that principle into evangelism every time. I was rather timid to use the law in some of my past encounters because of the possible persecution it could bring to me. The law is heavy-duty stuff, and I always preferred to make a non-confrontational impression on my prospects if possible. This is why I always downplayed the nature of God's Law and overstressed God's grace.

However well-intentioned I may have been, my positive presentations did not do much to change self-sufficient, self-righteous hearts. For all I knew, it may even have fostered it. I could have reasonably solved this dilemma if I had used the Ten Commandments in the beginning. They would have been the key to destroying my prospect's hopes for self-salvation. This act would easily make Christ-salvation more feasible to sell because the law would actually be driving my prospects toward grace! As Paul tells the Galatians, "The law has become our tutor to lead us to Christ, so that we may be justified by faith" (Gal. 3:24).

THE EXTRA BOOST

"Hell's Best Kept Secret" was an enlightening experience for my evangelistic knowledge, but it didn't end there. What I experienced next added to "Hell's Best Kept Secret" in a manner that supplemented its power. On the same webpage where I viewed the acclaimed message, there was also a video titled *God Has a Wonderful Plan for Your Life*. Since I had much time on my hands and was curious to watch another episode, I clicked on the start button and viewed the thirty-minute presentation.

In the previous video, Kirk and Ray presented a masterful, yet biblical, case on the necessary relationship between law and grace. In *God Has a Wonderful Plan for Your Life*, the two hosts describe the true meaning of the gospel message in a way that I never really thought of before. They debunk the popular practice of using the phrase, "God has a wonderful plan for your life" in gospel presentations. Although it is a pleasant thing to want to believe, the ideology has no biblical grounds. The believer's Christian walk is not a guarantee of riches, happiness, sunshine, and roses. Most times, it is filled with tragedy, hardship, confusion, and sometimes death. The preaching of the *Wonderful Plan* doctrine can lead many to a false notion of Christ, and indeed, many fall away from faith when they don't see rewards in this life.

It is through *God Has a Wonderful Plan for Your Life* that I came to learn about the prosperity theology for the first time. For those unfamiliar with this philosophy, prosperity theology (a.k.a. the health-and-wealth gospel) is a religious belief that centers on the notion that Christ blesses His believers with riches, health, and a happy existence if they come to Him in good faith. There will be no tragedies or stumbles in life as long as God is their banner. Christianity will therefore be about what people can get from God, and not the other way around. The prosperity message is a sly promise that has replaced the theology of law, sin, and repentance in the hope that Christianity will become more accessible, less controversial, and less demanding on the participant.

Although I've not been taught the prosperity theology, I have felt its tremors at various times in my Christian walk. It wouldn't be surprising to say that most of my past church comrades and pastors loved to preach about the love of God. They exalt the joy of the Lord to the point where, most times, they neglect the issues of His wrath and justice. This can naturally paint the image that we should present God's salvation to the lost in a manner that is non-confrontational and that stresses the happiness found in His name. However, this happiness is not the same happiness that prospects may surmise. Christians interpret this happiness as the joy found in eternal salvation, yet unbelievers link this promise to hedonistic pleasures of wealth, health, and success found on earth.

The video explains that the prosperity evangelism method can never bring about the repentance necessary to save someone. Christ mandates the virtue of self-denial, not self-fulfillment. The only way to bring sinners to a true understanding of what the gospel message is and what it requires is to match them up against the Law of God, the emblem of perfect righteousness. Unbelievers would therefore see that their predicament is not about happiness, but righteousness. People can only understand this righteousness through the law, which leads sinners to see their eternal dilemma and that they need to be rescued. This is what leads to the saving truth of the true gospel message. Such is the true joy that Christians are to seek.

Shortly after soaking in both of *The Way of the Master* episodes, I decided to make a firm commitment to use the law in my oral presentations. It's easier to say something aberrant for the sake of peace, but I would not be dissuaded. Now that I know much about the gospel and about false conversion, I can no longer return to my old strategies in good conscience. I must speak the truth in confidence and in love. I must use the biblical method to start convicting people, even if it is to professing Christians. Only the law can wake them up from their spiritual slumber.

I found the *God's Wonderful Plan for Your Life* video to be somewhat coincidental. Just a few days before, I uttered the same exact slogan to one of my prospects. While working on an episode of the TV show *Ghost Whisperer*, I was able to evangelize one of the principle actors at the end of the night. I walked up to the open trailer of Christoph Sanders, who plays the young Ned Banks, in hope of getting the good news to him. I was somewhat confident in my approach because Christoph and I had exchanged some friendly words earlier in the day.

I gave Christoph one of my customary *Good Person Tests*, and then said something I had heard one of my friends utter to an evangelistic prospect. It sounded nice, so I gave it a try. I told Christoph, "God has a wonderful plan for your life."

He looked at me with a slightly baffled expression, but he remained composed. He smiled and replied, "Oh, why thank you."

As I walked away from him, I gradually realized how paradoxical my slogan was compared to the content of the *Good Person Test*. I was talking about God's great, positive plan for this man's life, while my little tract emphasized righteous judgment as the Lord's only plan for unrepentant sinners. By the look of this scenario, I figured that I shouldn't ever mix the philosophies of two separate evangelistic organizations because often times the two can clash. *The Way of the Master* gives strong emphasis to the need for righteousness to save someone from damnation, while the God-has-a-wonderful-plan approach gives more of the prosperity gospel feel. You can already see an obvious discrepancy here that sends mixed messages about what the gospel is suppose to be.

After watching *God's Wonderful Plan for Your Life*, I fully regretted my words to Christoph. I say this not because I felt that it damaged Sanders' emotional wellbeing, but because it gave the wrong impression of the gospel message that I had passed on to him. From that day on, I never uttered the "God has a wonderful plan" slogan again. I revamped my style and became firmly fixed on the Bible's powerful method. Whether you want to brand it as another typical evangelistic method or not, I knew for sure that the law and gospel structure is a biblically based approach, as evidenced in Mark 10:17-31. It was a state-of-the-art weapon, and I planned to take advantage of it.

PIECING THE PUZZLE TOGETHER

About a month after my *24* job, I received a call to return to the production as the King photo double. This time we shot the scene in an outdoor facility a few blocks from the studio in Chatsworth, California. I was suited up in the same SWAT attire. The only difference this time was that I wasn't the only background artist present. There were about fifteen other extras with me, all playing cops. My role was still fairly exclusive in that I was a photo double, but I didn't have the same amount of intimacy that I had previously had with the principle actors. In fact, I wasn't used at all on this day! Apparently, the real King decided to show up to work, so they left me roaming the streets for nearly seven hours, without much to do except munch on craft service food.

I figured that I should use this valuable time to witness to some of the available folks around me. Being idle would not do much in building the kingdom of heaven. I had to motivate myself to make a difference in people's destiny. Every minute truly counts for the Lord. Unfortunately, the background players were not all present because they were on set, so I was alone.

Who should I witness to? I thought. It didn't take very long for the Lord to answer my question.

A few minutes later, a married couple strolled up to the set. Since the set was located in a casual, quiet suburban neighborhood, it was relatively easy for the residents to get close to the action if they stood a reasonable distance away so as not to interfere with the production. That's exactly what the husband and wife did as they stood right next to me on the street, gazing on to see if they could spot Waldo, or in this case, Kiefer Sutherland.

The Lord had apparently presented me with good prospects with whom to share the gospel. Even though they weren't employees of the production, I took advantage of the offer and immediately started a discourse with the two. They were glad to chat with me, thinking I was actually one of the actors on the show! How can you blame them, considering I was dressed in such stunning attire? The star struck spell worked to my advantage, and I soon proceeded to share the gospel message with them.

I primarily focused on the husband, Rudy, since his spouse turned her attention more toward the filming on set. I spent the first ten minutes discussing everyday topics with him, and then directed the conversation to the spiritual realm. As always, this stage of the evangelistic process requires the most courage. It's almost like jumping into cold water. However, once you do it, everything warms up from there.

I made my dive into the water by handing Rudy one of my *Good Person Tests* and asking, "Have you ever taken a Good Person Test?"

Rudy chuckled as he asked me what the small pamphlet was all about. I explained to him that it was a gospel tract, more specifically the Ten Commandments. I asked Rudy if he was familiar with God's Law. He said he was because he had a Catholic upbringing. However, Rudy didn't attend church anymore. In other words, he wasn't too spiritual.

I asked Rudy if he believed in God, to which he replied, "Well, yes. Some higher power you can call it."

My new friend was a Catholic-turned-agnostic. He surely wasn't born again, and I wasn't even too sure if he knew the gospel message. I began in the only way that seemed appropriate. I simply asked him, "Do you think you're good enough to go to heaven when you die?"

Rudy responded, "I would hope so, if there is a heaven."

This was the opportunity for me to take Rudy through the law and destroy his reliance on personal merit to enter heaven. I asked Rudy if he had kept the Commandments, or had he engaged in prevarication, theft, blasphemy, lust, and hatred. He admitted being guilty to all. After I posed the ultimate question about his theoretical destiny, Rudy concluded that he would end up in hell if he were to be judged in such a manner.

Although my prospect saw the logic in this scenario, he wasn't too concerned about his predicament. He claimed, "Well, I don't think God is going to judge me so harshly. I try to do good and make my way through life. I think I've made peace with my god. I talk to him whenever I can."

I informed Rudy that he had now broken the second of the Ten Commandments, which states that, "You shall not make for yourself an idol..." (Exodus 20:4). If you shape a god to suit yourself—a god to conform to your own sinful lifestyle—then that is called idolatry. I told Rudy that idolatry was serious in the Lord's sight. I pointed to 1 Corinthians 6:9,[20] which references that idolaters will not inherit the kingdom of Heaven.

Much like the Jews mentioned in Romans 10:3,[21] Rudy was somewhat ignorant of the righteousness of God and sought to establish his own. Therefore, I needed to make sure he understood the attributes of God's holiness and justice. I did so by literally explaining all the main points that "The Greatest Gamble" touched upon regarding God as an infallible judge in the courtroom; the futility of good works in bribing justice; and the human conscience that testifies to right and wrong conduct. These factors define

God's holy requirements, all of which proved that Rudy couldn't save himself.

In due time, Rudy became convicted that he might need a Savior after all. Now I knew he was ready to hear the awesome news of God's grace. I spoke to him about how Jesus rescued him from God's courtroom by paying off his eternal fine with His life's blood. Rudy broke the law, but Jesus paid his fine. That meant God could legally dismiss his case on Judgment Day. The resurrection further proved that Jesus' words about eternal life were true. I linked the famous John 3:16[22] verse with this entire equation to show how God's love was so marvelous. I finally informed Rudy that the only way for him to be saved was to repent of his sin and put his faith in Jesus. Only then would the Lord baptize his soul with the Holy Spirit and give him the righteousness necessary to enter heaven.

It took awhile for Rudy to internalize everything, but he caught on well. At that moment, he told me that he and his wife needed to return home to take care of some errands. He ended the conversation by making a comment that took me by surprise. He smiled a bit and said in a sincere manner, "Thank you for telling me these things. I learned a lot from you. You gave me many new things to think about. I'll definitely consider it."

This statement seemed contrary to his former position, which was why I was so astounded. He was humbled, and I knew much of it had to do with the effective use of the law. The Holy Spirit had worked through the law to reveal God's existence and His righteous requirements to Rudy. This in turn made grace even more real for him.

Before Rudy left, I gave him a couple additional tracts and invited him to contact me if he had any questions or concerns. He was glad to take my resources as he embraced me in good faith. After I endued him with a casual blessing, Rudy went back home with his wife.

I had never experienced anything like that before. Not only did I now have the courage to use the law in evangelism, but I also observed its ability to produce solid conviction in prospects that I had never seen before. Evangelism was suddenly more effective, and I knew I wanted to use my new God-given resource to speak to more unbelievers. At this point, I would do anything to ensure the success of my missions, even if I had to take on a technique that was originally difficult for me to use. As long as it was biblically rooted, the philosophy could only work in my favor.

The day on 24 was the first and last time I ever heard from Rudy or his wife. I don't know if the man ever made his peace with the Lord. Based on my interactions with him, it seemed as if he might have. I take peace in the fact that after my discourse with him, Rudy came one step closer to heaven instead of one step closer to hell.

HALF GLASS MADE FULL

Another astounding effect of the law of evangelism became evident when I worked on yet another episode of *90210*. The production took place in Los Angeles at a theater (the name of which I cannot recall). I played one of the waiters for a ballroom concert scene, which involved well over a hundred extras—most of them playing party students.

As I approached the end of the night, I was able to start up a conversation with the security guard assigned to the background holding room. He was a late thirties, rotund Hispanic gentleman named Luis. It didn't take me very long to get acquainted with my new friend Luis. During the hour-long talk we had, Luis filled me in on his family life, his childhood upbringing in some frightening parts of the city, his views on gangs, politics, as well as the perks of his job. The communication proved easy because he was fluent in English, with no accent whatsoever. It was obvious he had been born in the States.

Before long, I was able to get to the heart of the matter and bring up the things of God. I accomplished this through the usual means: handing my prospect a gospel tract as an icebreaker into the subject of faith.

I asked Luis, "Have you ever taken a Good Person Test before?"

The man chuckled and looked down on the pamphlet. I told him it was a gospel tract with the Ten Commandments. Luis said he was familiar with God's law because he came from a Roman Catholic family (much like Rudy). In fact, Luis informed me that his mother was extremely devoted to her faith, so much so that she would denounce Protestantism and deem it as the path to hell! I found his mom's belief humorous, yet I did not dwell on her spiritual case very long. I focused on Luis, asking him if he was still a practicing Catholic. He replied, "No." He said that he didn't believe in organized religion because of its flaws, hypocrisy, and the ritualism of the system. However, Luis maintained that he held his own personal beliefs about Jesus Christ.

This to me always represented shaky ground. I say this because not only did Luis fall away from church, but he might have adhered to an idolatrous view of Jesus, which happens when people formulate their own views on the Messiah. The fact that Luis knew Jesus from a Catholic background wouldn't help matters either, since its traditional views on grace and works differ much from that of biblical Christianity.

Like most other religions in the world, Roman Catholicism teaches that salvation is gained through a combination of faith and works. To be made right with God, the Catholic must have faith in Christ as Lord/Savior and participate in a lifetime's worth of rituals in order to maintain salvation, which includes baptism, confessions to a priest, transubstantiation, and other religious deeds. One has no guarantee of salvation and must continually work somehow to erase sin from his record. As you can see, this philosophy differs much from what the Bible says about salvation. Scripture states that salvation can never be worked for or purchased. It is a gift that comes through God's grace, or through faith alone (see Acts 20:21; Rom. 10:9; Eph. 2:8-9). One who practices otherwise would be calling God a liar and would be following a different gospel—one which does not save.

I began by asking, "If God were to ask you why you should enter heaven, what would you say?"

Luis replied, "I guess because I try to do good in life."

I then asked the foreboding question, "Do you think you're a good person?"

After Luis replied yes, I took him through the law as I did with Rudy. I brought up the very same five Commandments, to which Luis affirmed guilt in breaking all of them. I also illuminated an additional principle by asking him to recount all the times that he had broken God's law. With the example of only three transgressions a day, Luis would have been responsible for breaking God's Law over one thousand times in a year. If he lived to be eighty years old, Luis would have violated the law over eighty-six thousand times!

Luis knew from this portrait of God that if he were to die in his sins, he would be terribly guilty and end up in hell. I asked Luis if he knew what God did to save him from eternal punishment. Fortunately, my prospect knew pretty well. He made a general reference to Jesus' crucifixion, death, and atonement.

I affirmed his answer, yet I further explained God's grace and imputed righteousness just so he could see why his personal works could never get him into heaven. After describing the love of Christ exemplified through His death and resurrection, I explained what it meant to be born again and why men must experience rebirth to enter the kingdom of heaven, which is based on John 3:3. The process of regeneration not only absolves Luis of his sins, but it also gives him the righteousness necessary for him never to sin again in heaven. That is why Christ lived a sinless, perfect life—to give his sinless body (His righteousness) to Luis in exchange for Luis' sins. That transaction only occurs when a sinner invites the Holy Spirit into his life.

After I had finished with my points, Luis remained silent for a moment. I anticipated that he was going to reprove me or further interrogate the Christian tenet. Then he opened his mouth in subtle amazement, exclaiming, "You know, I have never heard anybody explain the gospel message to me the way that you did. Never has it made so much sense as it does now! Even pastors and priests whom I've known in the past didn't explain it as well as you did!"

Wow, I thought. Luis' statement represented exactly how I felt after I first learned the gospel message from *The Way of the Master* resources. This made me utterly joyful. I was glad that this tool helped open more eyes to the truth of God's salvation. I guess all the testimonies from the Living Waters materials were right! Law before grace truly does bring enlightenment to those who have never really understood the gospel message.

For the next ten minutes, Luis and I continued our discussion on Christology. We talked about everything from the Great Commission to eschatological (end times) issues. He was so convicted by the Holy Spirit calling to his heart that he asked if he could visit my church with his family! He suddenly desired to return to a congregation not only for his benefit, but also for the spiritual welfare of his wife and daughter. His family was not walking in the salvation of the Lord, so Luis figured this would be a great opportunity for them to be saved as well. I was quick to provide him with the necessary information.

The accounts of Rudy and Luis are some of the best examples of my evangelistic success in Hollywood. They also shed light on the question of whether the law is truly necessary in evangelism. From my experience, I give a resounding yes to this question. The law should not be used on broken sinners who admit their spiritual poverty, but it most definitely needs to be applied to people trusting in their own goodness to get into heaven. This represents most of the people you will meet on an everyday basis. I have learned this through hands-on experience.

If I had glossed over the law in favor of concentrating on God's grace (and maybe even extra-biblical notions of self-fulfillment promises), I would never have seen my prospects broken the way they became. They would not have been humbled by their sinful nature and they would not see why they needed Christ to save them instead of them being able to redeem themselves. They would not understand why their good works do not add to the salvation process. Most frightening, I might have even created false, unrepentant converts.

Now that I had experienced a dose of beginner's success, where would this turning point (or Pinch) lead me from here?

I can only say that everything went on a rollercoaster ride from here.

Chapter 11

TEACHER ABOVE PUPIL

DO YOU EVER wish you could have a clear-cut formula that works on everybody in every situation? Imagine that your films were so flawless that they garnered only positive reviews and no negative ones. Your multi-level marketing product was so irresistible that everyone signed up under you, and thus placed you on top of the company's commission ladder in a matter of weeks. Your basketball skills were so unparalleled that you were unanimously dubbed the greatest basketball player in the world. Your political strategies were so revolutionary that they brought together undivided support from the entire nation. Consider this interesting scenario. Your evangelistic tool is so life changing and convincing that everyone you talk to converts to Christianity. I'm not talking about spurious, superficial conversions, but real deal rebirths in the Holy Spirit! Fathom a religion that could actually sell to everyone it comes across.

Unfortunately, these desires seem all but contrary to reality. Whether you are in the business world, politics, or the arts, there is always a hostile view to a proposed concept, no matter how great it is. The same applies more so to religion and spirituality.

In the last chapter, I discussed how I used the Law of God in my evangelism to make grace seem more enticing. However, I must be dutiful to inform you that the law is not a magic formula that holds a one-hundred percent success rate. As much as it is robust, biblical, and invaluable, the law does not guarantee to bring lost sinners to the grace of Christ. This powerful method has won and continues to win many to true saving faith, but the results of this (and the gospel message in general) can only go so far.

In responding to such dilemmas, Jesus advises in John 15:20, "Remember the word that I said to you, 'A slave is not greater than his master.' If they persecuted Me, they will also persecute you; if they kept My word, they will keep yours also. But all these things they will do to you for My name's sake, because they do not know the One who sent Me." This line reflects the obvious truth that believers are expected to be treated like the Messiah. If people hate Christ, they will also hate the disciples. If people listen to Christ, they will also listen to the disciples.

Jesus, being God in flesh, was the most loving, good, and truthful man to ever grace this planet. Christ was the perfect evangelist, but sadly, even He couldn't convince everyone of the truth. Although Christians are summoned to be as passionate and diligent as possible in their life of witnessing to the lost, they are not expected to outdo Christ in terms of evangelical effectiveness. Followers will experience rejection, especially if they follow Christ's biblical methods.

The only way Christians can ever attempt to become greater than the Master or Teacher is if they cheat in the game. They accomplish this cheating by twisting the gospel message, presenting an incomplete view, or using non-biblical methods. In other words, evangelists distort the gospel message to make it as marketable as possible. Those who go around the Master's teachings might be perceived as having outdone the Master in that they have found a method that is more harmonious, more convincing, and more popular. This could favorably bring many to Christ in numbers, but it doesn't necessarily mean that these sinners are saved. In fact, most of them probably are not. If Christians rely on the power of the flesh rather than on the Spirit, God will not work in their favor. That's why Scripture declares that we must be faithful to His ways. We can never surpass the knowledge, greatness, and persecution of our Lord Jesus Christ, and we should never attempt to. It will only result in detriment to others and possibly to us as well.

Knowing this, I do not overestimate the power of my gospel presentation, thinking that it will win souls all the time. It is not me who wins, but the Spirit of God. All I can do is be faithful to His outlined ways, and He will take care of the rest if it is in His will.

The only question that remains is how many more lost souls my actions will bring into the kingdom. I have my entire life to find out.

The Little Tokyo Meeting

On one casual Friday, I had lunch with a couple of church friends at the Sushi Gen restaurant in downtown Los Angeles. I decided to arrive thirty minutes before my friends to obtain a table for the three of us, since the restaurant does not have a reservation policy.

As I waited in line before the restaurant opened at 11:15 A.M., I spotted a familiar face beside me. He was a

Japanese-looking gentleman in his late twenties, casually sported, and accompanied by his girlfriend. I recognized him to be an actor from a movie. I had a good idea of who it was, but I wasn't sure just yet.

With nothing much to lose, I candidly asked, "This may seem like a strange question, but are you an actor?"

He looked pleasantly surprised as he replied, "Yes. How did you know that?"

"Were you in the movie *Letters from Iwo Jima*?"

"Yeah, I was."

That was what I wanted to hear! I enthusiastically greeted the actor as he introduced himself as Yuki Matsuzaki. If you are unfamiliar with his credentials, Yuki was most known for his breakthrough role as Nozaki in the Clint Eastwood directed war drama *Letters from Iwo Jima*, playing the beloved companion to the main character Saigo (Kazunari Ninomiya). Yuki also had a noteworthy role in the *Pink Panther 2* as Kenji, and played a Japanese Imperial Soldier in *The Last Samurai*.

Although my encounter with Mr. Matsuzaki did not take place in the Hollywood work environment, I decided to include this account because this actor is still a part of the entertainment world. As long as I can relate a good story about anything pertaining to mainstream Hollywood, I am there! Yuki turned out to be a very interesting case. Other than Xavier Tash, Yuki was the only other actor I had an opportunity to engage in a deep conversation regarding Christianity.

Yuki and I began our chat in the secular realm, talking about films. It's only natural that I first questioned Yuki about his experience on *Letters from Iwo Jima*. I was very curious as to his professional relationship with Clint Eastwood, so I asked him about the director's supposed one/two take philosophy. He confirmed that everything was true regarding Eastwood's efficiency in filming. The director does, in fact, nag a shot in one or two takes, and then moves onto the next scene. I also learned that the director does not yell, "Action!" as most directors do before the beginning of a take. Rather, he motions or gently tells the actors, "Go," and then the game begins.

After finishing with our film talks, we quickly moved to the subject of acclaimed Japanese restaurants in Los Angeles. We talked about everything from sushi to izakaya. It was a fun ten-minute conversation, and I was tempted to keep it that way for the sake of peace, but I knew I couldn't cave in to such thinking, even for this casual encounter with the celebrity. For the sake of the Lord's kingdom and for Yuki's salvation, I needed to find out about his spiritual status, even if it seemed unusual to bring the subject up out of nowhere. There really is nothing more important than this. Looking out for a neighbor's eternity is the ultimate act of love a Christian can bestow upon a non-believer.

I quickly pulled out a *Million Dollar Bill* from my shirt pocket and handed it to Yuki, asking, "Have you ever gotten a million dollar bill before?"

Yuki laughed as he stared down on the tract, exclaiming, "What the hell is this?"

"It has a gospel message on the back. Do you have a Christian background?"

In a short matter of time, I learned that Mr. Matsuzaki did indeed have some religious upbringing. He reminisced on how he had attended a Catholic school back in his childhood days in Japan. Aside from that, he had no real knowledge or connection with Christianity. Essentially, he was not an active believer.

I asked, "What do you think is going to happen to you when you die? Do you think you're going to go to heaven?"

From there, the actor responded in a convoluted manner. He wasn't too certain if he believed in an afterlife. He described concepts of life and death that represented a jumble of metaphysics, relativism, and philosophical naturalism. I didn't completely comprehend some of his views and I didn't give them much thought. I knew it wasn't important to solve problems in these areas. Just as the Bible teaches, I needed to speak directly to the man's conscience in order to gain access to his soul. Only when he is convinced of his spiritual disease of sin and death will other issues become meaningless to him. Only then will he desire to obtain the cure that is God's grace.

I tried to examine Yuki's views regarding his own sense of goodness by asking, "If you were to stand before God and He were to ask you why you should be let into heaven, what would you say to Him?"

Yuki asserted that he didn't think God would ask such a question. He didn't know what the point of it would be, claiming that every human is so distinct that there could be no real criteria to determine such cases. It became obvious that Yuki's moral views were highly blurred and that he didn't understand the correlation between the voice of his feelings and the universal absolutes of right and wrong. He was the ideal candidate for a discussion relating to the law. I decided to proceed with the presentation, although it turned out to be quite a challenge with this man.

After I took Yuki through some of the Commandments, he suddenly cut into my flow by asking, "Let me ask you something, Steve. If God created the earth, and the earth is made of matter, and voice is a product of matter, and God speaks, then does that mean that God is made of matter also? It doesn't make sense."

This was one of the most bizarre things I've ever heard from a skeptic. Yuki attempted to stump me with some of these questions during our conversation, making it difficult for me to take him through the law and grace. It was actually a bit frustrating, but I endured patiently. I have learned that when you're presenting the gospel message, the prospect will at times try to get you off your rock and have you chase them down a shaky trail. The key is to answer their question quickly, then get back on your mark. I had to stay on course and finish the presentation. It is a conviction of the gospel message that saves, not arguments that center on the prospect's false notions. Once you can speak directly to the conscience, most arguments usually fall away, unless the prospect's concerns severely handicap his thinking.

After addressing some of his concerns, I proceeded to explain the gospel to Yuki, but to my agitation, the restaurant doors opened at that very moment! I felt slight panic as I knew I would be cut off at this point. I explained the message as quickly as possible while we moved forward in the line. I touched on everything from God's justice being satisfied to His love exemplified through the offer of everlasting life found in Christ. As Yuki, his girlfriend, Satomi, and I moved along in the procession, I shared the gospel message somewhat like a news reporter being held back by security as he attempts to relay an important message to a VIP. I knew that we would be separated after we were seated, and that's what happened.

To my relief, I didn't lose the man forever. After the meal, I was able to reconnect with the actor at his table. I gave him a couple of apologetic tracts before he left. By now, you would think that my proselytizing might have bothered Yuki, but it didn't. In fact, Yuki was still upbeat. He accepted my offer graciously and was open to reading my tracts. He even extended his hand of respect to both my church comrades before he departed with Satomi. This occasion didn't result in Yuki's immediate conversion, but nonetheless, I still rejoiced in doing God's work.

It's always pleasing to have personal encounters with celebrities, especially ones who are open to friendly conversations. I commend Yuki for the fact that he was one of the most genuinely down-to-earth and approachable actors I've met. I really wish more were like him in terms of welcoming people into their hearts and minds. It's a shame that the gospel message doesn't have much success in accessibility.

Yuki's mind seemed hopelessly cluttered, yet nothing is impossible to clean up. The Holy Spirit is the only one who can grant clarity, understanding, and ultimately faith. I pray that He will break through someday and speak straight to Yuki's heart so he may testify of God's truth.

From Truth to Deception

By the appearance of my evangelistic accounts, it seems imperative that a Christian be well versed in the art of apologetics in addition to knowing law and grace. I wouldn't disagree with that logic. In instances such as Yuki, in which skeptics can conjure up unanticipated issues of science, evolution, or other mind-boggling concepts, it is good to have at least a fundamental understanding of all the important oppositions that run rampant in the world. It will only make you better at what you do. An effective witness of Christ will always be studying, learning, and practicing his craft, much like a Samurai warrior or Olympic athlete does in order to achieve his desired goal. His education should never stop, but continue until the day he dies. This is what makes an effective evangelist. This is what defines an overall effective disciple of Christ.

If you thought my time with Yuki required that I exercise a good deal of extra-biblical knowledge, it was really nothing compared to my experience with another prospect I encountered in Hollywood. While working on the television show *Lie to Me*, I met a woman named Heather, who revealed that she was a Mormon. She sat across from me in the extras holding area. Earlier in the day, I had given this woman a *Good Person Test*. At that time, she was sitting at another table in the facility. When she was required to move to mine because the film crew occupied her previous territory, she started to chat with me about the tract I had given her in the morning.

Heather appeared to be in her late forties. She was a temperate, kind, and mellow-spirited woman who was a retired LAUSD schoolteacher. She never married and made her own way through life. I was fascinated when she said she was formerly a Methodist Christian before converting to Mormonism.

I initially expected it to be the other way around—a Mormon turning into a born-again Christian. This situation was a slight anomaly to me, so I asked Heather, "How did you go from being Christian to becoming a Mormon?"

Heather responded that the Mormon doctrine just made sense to her. She then spent the next five minutes expounding on her journey to the Church of Latter Day Saints. It began with a Mormon friend introducing her to the philosophy. Heather was slowly, but willingly, educated through the doctrines of the religion. She told me just about every main point of Mormonism: the history of Joseph Smith, the Mormon book titled *The Pearl of Great Price*, and the pre-existence of all people in the eternal realm before being born into this world. She even explained salvation by quoting 2 Nephi 25:23 (from the Book of Mormon), which states, "For we know that it is by grace that we are saved, after all we can do."

I knew most of this beforehand from my studies on Mormonism, but it was surreal to hear someone shovel it out, especially coming from a former Christian who thought this made more sense than the truth of the Bible. I didn't know whether I should think of this as funny or disturbing. One thing I did know was that I needed to steer this woman away from this heretical teaching, or she would end up in a whole heap of trouble when she died. Idolatrous views of Jesus will certainly not be rewarded. Satan somehow had a grip on her, and I needed to address it.

I asked Heather, "Do you believe that we are saved by grace or by works?"

She replied, "By works. We need to prove ourselves worthy."

Since Heather wanted to enter heaven on her own merits—by her works-based religion—I presented her with what she must do on her own, just as Jesus had done with the rich young ruler in Mark 10. I informed her that she must perfectly follow God's standard of holiness, the Ten Commandments, in order to be good enough to attain salvation. I took Heather through the law and she admitted her inability to keep the Commandments. Unlike Yuki, Heather was cooperative in answering my questions. By the end of the presentation, she knew that she was headed for hell.

I asked Heather if she knew what God did to save her from eternal damnation. Heather knew the exact answer, mentioning Jesus' death on the cross for her sins. This was a positive step in the right direction, but I continued to explain the gospel nonetheless, illustrating its link to the law and the fulfillment of God's justice so she could fully understand grace. The point was to show her that her good works are futile and cannot save her, and that Christ did everything for her already with His own righteousness. All Heather needed to do was accept God's gift. This gift can never be purchased but only obtained through faith in Christ's completed work.

I wished at this moment that she would have fallen on her knees and repented in sackcloth and ashes, but it didn't turn out that way. She remained steadfast in her beliefs. During the next ten minutes, Heather tried her best to defend the doctrines and the truth of Mormonism, exclaiming that it was the new revelation given to humanity. In other words, the Book of Mormon was sort of like the "new" New Testament. The former biblical revelation had been supposedly corrupted over the centuries, and it was "the prophet" Joseph Smith who restored the truth after having been visited by celestial beings. Smith recorded everything the "angels" told him and therefore produced the Book of Mormon. It sounds kind of like the story of Muhammad and Islam, doesn't it?

Already having explained law and grace to Heather, I knew I couldn't take her through the motions again. I needed to draw upon the well of my extra-biblical knowledge to highlight the truth of what I was advocating. Taking a Bible out of my duffel bag, I turned to Galatians and read to her, "I am amazed that you are so quickly deserting Him who called you by the grace of Christ, for a different gospel; which is really not another; only there are some who are disturbing you and want to distort the gospel of Christ. But even if we, or an angel from heaven, should preach to you a gospel contrary to what we have preached to you, he is to be accursed!" (Gal. 1:6-8).

Heather looked at me in slight perplexity as I explained my purpose in reading the passage. I said, "What I'm basically saying is this: Joseph Smith ran into angels that preached a message different from what's in the Bible. I'm sorry to say this, but those angels that Joseph Smith encountered were demons. Joseph Smith is a false prophet."

She immediately replied, "No, those weren't demons. Joseph Smith told the demons to be gone! Joseph Smith is a true prophet from God."

Heather pressed on with the issue of God's revelation in this world. She continued to defend the veracity of the Mormon books, and even exclaimed that the presidents of the Mormon churches were modern-day prophets sent by the Lord.

Heather pleaded with me, asking, "Tell me, what must I do to convince you of the truth? How can I convince you that this is the new revelation from God?"

I was speechless. The realization that this woman was now proselytizing me seemed ironic. I admit that her passion for her religion was admirable, only because it led to a sense of evangelistic zeal that nearly matched my own. I honestly wish more Christians had her same fervor in witnessing. It's sad that some non-Christians are more willing to die for a lie than most Christians are willing to live for the truth.

I mustered up my last attempt to try to persuade my prospect. Through other defense tactics against the Mormon doctrine, I attempted to show Heather the vanity of her works and her need to depend on grace alone. I even directed her to Paul's letter to the Ephesians that states, "For by grace you have been saved through faith; and that not of yourselves, it is the gift of God; not as a result of works, so that no one may boast" (Eph. 2:8-9). After an endless game of spiritual ping-pong regarding faith and works, the trinity of God, and salvation, a PA finally encroached on our territory and called us to the set.

I didn't have the opportunity to talk with Heather again after that. I don't know how much of an impact I made on her train of thought. I can only hope that it at least planted a seed, and that our faithful God will help it flourish through the influence of other people. It's depressing that a once-professing Christian wound up on this path; not through rebellion, but through honest deception.

The Sovereignty of God

Sometimes evangelism can be discouraging. You may possess all the right tools, all the knowledge, and the most potent weapons in the universe, but they will not always lead you to your desired outcome. Most times they will probably fail you. Does that mean our efforts are in vain? Absolutely not! Jesus calls us to be obedient slaves in seeking out the lost. If it is in His will, He will draw the unbeliever to salvation through the working of the Holy Spirit.

Jesus spoke these words while praying to His Father in heaven, "I have manifested Your name to the men whom You gave Me out of the world; they were Yours and You gave them to Me, and they have kept Your word" (John 17:6). This is one of numerous passages that illustrate the principle of God's divine election of the saints. The Father leads believers to Christ. God chose them before the foundation of the world and then wrote their names in the Lamb's book of life. Jesus says that, "no one can come to Me unless the Father who sent Me draws him" (John 6:44).

Because God has preordained these things, does this mean that we should not evangelize? No. Human responsibility works in conjunction with God's sovereignty, whether it is in the issue of evangelism or sanctification. We should never presume God's plans, especially with regard to the sensitive issue of election. The Lord calls us to be active witnesses for the lost, and one day we will give an account of our actions at the Judgment Seat of Christ, which is described in 1 Corinthians 3:13-15.

The Judgment Seat of Christ is an event in heaven where God will distribute blessings and rewards to Christians based on their level of sacrificial service to Him. Revelation 22:12 shows that this happens immediately after the rapture of the church, or when Christ comes to take Christians out of the world before the Tribulation period begins for remaining unbelievers on earth. This is why Christians must always be laborious in their efforts to reach the lost and be ready for the Savior's imminent return. Failure to do such things will undoubtedly lead to diminished eternal honors when that day comes.

Though there are no magic formulas to bring everyone to salvation (except for the will of the Holy Ghost), we can live with the hope that such a trend will not last forever. One day there will be no more dissension in the land of God. When Christ establishes the New Heavens and the New Earth, His rule will win the allegiance of the entire world. His desires will motivate everyone to participate in His plans. His abilities will captivate everyone to proclaim Him to be the greatest star ever. Most importantly, His love will draw the hearts of every man and woman toward unbreakable peace.

Until then, I will just have to work to the best of my ability with what the Bible teaches me. That's all I've really got. Whether my mission succeeds, fails, draws praise, or induces criticism, I can be at peace with knowing that if I follow the Lord's ways, I will always be a winner.

As Romans 8:31 states, "If God is for us, who can be against us?"

Chapter 12

THE LONE RANGER

I T'S NO SECRET that Jesus' ministry had its share of opposition, most characteristically from the teachers, scribes, Pharisees, and other religious leaders of His time. As much as His words shone like a beacon of light to some, to many others those words reeked like an unwelcome stench. I'm not just talking about the genteel religious authorities. It seems as if the obstacles of the Messiah's statements had turned away even the commoners who had once committed themselves (at least superficially) to the Lord Jesus' will.

Following the Bread of Life discourse, when Jesus painted the portrait of Himself as the ultimate truth and the only food that gives life, the Redeemer's disciples could finally go no further. They caved in to the pressure of the demands expected of those who follow Him. "Therefore many of His disciples, when they heard this, said, 'This is a difficult statement; who can listen to it?' But Jesus, conscious that His disciples grumbled at this, said to them, 'Does this cause you to stumble? It is the Spirit who gives life; the flesh profits nothing; the words that I have spoken to you are spirit and are life" (John 6:60-61 and 63). The passage then goes on to explain that, "as a result of this many of His disciples withdrew and were not walking with Him anymore" (John 6:66).

Though this text was intended to highlight the theme of God's divine election of the saints through Jesus' earthly separation of the sheep and goats (true and false disciples), it also comments on an interesting point that would become timeless thereafter. The teachings of Christ, especially those truths that are not readily pleasing to the ear, prove offensive even to believers. Most followers of Christ will do whatever they can to downplay the difficult nature of Jesus, whether they are soundly saved or not, even if they have to employ euphemisms to make the Messiah's words more accessible or less disconcerting to the fellowship body.

When it comes down to the main incentive, it's really all about peace, sometimes even at the expense of somebody's eternal welfare.

A Soldier on the Attack

During one of my phone conversations with Jonathan Khan, I learned that my name had garnered a negative impression from some of the people on set, even among some professing believers. Jonathan filled me in by recounting a recent job in which he worked with Paul Kwak. All three of us are intimately familiar with each other, although we've never officially collaborated on the same project as a trio (I pray that we will someday).

During the production, Jonathan met a female background actor who claimed to know Paul and me. *How interesting*, I thought. I didn't know who this person was, but I nevertheless asked Jonathan to elaborate on the story.

Jonathan mentioned that as he conversed with this woman about Christianity, she said she, "didn't like the way Steve shared the gospel with people," and that she liked Paul's approach much better.

To my relief, Jonathan defended my cause. He informed this woman that Paul didn't use the law in evangelism, which is why his approach was entirely inoffensive. I'm not attempting to discredit Paul's evangelistic effort in any way. I'm merely trying to prove my point that the gospel message, when presented in its unadulterated form, is naturally offensive to many unbelievers. That is why Christians shouldn't be too surprised or dismayed if they get negative feedback for their truthful gospel presentation.

With that in mind, I must ask that if Jesus was such a kind and loving man, why did some people hate Him so much? It is because of what He said. He testified to the truth that their works were evil, that there is a day of justice coming from a wrath-filled God, and that a person can be saved from his bondage to hell only through the Son of Man. He convicted people of their sin by presenting God's righteous standard against theirs to defeat their hopes of self-merited salvation. We know from human history that when a person's pride and self-worth is severely challenged, people can become quite touchy!

Following the Messiah's footsteps of evangelism would naturally lead me to the same results, which is why I wasn't entirely disheartened that someone didn't like my evangelism approach. When I present my messages, I anticipate that some will become convicted toward repentance and gratitude, while others will become more convicted toward self-righteousness and alienation. It's interesting to know that my infamous reputation had even spread to the far corners of the extras' gossip circle. I knew that a substantial part of this came about because of my infamous gospel tracts.

CALLING CARDS

It's a habitual practice of mine that at the end of a work day I pass out tracts to every background artist standing in the check-out line. Since I can't witness verbally to every single person in a given day, I figured that I could at least give them a tract and pray that God would plant a seed or maybe even lead these people to immediate salvation. One should never underestimate the power of a gospel tract. Tracts have led many people to salvation in the past and continue to do so every day. If you don't have an opportunity to communicate with someone, then you can at least hand them something to read in their spare time. It's always better to give them something rather than stand back and do nothing. It's possible that the person could be living his very last day on earth, and that your influence may make a difference for his eternal destiny.

During my three years in the acting business, I distributed tracts to well over one thousand Hollywood players. This end-of-the-day tract dissemination was something that Jonathan didn't even think about. After I informed him about my practices, Jonathan also started to hand out tracts to every person in the clock-out line. I guess there are some things that even mentors can learn from their students.

As you may already know from my predicaments with such stars as Sutherland, Spelling, and Woods, gospel tracts have helped me reach many people with whom I would normally not have a chance to communicate, and a good number of these people actually liked them. I worked on a Rhapsody music video commercial in May of 2009, where I was able to give another one of my tracts to the production's lead star, Rob Thomas. For those who are unfamiliar with this name, Rob Thomas is a famous rock/pop singer who was well known for his association with the band Matchbox Twenty back in the 1990s. He is a solo artist now, but is still successful from what I understand.

Mr. Thomas was surprisingly courteous and approachable. I exclaimed to him how I appreciated his music. He was encouraged and thanked me for my support. After that, I was quick to hand Rob a gospel tract. It's funny to mention that he didn't merely take it and say thank you, but actually opened the tract and started to read the first page with great interest.

As I stood in front of him in this awkward moment, I said, "Oh, don't feel pressured to read it in front of me if you don't want to. You can read it in your spare time."

The musician nodded his head and replied, "Alright, I sure will."

Mr. Thomas then took off with his trailing assistant. It was interesting to see him still perusing the pamphlet as he walked off down the street. I think he was the only celebrity I met who was this interested in reading the gospel tract I handed him. It is through times like this that I fervently ask the Lord to cause these gospel tracts to have an impact and bring the recipient to salvation.

It would be great if everyone reacted with the same sense of excitement, curiosity, and interest that Rob Thomas displayed. Unfortunately, that's not always the case. Even if you hand out the most ostentatious, eye-popping, and cutting-edged tracts, they will oftentimes be met with indifference and even antagonism. Why? Because the power of the gospel message will burst out of the tracts and run straight through their hearts. Regardless of medium or deliverance, Jesus' words ultimately repel impenitent sinners.

TURNED-OFF BELIEVER

In the month of May, I worked on a feature film titled *The Roommate*, which was shot in downtown Los Angeles, in which I played a college bar patron. It was one of those rare days when I was never actually used, but it didn't matter much to me. It may seem unusual that an actor didn't care whether his face is plastered on the big screen or not, but I was really a missionary disguised as an actor. My real pay came from accomplishing the will of my Father in heaven. His will was that I seek and save the lost.

I verbally proselytized a couple of the background folks on this day, but I was unable to get to the rest of the crowd. So I reached them with the printed medium—tracts. This always proved to be a fast and easy way to get the gospel message out to a large crowd. When it came time to sign out, I distributed *Million Dollar Bills* to nearly every background artist in the checkout line. There were close to a hundred background players on this job, so I passed out quite a load. Although most of them respectfully took my offering, a few actually returned and shoved the tract back into my hands after reading them. Such an act wasn't entirely new to me, as I had experienced rejections like this a few times in the past. I didn't enjoy it, but I was prepared to take it because I knew it was part of the job. I had to be ready to receive the heat as well as the praise.

As I neared passing out my last tract, a surprising thing happened. A young woman marched up to me with the *Million Dollar Bill* in hand. Her face showed concern, yet it was plastic in reality. There was more of an inner sternness and condescension in her as she lectured me with these words, "Let me tell you that I love Jesus too. You see these people handing them back to you. They're doing so because they're feeling condemned. I make relationships with people so that they come to Jesus."

She once again accentuated her point by declaring, "Make relationships. Think!"

I stared blankly at her as a million thoughts raced through my mind. I felt confusion, concern, and irritation all at the same time. Before I could respond, she turned and marched away from me, back to the sign-out line. It took a few seconds for me to internalize the reality that I had been insulted by a fellow Christian. It's bad enough that I get persecuted by non-believers on a near-regular basis, but to receive the same treatment from a believer is utterly confounding and disheartening.

It's sad to say that this woman did not have a solid understanding of God's truth. If she did, she would have supported me and not condemned my actions. Nowhere in the Bible does it mention that you must form a long-term, meticulously-planned friendship with someone in order for them to be saved. Rather, it illustrates the opposite. The disciples often preached in the marketplace and synagogues, being quick to share the gospel message with people they didn't know and people they would never see again. Most of the apostles were assaulted, beaten, and killed for their efforts. Religious persecution is a natural part of doing the Lord's work, and it should not be looked upon as a fault on the Christian's effort.

So why would the apostles evangelize in a manner that seems counterintuitive to our postmodern methods? Because they knew the gospel message was the power of God that led to salvation and that it would not come by the strength of human ingenuity. This is why they were bold enough to speak to dozens of strangers at any given moment. If they had restricted their game plan to just forming relationships with sinners and sharing the gospel with them over the course of a few years, then the rate of the kingdom expansion would have progressed too slowly. I probably would not have been a Christian today if this were so!

Let me mention that I am not against friendship evangelism. I support it because it can prove highly beneficial to the one being ministered to. It can pave a smoother path for your love and testimony to break through to a friend's heart—an advantage that strangers would otherwise not have access to in such a brief time span. Yet, if you compartmentalize evangelism into this one set mode, then you are limiting your potential to influence many others who also need your help. There are multitudes of strangers we see all around us every day, and these are the lost sinners that we have an obligation to reach out to—whether we are comfortable seeking them or not.

This is the essence of the Great Commission. This is what it means when Jesus commands us to deny ourselves and take up our cross daily.[23] In doing so, we will undoubtedly suffer pain, and some of us may even lose our lives. Yet the Bible says that it is an anticipated outcome, because Jesus suffered the very same fate.

I don't know if this woman is truly saved or not; whether she is following the true gospel or a counterfeit one. I only hope that she will study the Word of God more carefully and take courage in reaching out to the multitudes with radical love. Only then will she see the heart of a Christian missionary in this world.

Only then will she realize that persecution is not a curse, but the blessing of God falling on her life. Paul gloriously declared, "For to me, to live is Christ and to die is gain" (Phil. 1:21).

Hollywood Confidential

If it appears that my image is becoming increasing unfavorable within the society of background players (Christian or non-Christian), then this next account should serve as an even greater surprise. While working on an episode of *Chuck* for a downtown Los Angeles night call, I met an extra named Chris, who was a Roman Catholic apostate. He was somewhat of an agnostic, and non-religious in every way.

After familiarizing myself with Chris for a little while, I attempted to explain the gospel truth to him. At times, I even presented a clear distinction between the foundations of biblical Christianity and Roman Catholicism. Unfortunately, the seeds fell on hardened soil. He casually shrugged everything off and even attempted to pick my brain by asking convoluted questions in the hope of crippling my position. I confidently answered him in every respect, although I wasn't too sure how much closer it brought him to the doors of heaven.

After a few additional minutes of debate, Chris dropped a bombshell when he claimed to have recognized me. He mirthlessly stated, "I think I know about you. You're the guy who gave that religious stuff to James Woods, right?"

Chris mystified me by this declaration, as he had not come across my path before this day, and I was certain he wasn't there on the day I met with James Woods on the set of *Shark* at 20th Century Fox Studios. Even if he was there, he couldn't possibly have known about this incident because no background artists were around me at the time.

I asked Chris, "How do you know that?"

Chris responded, "That is the story that has been circulating throughout Hollywood."

Chris smirked and walked away from the conversation. He left me dumbfounded in this revelation. As much as I was disappointed not to have helped Chris see the light of the truth, he intrigued me by his final words. My gig on *Shark* took place quite awhile back, yet I began to fear the repercussions of my actions once again.

Apparently, what happened at *Shark* did not stay at *Shark*. Either James Woods or the rattled production assistant spread the news regarding the antics of one Steve Cha. I was suddenly a targeted man, an infamous name, the Christian freak that every film industry heathen needs to be on the watch for.

It's intimidating to think that my Christian reputation had already caused a stir in the background artist community, but for it to also blaze like fire into the deeper realms of actors and crew members gave me a real reason to be concerned. This is especially true considering its heat had fallen on a distant background artist like Chris. Should I be in fear for the safety of my Hollywood career?

Regardless of what may have happened, I was prepared. I knew that danger would surface sooner or later. I needed to be faithful to my Lord's calling. Only then could I exercise trust that He would provide for me in times of my needs. Whether I am loved, hated, happy, grief-stricken, rich or poor, I will glorify my God and not the world.

As Peter states, "Beloved, do not be surprised at the fiery ordeal among you, which comes upon you for your testing, as though some strange thing were happening to you; but to the degree that you share the sufferings of Christ, keep on rejoicing, so that also at the revelation of His glory you may rejoice with exultation. If you are reviled for the name of Christ, you are blessed, because the Spirit of glory and of God rests on you…therefore, those also who suffer according to the will of God shall entrust their souls to a faithful Creator in doing what is right" (1 Pet. 4:12-19). I continue to seek for His boldness as I journey through the entertainment industry. Whether it is to an extra or a principle actor, I will do what the Messiah did and speak the gospel message in truth and righteousness. It may cause animosity from both believers and non-believers alike, but His words represent life.

What else really matters?

Chapter 13

TOP DOGS

W HEN ADORING FANS approach renowned celebrities, the first thing the celebrities expect to give is either an autograph or a personal picture. If they are in a good mood, stars will spend an additional minute engaging in a brief, but friendly, conversation with their followers. Although this is a stereotypical image of the conduct between celebrity and fan, it has stood the test of time, proving true in almost every situation. It is one of those living clichés that can never be exhausted.

How can fans really help their actions if they are standing right in front of their idols? It's natural to be ecstatic and to want something from the actor to keep forever. I guess this is especially true if one views actors and actresses as exalted beings who dispense the highest hopes in life rather than being morally bankrupt sinners in need of hope themselves. In reality, many of them are the ones who really should be receiving godly hope rather than dispensing their own futile versions of it. This is where the gospel comes into play.

The only person I've met thus far who has been able to think outside the box and give God priority in such circumstances is Jonathan Khan, as evidenced by his past experiences with Steven Spielberg, Will Smith, and other big-name stars. He was the one who directly inspired me to give up my own personal agenda when meeting my share of celebrities in order to advance the gospel. In essence, Jonathan showed me what it means to live out radical faith in this world instead of simply going through the motions. There is nothing gloomier than living a spiritual existence that is conventional, unchallenging, and most importantly, devoid of passion.

Until now, I've described some of my witnessing encounters with various celebrities. Some of them you may know and others you may not. Although there are still many prominent names with whom I desire to share the good news, I have been fortunate enough to do so with two other very popular names in the industry. Although I can't say they compare to the likes of Steven Spielberg and Harrison Ford that Jonathan Khan worked with, they were some of the closest I got to in my professional career.

As exciting and privileged as these opportunities were for me, they also ran major risks. My noble efforts cost me something at the end of the day. As I learned from Jonathan's past, the bigger the name, the worse the damage.

THE JESUS NETWORK

In November of 2009, I worked on the film *The Social Network*, the Oscar-nominated drama directed by David Fincher (*Seven, Fight Club, The Curious Case of Benjamin Button*). The day's shoot took place at the Ebell of Los Angeles building in West Hollywood, where we shot a university recital scene. For those who have watched the film, it is the scene where a group of tuxedo-clad students sings an a cappella rendition of the *All-4-One* song, "I Swear." I sat behind Max Minghella's character, Divya Narendra, who jolts out of the room after learning of the Facebook launch from his female friend's notebook computer.

The day turned out to be a typical twelve-hour shoot. The confounding part was that there were only two scenes scheduled on the call sheet and it still occupied the entire twelve-plus hours. As I learned at the beginning of the day, the director was known for doing innumerable takes for his shots. Fincher had captured fifty-two takes for just one shot the day before. I've never heard of a director who demanded so many takes for a single shot. Based on this work schedule, I could have been on set for possibly twenty hours! At this moment, I envied, in a slightly humorous way, not being on a Clint Eastwood production, but fortunately, Fincher didn't go to the extreme on this particular day.

Before I stepped onto the set, I researched the cast and formulated my plan for whom I was going to evangelize. This is what I always do when I arrive to do a film or television show. I do this to be better equipped with knowledge and preparation so I can approach each individual actor/celebrity in a way that would allow me to communicate with them more knowledgeably. Unfortunately, *The Social Network* didn't have an all-star lineup on board, so my options were pretty limited. Aside from the acclaimed David Fincher, the only other person I could have witnessed to was Justin Timberlake, but the singer didn't have any scenes scheduled for the day, so he was not an option. I concluded that Mr. Fincher was going to be the one and only candidate of the day.

As with some of my other specialized prospects, I was required to exercise discernment when it came to knowing when to approach the director at the appropriate time.

Sometimes I would evangelize the prospect during the day, but most of the time it took place after the sign-out process. I actually sat next to Mr. Fincher during lunch, but I was not able to witness to him then because he was involved in a deep conversation with a staff member sitting across from him. I had no choice but to perform my duty at the end of the day.

My plans took a bit of a stumble when I signed out an hour before the official wrap time that night. The production eliminated a group of background artists because they were not required for the final shot. I was one of the artists released. Although I still could have evangelized since I was off the time clock, the rest of the cast and crew were not, which made it difficult for me to meet up with Mr. Fincher. To witness to him required that I step up to him in front of the entire film crew on set and make my presentation about Jesus. You can probably surmise that this would cause the film crew to pounce on me as the angry Jews did on Peter, Paul, and the rest of the apostles in the book of Acts.

By the grace of God, an opportunity presented itself. As I lingered close to the shooting facility in the hallway, Mr. Fincher stepped off the set temporarily to retrieve something from another room. I thought this would be the best time. My heart pounded with nervous anticipation as I waited outside the room. Within a few seconds, David walked out. It was just he and I in the immediate region.

I boldly exclaimed, "Oh, Mr. Fincher…"

The director looked directly at me. I said in an ecstatic manner, "I was just about to take off, but I wanted to say that I really loved *Zodiac*. It was an awesome movie."

At this point, I didn't know how he would react. I didn't know if he would be appreciative, lukewarm, or antagonistic. From what I had heard from Paul Kwak (who worked on *The Social Network* a week prior), the director seemed like a stern, serious, and exclusive man. Because of this, I didn't have high expectations of friendliness when I stood in David's presence. Yet, I still acted courageously in stepping up to him. I was more concerned for his salvation than for my reputation. The fear of the Lord must always be greater than the fear of man.

As it turned out, I had nothing to fear. After I gave him my compliments, the director's face slowly expanded into an amazed expression as he proclaimed, "Oh, so you're the one who likes my…" David chuckled and said, "Nah, I'm just kidding you!"

I was very relieved. I continued in an aura of excitement as I replied, "Yeah. I just want to say once again that I really liked *Zodiac*, as well as all your other movies."

"Oh, why thank you. I really appreciate it."

The director extended his hand and I shook it with glee. I was now ready to move on to the Jesus matter, which was to bestow upon the director a tract. This time, it was not going to be a mere *Good Person Test*, but a copy of "The Greatest Gamble" DVD! I retrieved the resource out of my jacket pocket and asked Fincher, "I'm curious, have you ever heard of a show called *The Way of the Master*?"

The director shook his head. I then asked him, "Do you know the actor Kirk Cameron?"

David shook his head again. I was somewhat surprised that the director was unaware of Mr. Cameron. I thought almost everyone in Hollywood knew who Kirk Cameron was, especially the older generation.

I made sure by asking Mr. Fincher, "Have you ever heard of the television show called *Growing Pains* from back in the 80s? He was one of the teenage cast members."

It seemed as if a light bulb flared inside of the director's head as he exclaimed, "Oh yeah, I think I remember!"

"Okay, well check out this DVD. This is his reality television show called *The Way of the Master*. It's one of the episodes called "The Greatest Gamble." It's about playing Russian roulette in Las Vegas."

Mr. Fincher looked astounded. He asked, "Is it real?"

"Well, I guess that's what you have to find out."

"Thanks! Is that your name on this sleeve?"

"Yes, it is."

"Cool. I'll take a look at it."

Mr. Fincher walked back to the set with the DVD in hand, still gazing down on the cover as he read, "*Way of the Master...*"

I found this encounter to be a bit humorous, but I was glad that Fincher had a bright attitude. It gave me more confidence that he would be open to the gospel message found inside. It's hard to predict whether people like him would be receptive if I had candidly declared such tracts as Christian material. I guess what was important was that he took it and considered watching it. It shows that sometimes in life it is necessary to present attractive bait so prospects are willing to swallow the bitter medicine. In this case, it was Russian roulette in Las Vegas. What can be more gratifying to a sinner's appetite than this tagline?

For an entire week afterward, I wondered whether the DVD had affected David Fincher's life or not. I may have received a clue to this question about two weeks after my time on *The Social Network*. As I returned from an overseas vacation in December, I checked my voicemail and discovered I had received one message from the Screen Actors Guild office. The department assistant wanted to speak to me regarding "a matter" on the film *The Social Network*. She was vague on the details but asked that I return her call.

Oh, no, I thought. *This must be about my meeting with David Fincher.* I knew they would question me, but I wondered how damaging the results would be. Would I be reprimanded? Or possibly even terminated from the acting union? Then again, it may not even be about the David Fincher situation, but what else could it have been about?

I dutifully returned the assistant's call the following day. She didn't receive my message immediately, because she was out of the office that morning. She did eventually get in touch with me the next day, but when it happened, she said that she couldn't remember what she wanted to talk to me about. She just told me to be at peace before she hung up. That marked the end of any personal connections to *The Social Network.*

I still wonder to this day what piece of information slipped this woman's mind. Had I actually picked up the phone when she first contacted me, I would have known, but now it will forever remain a mystery.

I guess in many ways this could be a good thing.

HERO TO A HERO

During my entire career as a background artist, I had been associated with nearly one hundred different television productions. For a good number of them, I worked only once and never returned. However, there were a few where I received recurring jobs. Such examples include *90210*, *CSI: NY*, and *How I Met Your Mother*. One of those that couldn't seem to get enough of me was the NBC hit series *Heroes*. I worked the show ten times in less than two years.

The number officially changed to eleven when they called me back to another episode of *Heroes* in the summer of 2009. This particular gig was novel because I was finally going to work with a new cast member. In the past, I was almost always placed alongside the same two actors:

Masi Oka (who played Hiro Nakamura) and James Kyson Lee (Ando Masahashi). Since these two principles were constantly involved in Asian settings, the show always needed me to help fill in the background. Based on the low ratio of Asians to Caucasians registered with Central Casting, you can surmise why the company would recycle Asian talents for the job.

This time, Masi and James were not around. Instead, we got one of the main actresses, Hayden Panetierre, for the day. This young woman plays Claire Bennett, who is one of the main characters on the show. It's no secret that Hayden is one of the most popular cast members on the lineup. That is why I figured this prospect would be a golden one. I didn't know if she was a Christian. Nevertheless, I was determined to act. This would surely be a great opportunity to be a spiritual hero to a fictional one.

The production took place in the Sunset Gower Studios in Hollywood. I was part of a cafeteria scene, in which college students study around various tables while Hayden's character converses clandestinely with one her friends. It was an easy day for the extras. In fact, the whole atmosphere was somewhat laid back, which worked well to my advantage. This made it easier for me to get the gospel message across to the actress.

The golden moment came after Hayden finished her scene rehearsals at the cafeteria site. I stood against a building wall, at a distance from the shooting location to my left. The actors' honey wagons were on the direct opposite to my right. After finishing a chat with one of the PAs, Hayden walked away from set toward the wardrobe trailers. That meant the actress had to cruise right by me in order to get to her destination. The great thing was that no one else was in the immediate proximity.

As I previously mentioned, I always felt more comfortable dealing with the principle actors at the end of the day so as not to risk my job or at least my reputation during the twelve-hour work shift. In this case, my day had just begun, yet here was Hayden, moving closer to my direction, with no PAs looming around.

A few thoughts percolated through my head. *Should I act now? What if I get into trouble? Will this chance ever come again?*

I thought that maybe I should wait. I might get another opportunity at the end of the day. As she got closer, I knew I couldn't take that risk. Maybe there wouldn't be another opportunity. This could be a Woody Harrelson botch all over again, so I decided to grab this opening.

I stepped up to the side of Ms. Panetierre and exclaimed, "Oh, Hayden!"

The actress stopped in her tracks and turned her gaze toward me. In somewhat of an ingenuous and fawning approach, I explained to Hayden, "I wanted to introduce myself and say that I'm a fan of your work."

Hayden sported a curious, yet slightly paranoid, expression as she asked me, "Do you work around here?"

I replied, "No. I actually work with you on the show, but I wanted to say that I used to watch your shows on the Disney channel with my little sister."

Upon hearing this, Hayden's face brightened up tremendously and she smiled gleefully like a child. I guess the word Disney truly does bring out the magic in people's behavior! God bless the company in that aspect.

Hayden extended her hand to me and introduced herself. I shook her hand and told her my name. We engaged in a chat, although it was a brief because she needed to return to her honey wagon to change into her scene apparel.

As Hayden finished the conversation, I quickly handed her a *Good Person Test*. She looked down on it curiously and asked, "What is this?"

I replied, "It's a Good Person Test. It has the Ten Commandments."

Hayden flipped through the pamphlet a bit. She asked, "How are you affiliated with this organization?"

"Oh, I'm not, actually. I buy these and give them out to help people."

The actress nodded. She sported a mischievous grin as she stated, "I don't think I'm a good person."

This was the direct opposite response from Diablo Cody. Hayden impressed me by her confession. It was original and brutally honest. Even the worst sinners I've met proudly proclaimed their own goodness, despite their obvious failure to keep the moral laws of God. Yet, Hayden was sincere about her moral condition. I can only imagine what she must have done to affirm this.

I said, "Okay. Well, read through it when you get a chance. It has a great message."

She replied, "I sure will." Hayden continued to chuckle as she walked back to her trailer with the tract in hand.

A few beats later, a couple of background players walked up to me from a distance and asked, "Hey, I saw you talking with Hayden over there. Did you actually give her something? What did you give her?"

Some additional extras huddled up to me as well. They all asked, "Yeah! What did you give to her? What did you give her? Tell us."

Oh great. I guess I have to do some open air preaching now, I thought.

Before I opened my mouth, the production assistant, Mus, came over and called us to the set to begin work. Thus they had no choice but to abruptly drop the subject. It was somewhat of a relief for me, although I was prepared to stand up for the Lord if required. This in itself would have been another standout moment of the day had it actually happened.

We marched toward the cafeteria in unison, but my troubles did not totally disappear. They resurfaced from another angle. Before I entered the cafeteria, PA Mus motioned me aside from the rest of the flock. I sensed that he was going to give me a warning regarding my moment with Hayden, and I was right.

Mus asked me, "You know what you did was wrong, right?"

I shook my head in a naïve manner. Mus explained, "Talking to Hayden. That's something you cannot do. That's a big no-no. I'm going to be cool about it this time, but don't do it again, okay?"

I nodded firmly as Mus patted me on the shoulder. This gesture showed me that Mus wasn't angry with me. He was just trying to keep me out of trouble by gently warning me. I was lucky because most other PAs would have poured their personal wrath upon me for breaking set laws. This shows how seriously they guard the barriers between principles and extras.

I took advantage of this act of charity by behaving for the rest of the workday. I remained silent, hoping that the PA, the film crew, and even Hayden herself would not come marching back to me and give me a piece of their minds. I was able to get through the day with no more controversies. At least that's what I thought until the sign-out process.

Bitter Aftertaste

After the day's production wrapped, I went about my habitual practice of distributing gospel tracts to every extra.

This time I exercised a little precaution in that I performed my activities out of the PA's view. I was able to give out my *Million Dollar Bills* to most of the departing players. Although I anticipated a few rejections, I was glad that most everyone accepted my gift.

After I dealt with my last prospect, I returned to the line, which was now empty, so I could sign out myself. The PA (who happened to be a different person) asked me in a disgruntled manner, "Where were you this whole time? I was about to leave. Didn't I tell you all to wait in line and not stand around? Did you follow directions?"

I replied, "Oh, I'm sorry about that."

"Where were you?"

"I was in the back over there giving out some stuff."

The PA looked aggravated. He remarked, "You better watch out when doing stuff like that on the lot. You could get into major trouble. Did you know that?"

I replied, "In the past, the PAs were cool with it as long as I did it after work."

"Well, not here. I don't care if you do your thing on the street or outside the facility, but here it can be a big problem. I'm warning you right now."

I nodded to placate his anger. The PA signed me out grudgingly and handed me the employee's copy of the voucher. As I took it, I held up a tract and asked kindly, "By the way, would you like one of these yourself?"

The PA sighed at my offer and asked, "Did you hear any of what I just said? No, I don't want one. Tell me your name."

I replied, "Steve Cha."

The PA said nothing more as he marched away back to the honey wagons. I didn't know why he wanted to know my name, but I didn't dwell on it much. Though I felt the uneasiness that accumulated from my whole day's worth of evangelizing, I returned to my car in the Gower Studios lot and prayed wholeheartedly for the salvation of everyone I encountered.

That day on *Heroes* proved to be the most active ministry work I've ever conducted on the show out of the eleven times I was assigned to it. Unfortunately, it was the last time I ever worked for *Heroes*. My streak with the program mysteriously ceased after that. No longer did it become one of my recurring gigs.

I guess now I knew why the PA wanted to know my name. It seemed that they blacklisted me from the NBC television series because of my religious activities on set. It was a small tragedy, considering *Heroes* was the first show I'd ever worked on as a background artist. Not even their need for Asian-American actors led them to seek my services again. That's how powerful the gospel works in convicting sinners. It will lead people to either thank the messenger or kill him off.

This had become a sad and even scary realization. Was this *Heroes* incident a sign of more dangers to come?

I needed to prepare myself for the possible storms ahead. Although I had already gone through some pains and distress during my two years in the film industry, in the spiritual, personal, and professional realms, I knew there would be more obstacles coming my way.

The question was whether I could take it. Could I be as valiant as Jonathan and continue to bear even harder bashings? Was I motivated to continue preaching in the film industry to all lost people?

I knew things would most likely not get easier from this point on.

Chapter 14

THE DAYS OF NOAH

APOSTASY. GLOBAL WARMING. The World Trade Center. The suffering world economy. Diminishing natural resources. The Haiti earthquake. The Japan tsunami. Iran and Israel's deadly conflict. It's undeniable that there are countless problems abounding in all corners of this earth, whether in politics or in human behavior. What is even more disheartening is that men are trapped in the puzzle of not being able to explain why these things are happening.

Movies like *Armageddon*, *Deep Impact*, *The Day After Tomorrow*, and *2012* popularized the notion that the world is coming to an end very soon. Of course, these films are nothing more than popcorn fiction. Yet, their underlying themes are based on true-to-life premises that stand as viable threats to our civilization. The ozone layer dilemma, the rise of sea level, increasing epidemics, and nuclear weapons are some of the indications that our age is much more at risk of annihilation than it has ever been before.

Are these escalating horrors merely coincidental accidents? Has the world always been this bad? Could these occurrences signify the end of the world as we speak? In other words, are we the final generation that Jesus spoke of in Matthew 24:3-51—the generation that will inevitably be part of the Tribulation as prophesized in Revelation, Daniel, and Ezekiel?

It is interesting to note that when most people theorize about the end of humanity, they usually point to physical occurrences as the main indication of this calamity, whether by a meteor shower, a one-hundred-foot tsunami, or a disease that plagues everyone on the planet. The Bible mentions that horrific natural maelstroms will coincide with, if not at times be caused by, declining moral behavior in the last days. In other words, the state of lawlessness in the world will be the direct indication that the end of the age is soon approaching. It is the immaterial tsunamis, earthquakes, and epidemics to which we, as a collective people, must desperately take notice.

In a modern society that accepts blasphemy, homosexuality, prevarication, narcissism, and fornication as new trends, it is easy to believe that all is well in the course of the world, especially if we grew up learning nothing but the acceptability of these godless behaviors. We are dubbed as good people as long as we don't murder, steal, rape, or break any serious civil laws in our country. That is our subjective standard. It may appear pathetically low compared to religious bars, but it is nonetheless accepted. However, this human criterion is not what Scripture affirms as the universally binding one.

God's Word gives us a clue that moral conduct was held in much higher esteem in Jesus' day than in our current twenty-first century. Timothy declares that in the final times, "Men will be lovers of self, lovers of money, boastful, arrogant, revilers, disobedient to parents, ungrateful, unholy, unloving, irreconcilable, malicious gossips, without self-control, brutal, haters of good, treacherous, reckless, conceited, lovers of pleasure rather than lovers of God" (2 Tim 3:2-4).

Although people have been sinning since the beginning of time, they have not done so at the rate and intensity that we see all around us now. In fact, people used to get stoned to death if they were caught using the Lord's name in vain and committing adultery. That is how strictly people upheld God's Law in the past. Yet in our modern times, it is actually a fad to use God's name in vain, in both media and everyday language. Fornication is no longer a taboo, but considered by many to be a form of recreation. People long to lose their virginity, and if they don't do so by a certain age, they are dubbed as losers. By the look of this new shift, we must conclude that something has gone seriously wrong. This is anything but normal.

This new form of ungodliness has sent its shock waves to nearly all parts of the world. Not surprisingly, the region where its affects can be detected most is in the entertainment industry—Hollywood. It was here, during my three years as a background artist, that I saw a glimpse of what Jesus was talking about.

The Lust Bunny

One of my earliest jobs with Central Casting (before I became an active witness) was in the feature film, *The House Bunny*, starring Anna Faris. It was a three-night call that took place in South-Central Los Angeles. In one of the neighborhoods, we shot the backyard tiki party scene found about two-thirds of the way into the movie. I played one of the frat guys who filled in the atmosphere for the party scene.

This was a memorable project for me in many ways. First, it was my first film assignment. Second, it was the first time I had worked a night call for more than one day in a row (it was also the last time I ever did it). Last, it was one of the most sexually alluring work atmospheres I had encountered.

The principle actresses, Anna Faris and Emma Stone, as well as the rest of the female background artists, were clothed in scanty outfits for the entire shoot. It is easy to surmise that I was tempted sexually for three consecutive nights. I do not deny that my physical side admired these things, but the Spirit within me grieved at what was being flaunted around me. In addition to the raves, the alcohol drinking, and the entire secular entertainment, I was living in a sin city for a brief period of time. Although these things were fictional in that they were part of the film's storyline, I was stunned to learn that its reality was evident in the lives of the people around me.

One example I never forgot was the life philosophy of an extra named Russell. While waiting in the holding tent situated on a neighborhood sidewalk, I was involved in a three-way discourse with two other gentlemen—one being Russell and another guy named Justin. Russell was the one who did most of the talking in our group. He was a late twenties Caucasian male who had originally hailed from New York City. He was an upbeat, sociable, and humorous man who loved to tell sarcastic jokes.

Russell began his story by explaining a little about his background. He then dropped the bombshell on his moral state by glorifying his sex life. I'm not talking about sex with a spouse, but outright fornication. Russell was very graphic in describing the entire arsenal of women he had fornicated with, from all ethnicities and ages. The sad thing was that he didn't feel conscientious about it at all. He fully reveled in it. He even added that his current girlfriend gave him action every single week, and this was the reason why he was holding onto their relationship! It surely wasn't the real, self-sacrificing agape love that is often mentioned in the Bible.

I thought Justin might have been surprised to hear such an anomaly, but he wasn't. He condoned Russell's actions and even provided encouragement for them. Justin did not see such things as immoral, sinful, or even off-balance. He viewed fornication as harmless and something to aspire to. I shouldn't have been that surprised, as Justin's view matches those of many people in our current times.

I am not using this example to condescend them with judgmental views. They have not said or done anything that I have not done in my life too. There have been numerous times when I have been guilty of lusting for women and desiring to fornicate with them as well. I just mention this situation to show the sad reality that Hollywood and the world around us is oblivious to its moral condition. Sin has become so highly ingrained, exercised, and justified that people have become immune to its negative effects.

In an interesting turn of events, Russell started to discuss the functions and history of the planet. I don't remember how this came about, but I presume that it had to do with him linking sex to natural evolutionary behavior. Russell delved deep into the topic as he shared his beliefs on the subject. I knew this couldn't be good for everyone listening, so I asked Russell if he believed that God had anything to do with creation.

Russell balked at the idea of God running the show. He was pretty quick to address his pessimistic views on religion and how he thought the whole system was contrived. Although he did believe in some vague higher power, Russell surmised its only role was to guide the evolutionary process throughout millions of years (theistic evolution). He was even bold enough to assert, as fact, the theory that all men descended from Africa one hundred thousand years ago. Thus, he joked that we were all "niggers" at one point.

This is one of the most stereotypical, if not inane, views of human evolution found in school textbooks, but I wasn't flabbergasted that Russell clung to them. He was an unrepentant sinner who loved his sin. Therefore, the Word of God was naturally revolting to him. Jesus told Nicodemus that, "Everyone who does evil hates the Light, and does not come to the Light for fear that his deeds will be exposed" (John 3:20). Sinners like Russell would do anything to remain in their life of darkness, so they adhere to an ideology that debunks moral absolutes and accountability to God. There is no more appropriate philosophy to carry out one's life of moral freedom than the theory of evolution. Some of its doctrines may not make much sense in the light of intense scrutiny, but that doesn't matter to a person as long as he/she can do whatever it is that pleases him/her in life.

Such a philosophy is one of the deadliest opiates in America today.

NEW AGE DOMINATION

Russell is one of the more colorful examples of the industry's godlessness, yet I have met more like him who are headed down the wrong path in many other ways. It grieves me that immoral behavior is not the only thing I have to face each time I step onto a film or television set. There are also the other factors Jesus warned about in addition to men's abandonment of universal laws in the last days.

Timothy declares that, "In later times some will fall away from the faith, paying attention to deceitful spirits and doctrines of demons, by means of the hypocrisy of liars seared in their own conscience as with a branding iron" (1 Tim. 4:1-2). Concerning the generation living at the time of the Antichrist, Thessalonians also states that, "God will send upon them a deluding influence so that they will believe what is false, in order that they all may be judged who did not believe the truth, but took pleasure in wickedness" (2 Thess. 2:11-12).

First Timothy 4:1 and 2 Thessalonians 2:11 reveal that apostasy and false doctrines will be rampant in the final moments before Jesus' return. Many professing believers will be falsely converted while others will depart from the faith entirely, giving heed to ungodly philosophies that cater to their sinful hedonism. The power of Christianity will rapidly dwindle in the final generation leading to the appearance of the Beast and the Tribulation period.

Aside from their immoral practices and beliefs, background artists and film crew are often steeped in philosophies that run contrary to the will of Christ. It wouldn't be surprising to observe Hollywood people reading books on New Age spirituality, pantheism, and Eastern religion. Out of the hundreds whom I've met and observed on set, I've only seen two people read books on Christianity, and these books weren't even the theologically dense ones that serious followers read to grow in discipleship. They were somewhat like the universal, self-help type books that would be popular with prosperity gospel lovers and even people of other religions. Any piece of literature that does not confront sin but rather speaks on self-indulgent, exotic wisdom is in pure fashion among groups in Hollywood.

This trend has even made its way into the actors' circle. When I worked on the feature film, *Fame,* in January of 2009, I observed one of the principle actors, Paul Iacono (who played Neil Baczynski), reading the popular New

Age book, *The Four Agreements* (by Miguel Ruiz) in his downtime. I felt discomfort as a Christian as I watched those false life doctrines pumped into the young man's heart. I figured Paul wasn't a Christian, based on some of the things he said, so I knew he had no solid defense against falsehood. The sad thing was that I couldn't do much about it at the time because of the authorities all around him.

The only relief I experienced that day was learning that the other two principles, Kay Panabaker and Collins Pennie, declared themselves Christians. Before shooting one of the takes, Collins, Kay, and the other principle actress named Ana Maria Perez de Tagle, engaged in a hearty conversation about casual subjects. Suddenly, Collins mentioned his association with a Baptist church. He then asked Kay what church she attended. Kay responded that she was part of a non-denominational ministry, while Ana Maria said that she attended a Catholic church.

Interestingly, I gave Kay a *Good Person Test* the day before (since my commitment to the film was a three-day call). I didn't know that this young woman was a believer. I was glad I found out the following day when she affirmed it during her chat with Collins. It seems as if my tract went to waste, but I was excited about the fact that she was a Christian. It brings me more joy when people are already saved than if I have to work on them in their lost condition.

This small Christian fellowship is one of the rarest occurrences you will ever see on a film set, especially amongst an actor's circle. It truly made me wish everyone else in the industry were like them: the extras, actors, the production assistants, directors, and the producers. It would be a more pleasant work environment, but that is just wishful thinking. My observation on *Fame* was the last time I ever saw such a thing, at least on the crewmembers' side of the playing field. Not even the extras that day on *Fame* were Christians. So you can probably guess I wasn't participating in any spiritual discussions in the holding area unless for proselytizing purposes.

It grieves me to say that non-Christian book readings and discussions are not the only dark activities that affect the lives of these industry people. I once heard from Jonathan Khan that he observed people practicing astrology, horoscopes, and tarot card reading in the work environment. When Jonathan worked on the Spielberg film, *The War of the Worlds,* in early 2005, he even spotted a Scientology booth on the set, undoubtedly positioned there by the lead actor, Tom Cruise.

Scientology, as well-intentioned and harmless as it may seem, is another one of the world's opposing forces to Christ's gospel. It is a self-help religion with pantheistic and idolatrous influences similar to those of New Age. It is another one of the religious trends hot in Hollywood today, and it must not to be taken lightly by Christians since its teachings clearly do not lead people to the saving knowledge of Jesus Christ.

Although I have yet to personally see some of these things practiced on set, I don't have any doubts as to its plausibility. I believe Satan is laboring as hard as possible to entice whatever people he can to follow the wrong path before his day of destruction arrives. It will only be a matter of time before his work starts to flourish in the professional environment, especially those utterly devoid of God's shield to begin with. Yet, Hollywood seems to be at ease with this daunting reality.

I can say with confidence that Hollywood condones most every religious pastime except biblical Christianity.

DARKENED MINDS

Although Jonathan and I have obtained different scenarios and perceptions from the set, the one thing that both of us can testify to by experience is the fact that Christianity is the most anger-instigating religion in all of Hollywood. Mr. Khan recounted instances when he met elderly women who appeared to be humble and affable on the surface, but upon presentation of the law and the gospel, everything changed swiftly. The eyes of these sweet old grannies turned from puppies into snakes as they lunged out at Jonathan with sharp fangs. It didn't matter whether Jonathan was kind or not. These people just didn't want to hear the truth, and that's what God's light does to hardened sinners, regardless of their age, gender, or ethnicity.

When I mention that tinsel town tolerates most every religion except Christianity, I really do mean it. If you were to talk to these people about Buddha, Muhammad, Krishna, or even teachers like Socrates and Gandhi, they usually will not react with such rage. Sometimes, spiritual teachers like these might even fascinate them. However, when you mention the name Jesus, it immediately strikes a nerve in these industry people and causes them to go on the offensive.

As supernatural as this may sound, it is the truth. Incidents like these merely prove that Jesus Christ is the only way to salvation. Satan is blinding the hearts of men and women so they will not know the truth of the Messiah's exclusive claims. That is why these industry people don't take offense at the other teachers and philosophies. Satan gives these people no real reason. These other religions lead straight to damnation, and there should be no stopping that motion on the Devil's part.

I had an opportunity to experience this personally when I talked with a background artist on an episode of the television show, *Numbers*. His name was Wade, a man in his early twenties who was a recent arrival to Hollywood, looking to make it big in the industry. I first met him after the production positioned him beside me for a university hallway scene set in one of the soundstages of the Los Angeles Center Studios.

Later during lunch, I overheard some of Wade's conversation with another extra, in which he actually touched a bit on his faith. He mentioned that he had a Christian upbringing. I figured this was good news, until he expressed a little uncertainty about the Bible's veracity, authorship, and doctrine. I suddenly sensed that I needed to get to know a little more about his religious beliefs. He may have come from a Christian background, but that didn't necessarily mean he was saved. I always needed to be as attentive to Christians as I was to unbelievers.

I approached Wade in the halls of the soundstage after lunch to bring up my concerns. With curiosity as well as compassion, I asked Wade to elaborate more on his Christian background. He informed me that he grew up in a Pentecostal church in Texas. However, he had been studying other religions as of late. He wanted "to know more of what's out there in the world." In other words, he was attempting to discover whether his Christian religion was really the right path or not. I knew this wasn't a good sign. Only the heart of an unsaved man can entertain such curiosity.

I'm not condemning the practice of Christians trying to gain knowledge of other religions and philosophies. Most times, believers will need to understand the combating forces so they can effectively defend their faith. Christians need to understand other religions so they can enlighten those who have been deceived by the false teachings of this world. However, I didn't sense this was Wade's motive.

I asked Wade, "So you mean you're researching this stuff so you can know how to better defend your faith in public, right?"

Wade responded, "Well, yeah. I just never did this before and I want to see what else is out there."

His disinterested response showed me that it was unlikely that Wade was saved. He was about to leave Christianity because of Hollywood's influence and venture into a land where he would most likely never return. I knew I had to help him.

I asked Wade, "This may sound strange for me to ask, but do you have any assurance that you're saved? What I mean is, are you born again?"

Wade looked baffled. He replied, "I was baptized in high school."

Wade had not understood what being born again meant. He thought being born again was nothing more than being baptized in water, which led to salvation. The Scripture clearly does not mention that someone must be physically baptized to be saved. It does, however, speak about the baptism of the Holy Spirit.

The water (much like circumcision from the Old Testament epoch) symbolizes the outward covenant of the inward transformation. In and of itself, it is not the means to salvation. If it were, then the Word of God would be teaching that salvation is merited by rituals (or works). Ephesians 2:8-9[24] would clearly be wrong. Outward covenants of baptism or circumcision would mean nothing if the inward man is not regenerated (or reborn). Spiritual rebirth is what it means to be born again. It is when God imputes righteousness to the sinner's account by the Holy Spirit. The man's old self dies and his new self comes to life. This is the second birth that Jesus spoke about to Nicodemus in John 3:3.[25]

I explained this doctrine to Wade as he listened intently. I figured that afterwards I needed to take my prospect through the law to see if he truly understood salvation by grace, so that is what I did.

I took Wade through the Commandments, and he admitted to lying, stealing, and blasphemy. He admitted his guilt in not upholding the precepts, as did most other people I had evangelized in the past. When I finally got to the seventh commandment about adultery (or lust), something unexpected happened.

Wade stopped me in my tracks. Flustered, he asked, "Why are you asking me these things? I get it! Get to the point. What is it that you're trying to say or prove?"

I was a bit speechless at his reaction. This was the first time anyone had ever gotten defensive toward my use of the law, though I took great effort to be kind and sensitive in my presentation. Although people in the past have tried to interrupt me and assert their constructive opinions during my momentum, never had anyone been as personally offended as Wade had. In some ways, I should have anticipated it would happen sooner or later. It was actually a relief that I hadn't received more cases like this, especially in light of the fact that Jonathan Khan faced them all the time.

Attempting to alleviate the tension, I explained to Wade that I took him through the law to show him his true moral condition and need for a Savior. I explained the validity behind the gospel message, what characterized the other world religions (in terms of grace vs. works), and why Jesus was the only way to heaven. I ended by accentuating the importance of being born again by repenting of sin and trusting in Jesus Christ alone for salvation. I informed Wade that although I wasn't sure about his eternal state, he needed to take heed to the gospel message. I told him that I cared about his soul.

Wade silently gazed at me. He nodded and stated respectfully, "Okay. Thank you very much. I appreciate it."

With that, the man simply turned and walked away. I wasn't sure if Wade meant what he said or not. It's possible he may have harbored some animosity toward my actions. In any case, my proselytizing rattled his cage, as he never looked at or talked with me in the same manner again.

I knew Wade's journey toward the truth couldn't possibly get any better from this point. The fact that he was peering into other beliefs was an indication that he was going to be another one of the many apostates in this generation. As with most players in Hollywood, the spirit of the antichrist had brainwashed Wade with the temptations of seducing doctrines. The Hollywood revelries, blasphemies, fornication, and self-aggrandizement could do nothing but aggravate the process.

All I can do is pray for people like him, that they will stay strong and not backslide. Even if he does, I pray that God will convict him so that he may repent for the first time and be truly born again in the Spirit.

WEARIED MESSENGER

Although I took pleasure in fulfilling the Great Commission for God, the role started to take its toll on me. Having to deal with people like Wade and an entire range of other challenges every single workday caused sporadic moments of stress, anxiety, and discouragement. Martyrs would deem me lucky that I was not being pulverized, stoned, or burned at the stake. Yet, even light persecution such as resentment and verbal confrontations had been enough to sink my spirits.

After being in the industry for more than two years, my mind started to lose patience. The blasphemies, swearing, cursing, crude jokes, unruly manners, and ungodly practices on the set caused me to suddenly dislike Hollywood. The temptations became a nightmare and even a hindrance to my spiritual goals. Just gazing at the content being acted out for the television storylines made my heart ache.

I find it a travesty that the industry doesn't have very many wholesome programs as they had a couple decades back. I'm not saying that every television show needs to be about a Bible topic. I'm only hinting that it would be nice if more entertainment programs actually promoted good human virtues rather than degenerative ones. You can hardly find a show anymore that doesn't use the Lord's name in vain and glorify violence, sex, and materialism.

Regardless of how I felt about Hollywood philosophies, I decided to keep my head up high. I continued to cooperate with the Spirit day by day, to be serviceable in the industry, and to expand God's kingdom if the opportunities allowed. There were plenty more souls that needed to be won for Christ, so I needed to be on duty for my Lord.

Little did I know that my missionary efforts would soon run into detrimental results—trouble that would place my job in serious jeopardy.

Chapter 15
. . . .
ONE HARD BLOW

ON OCTOBER 9, 2009, I was assigned to work on the television show, *Better Off Ted*. I didn't know much about the production other than the fact that it was a relatively new show. Aside from that, there was nothing novel about the nature of my gig. It was another one of the Central Casting's television line-ups. It was in a familiar location of Los Angeles Center Studios. It had a dreadfully familiar call time of 6:30 A.M., and it was an AFTRA show. As comfortable and unmemorable as this job initially appeared, it actually turned out to be one of the most conspicuous ones in my life. On this day, I suffered a disheartening sting that affected me for a quite a while.

It all began as I first arrived at the location for my 6:30 A.M. call time. This was a rare occasion when I was late because I got lost while looking for the studio stage. It seemed as if I was already off to a poor start, yet the PA was gracious enough to overlook this minor mishap. He directed me to grab breakfast quickly at the catering zone one block away. I faithfully complied with his request. Who wouldn't agree to eat free food?

Since the meal wasn't served via buffet line, I was required to order my food directly from a catering truck and wait for it to be prepared from scratch. To my advantage, I didn't have to wait long since the only other person in line was a female staff member. We casually recognized each other as we waited for our meals in front of the vehicle. Within five minutes, my order of French toast came out. I reached up to the elevated window slot to retrieve my food from the server. I didn't leave without also handing a *Good Person Test* to my prospect in the truck. Although I couldn't engage in verbal proselytizing, I knew I could at least influence him through the written mode. It's always better to give them something rather than nothing.

After spending about fifteen minutes eating my breakfast in the adjacent dining room, I returned to the shooting stage, where I was immediately greeted by a PA named Jason. Initial encounters are usually cordial, but it did not turn out to be the case this time.

Jason asked me in an annoyed manner, "Where were you? I made an announcement earlier. I needed everybody here."

Jason had apparently delivered a corporate speech that required the presence of all the background artists, of which I was not aware. I was obviously not there because I was eating at the dining hall. I apologized to Jason and informed him that it was a miscommunication on my part. Although he was a bit flustered, the PA overlooked my mistake and recapitulated his previous announcement to me. It turned out to be nothing more than performance procedures for the shots.

Just when I thought this was the last of Jason's concerns, the PA raised a personal issue that took me by surprise. He asked me, "I'm just curious, were you passing out religious pamphlets to people earlier today?"

This was a surprise because I hadn't distributed any tracts to any of the film crew or background artists yet. The only person I gave a tract to was the server in the catering truck, but I doubted he reported such an incident to the production staff. The catering crew is almost entirely independent of the television side. Whatever protection that would be offered to the production employees would not apply to the food servers.

I seriously pondered who might have reported my actions. Was there a secret spy? Did somebody recognize me from a past gig? Or could it have been another person who was passing out tracts?

I replied to the PA, "Only to a catering truck server."

Jason said, "I'm just letting you, please don't do it on this set while we're working. We have a religious harassment policy here that we need to stick by. I can't get into any trouble over this issue. I don't have anything against your religion; I'm actually a religious person as well in my own way. Just keep your religious stuff to yourself. Unless somebody personally inquires and wants to know more, then I can't do anything about it. Then you can hand them the materials. Otherwise, keep it out of sight. You understand what I'm saying?"

Jason's words went against my duties as a Christian ambassador, but I complied for the sake of agreement. The PA was glad to hear my affirmation as he patted me on the shoulder and took off. Though Jason thought he had resolved the issue, it turned out to be a partial compromise on my part. In my mind, I agreed to keep my vow up until the point where I would officially sign out. Then the game was on again. I really had no choice since souls were on the line.

A SECRET CONVERSATION

This set was no different in terms of Hollywood moral conduct. I once again had to put up with the foul language, blasphemy, crass jokes, and ungodly ideas spilling out all around me. It was a headache, yet I endured for the sake of the greater good, which was to relay the gospel message to the unsaved. Ironically, this was the very idea that Jason was attempting to subdue in the first place. I made sure my time on set would not be fruitless. I was going to advocate the gospel message in some form or another by the time the day was over.

An unexpected opportunity arose during the filming of an office scene, when I met a gentleman in his early fifties named Seth. They positioned Seth beside me at the office table, apparently portraying one of my colleagues for a corporate meeting. During one of the breaks between takes, Seth playfully read off a prop magazine. The sentences didn't make much sense, obviously because the production staff typed up random words merely to fill blank space.

Seth read the words rapidly, which sounded like gibberish. He then concluded, "Wow, this is like speaking in tongues."

Did he just mention a religious term? I didn't know if this man was a fellow believer, but I figured I could use this as an icebreaker to find out. I asked Seth, "Do you know what speaking in tongues means?"

Seth replied, "Oh yeah. It's the practice of speaking in an unknown language. At least that's what they call it in the Christian world."

I asked Seth if he had a Christian background. He replied that he had, but he no longer practiced any religion. His reasons for backsliding were typical, but nonetheless indicated a recurring problem in Christendom. He departed from faith due to the apparent hypocrisy of the church. He elaborated on this statement by recounting personal stories of pastors/priests who exploited congregants in his community in order to become wealthy. When their evil deeds were exposed, it gave Seth a foul impression of Christianity.

I didn't fully blame Seth for being alienated, but at the same time, it was unfair to assess the content of the Bible by what men did in their sinful state. If Scripture was an exact representation of what corrupt leaders taught or did, then Seth, the world, and even I would have reason to abandon faith. It would be utterly corrupt and not worth being associated with. Yet, Jesus taught something completely different, which is why it's tragic when backsliders equate fallen human conduct with the content of God's Word. What is even more disappointing is when skeptics don't even analyze the Bible to see if their faith is worth continuing.

In any case, I had to work attentively on my prospect. I wasn't able to continue the conversation because we resumed filming, but I did get an opportunity to evangelize Seth during a ten-minute break outside the soundstage. I approached him as he was smoking a cigarette near the stage door. It was a frank approach, but the only thing that came to mind. I had already built a slight relationship with him back on the stage, so my presence wasn't entirely awkward.

I candidly asked Seth what he thought was going to happen to him when he dies. He suavely replied that he was probably going to move on to a better place. He obviously implied a heaven of some sort. I then asked Seth if he thought he was a good person, to which he confidently replied yes. I took him through the law. Predictably, he admitted his guilt to lying, stealing, blaspheming, and so on. This furnished me with hope that God would open Seth's eyes to the truth, logic, and heart of the gospel message.

It was not meant to be. A PA burst out of the stage door and interrupted the conversation by calling us back onto set. Seth immediately walked away from me and marched onto the stage. I had pretty much lost my opportunity to share the good news with him. Even if I were to reignite the motion of the law with my prospect later on (that's considering if there was time for another dialogue), it would not have as much of an impact as when I did it the first time. The conviction under the law would have already been dissipated. I was willing to re-start my conversation with Seth, but he would probably not be inclined to speak with me again since I revealed myself to be a Jesus freak.

I made one last attempt at the end of the day. After signing out, I approached Seth and told him about the purpose of my bringing up the Ten Commandments earlier in the day. I informed him that God's Law was the standard by which He was going to judge humanity on Judgment Day, and that I was deeply concerned about his eternal wellbeing.

Seth smiled and stated, "That's where you and I disagree."

With these last words, Seth turned and walked away from me. I called out to him with a final plea, "Just remember that tomorrow is not a promise for any of us."

Seth did not heed my prophetic warning. He didn't even turn back, but continued to walk on complacently in his path. It was a doomed one, as I saw the man walking away from God and straight through the gates of hell, but there was nothing more I could have done at that point. It was basically up to the Father now to draw my prospect toward the Son. I just find it sad that Seth didn't come to true faith when he had been actually involved in the Christian community years before.

AFTER-JOB TERMINATION

Just when it seemed like my task was over, and Seth was going to be my final one for the day, an even graver problem manifested. I guess you can say that I instigated it, but the results were unexpected, especially given that I was no longer on the time clock.

As I was about to leave Los Angeles Center Studios, I gazed around to see if there were any people I could have given tracts to. The only person in sight was a female crew-member who was concentrating on reports at an outdoor table. I casually approached her, extending a *Million Dollar Bill* as I asked, "Have you ever gotten one of these before?"

The woman glanced at the tract quickly and replied, "No, thank you."

I made one last attempt to get her to take it by joking, "You can spend it if you want."

The woman looked up from her reports again. She took the tract this time, but gazed upon it with skepticism. I chuckled and informed her that I was merely joking. I told her that the *Bill* contained a gospel message on the back. The woman started to read the message. Slowly, but surely, her eyes molded into a glare. It very much resembled the snake eyes I mentioned in the last chapter, regarding those chameleon sinners whom Jonathan and I encounter on occasions.

The woman coldly asked, "Are you aware that you're not supposed to do this at work? That we have policies regarding religious harassment?"

Trying to look naïve, I replied, "Well, on other sets they usually don't care after work hours."

"Who else did you hand these out to?"

"You're actually the only one I gave it to so far."

I knew the woman was fuming inside, so I extended my hand in friendship and introduced myself. She continued to stare down as she shook my hand half-heartedly, more out of duty than out of true hospitality. With nothing more to say, I gave her my farewell and walked away.

I had a bad feeling about what I had done, but I continued to keep my composure. I walked three blocks to the main building, which housed the escalators that led to the parking structure underneath. As I approached the glass doors to enter the lobby, Jason, the PA, ran up to me from out of nowhere. I was stunned at the realization that he had chased me all the way to the parking lot, which was a good three blocks distance!

Jason pulled out the *Million Dollar Bill* that I had handed the female crewmember a few minutes earlier. My heart raced with anxiety as Jason asked in shock, "Steve, what is with this? Didn't I specifically tell you that you couldn't give these things out on this property? Did you not understand what I said?"

I replied, "I thought you meant only during work hours."

"No. You heard what I said. I said you couldn't pass these things out at all on the property. Even though you may not be working anymore, we are still on the clock. We have a rule here that says you cannot force your religion on somebody in the work place."

"I didn't force my religion on them. I was merely sharing it."

"No, you can't do that. I told you this already. I mean, do you understand what I'm saying? Is everything processing okay in your head?"

The PA interpreted my actions and responses to signify that I was possibly retarded. Though he treated me like a monkey, I kept my demeanor in check for the sake of Christ.

Jason continued with his denunciation by stating, "Look, like I said, I have nothing against what's written on the back of this bill. There is a time and a place for everything, but you blatantly disobeyed orders with what you did. Do you ever want to work for this show again? Do you still want to work in this industry?"

I replied, "Yes, I do. But I feel that this is discrimination against my religion."

"It is not discrimination! If our work had a policy against using foul language, then we would have to abide by it. This is just a rule to protect everyone."

I sensed that Jason had had enough of me. He remained silent for a beat, deciding on what he wanted to do with my situation. I was hoping that he would just let me off with a warning, much like the PA on *Shark* did. However, mercy was not on my side this time.

Jason finally opened his mouth and declared, "You will not ever work for this show again. I'm going to report this to Central Casting."

The PA turned and marched away from me. As I stood in the lobby, I tried to process what had just occurred. I came to the realization that I had just been off from the show. On top of that, my name was about be reported to Central.

Before Jason could disappear from sight, I called out to him and asked, "Do you still want that bill?"

Jason replied, "Yes. I need it."

I didn't fathom that Jason was going to retain the tract purely for his pleasure or for religious curiosity. He was going to deliver it to Central Casting as evidence of my guilt. I didn't know what to think at this point. This was unprecedented for me. I felt bewilderment, concern, anger, and self-pity all at the same time.

What's most upsetting was the fact that these crew members were free to use the Lord's name profanely, yet I wasn't liberated to share His name positively. Hollywood can boast about their sins, yet I wasn't free to tell how they can find forgiveness for them. As you may know, I hinted at this point during my conversation with Jason. I could have pushed it further and threatened legal ramifications, but I decided not to for the sake of not showing a vengeful spirit.

As I drove home, I suddenly realized who might have reported my tract distribution to the server earlier in the day. The same female crewmember who waited in line with me for breakfast must have been the same woman to whom I gave the *Million Dollar Bill* at the end of the day. It made perfect sense, since she was the only one who could have spotted me in action. She was also highly knowledgeable about the religious harassment policy that they supposedly maintained on set. Last, her sensitivity to the issue made it likely that she was the one who relayed the message to Jason before the workday began. No one could have been so convinced to address such a topic unless it would make her satisfied.

I could have complained about the situation further, but it seemed futile. What's done was done. Now I needed to figure out what to do with the dark cloud that suddenly loomed over my future.

THE FADING DREAM

For the following days and weeks, I was out of the work force. No calls came in from Central Casting or from my calling service, Extras Management. This period was one of the longest professional droughts I had experienced throughout my brief career in the acting industry. The unemployment may have happened because of the shortage of gigs or lack of demand for my particular category. Yet I had a good sense it happened because of my proselytizing on *Better Off Ted*. The production reported my actions, and I was apparently being penalized from Central Casting.

Although I was not technically fired from *Better Off Ted*, I suffered a fate that bore nearly the same repercussions, if not worse. It was almost as if the job terminated me. The only difference was that they fired me after work hours (if that makes any sense).

Was my Hollywood career actually over? Although I wouldn't have liked to think so, it started to look more likely as I learned of another interesting reality when I spoke with Jonathan Khan. For the first time, Jonathan informed me that he wasn't being called from Central Casting to work much anymore. He told me that the *Little Fockers* production had recently ousted him for his on-set missionary duties. Then some time later, Jonathan was terminated from his calling service, Extras Management. Jonathan has had to move on to another line of work to support himself, moving furniture as an independent contractor.

It seemed that after nearly a decade, industry had finally blacklisted Jonathan from Hollywood. I knew that it was going to happen eventually. It's just surprising that Jonathan was able to stay in the game as long as he had. Such a miracle can only happen because of the sovereign power of the Lord. Now it seemed as if God was calling Jonathan away from the entertainment industry and to a new path. I have yet to witness what will become of Mr. Khan, but I know that God is unfailing in His plan. He will lead Jonathan to do greater things for the glory and honor of His holy name.

The question now was if I was going to be the next to die gloriously on the battlefields of tinsel town. It seemed likely. If not now, then somewhere along the line I would go down in flames. Yet, if Jonathan and I were to be removed from the industry, who was going to preach Christ in Hollywood? Who else was going to evangelize with the same passion, conviction, and truth that we constantly presented at the altar?

Based on my observations from the set, there weren't many who do what we do. There are some Christians scattered around, but none of them are bold enough to take a stance for God and His missionary mandate. Many of them are not even passionate enough to pick up a Bible from time to time, let alone attend church. If Jonathan and I were banned from Hollywood, that would leave only Paul Kwak for the task, and he didn't even specialize in that particular area.

Now that I reminisce about my former self, it's unbelievable how I came to my current position in life. My flesh grieved for turning away from my ambitious, self-serving, and goal-oriented philosophy of being an established film director. I could have continually devoted myself to making films, but publishing healthy connections, and working hard into the industry. At times, I wish that I had. I could have gained the world and made my dreams come true. I could have been living the good life. In the words of Terry Malloy from the Oscar-winning film, *On the Waterfront*, I could have been a contender. In one false move, I pretty much threw it all away. Because of all that, I lost what I could have achieved. A part of me cried out, "What have you done?"

Indeed, what had I done? My eight years of dreaming and planning since high school was flushed down the gutter because of inclinations that had nothing to do with film or entertainment. In fact, they ran entirely contrary to the success of my goals in the industry. I suffered, and now I was nowhere in this world. I had nothing in life.

This reality testifies to how much God changed me two years before. Prior to early 2008, I wasn't denying myself for the glory of God. Whatever spiritual life I had before then only served as a pastime and an emotional boost for my state of mind. Now the Lord had consumed me and caused me to be obsessed with Him. He enraptured me to love what He loves and hate what He hates. I loved Him to the point that I would follow His every literal command in the Bible, even if it meant sacrificing my safety, my ego, my time, and my film directing goals. Jesus Christ became my all in all.

Even though I would like to continue with my industry goals, I cannot do so at the expense of my Lord's will. I cannot stop spreading His message to sinners. I love people too much to do so. I love my Lord too much that any opposing force hurts me. Day and night, my heart's desire is to glorify His name. I no longer pray for God's help in carrying out my physical desires and goals, but for His aid in making His kingdom expand endlessly through my service. My heart had now become one with God's. Since 2008, the Lord has truly answered my prayers and given me the true desires of my heart.

After so many years, I finally came to realize the meaning behind Jeremiah 29:11,[26] as well as the prayer principle of John 14:14.[27] The plans that God had for me were not for my personal happiness, comfort, and glory, but to benefit me spiritually, even if it involved suffering, pain, and confusion. As long as I would be willing to follow, the Lord would guide my life in a manner that would affect me eternally for the better and promote His glory to the highest. Whatever desires I prayed for, it should be for His glory. This longing could only occur if my desires were identical to God's. As a Christian, I wholeheartedly testify that this is a beautiful feeling. It is fulfilling, satisfying, and peaceful in every way. It truly makes a person feel that life is worth living.

Times were tough with unemployment, but I continued to have faith in my Savior. I prayed that my labor would not be in vain but would produce fruit. As much as my efforts may be bearing eternal blessings in heaven, I hoped to have at least seen a hint of it on earth. I desired to witness some changes happening in the industry as a result of my influence. I longed to see my efforts blessed so I could continue to contribute monetarily to the cause of the gospel. I felt it was just a matter of time before God lifted me back up on my feet so I could stand in victory over Satan's tactics.

Hope was the only thing that could keep me going now.

Chapter 16

A BLAST FROM THE PAST

T IS NO secret that most of the celebrities I evangelized to happened to be one-shot deals. I would witness to them once (through a tract and/or verbal proselytizing) but would never see or hear from them again. It was not for me to know what became of their spiritual fate—whether they became regenerated in the Spirit or stayed hardened in disbelief.

Though most of these cases will remain a mystery to me on this side of life, I was able to get a glimpse into one. What I mean is that I was able to reconnect with one of the past celebrities with whom I had a chance to share the Christian faith. However, I did not meet him on the grounds of the work environment. The setting didn't even have to do with the entertainment industry or Hollywood. The rendezvous came about because of the influence of a mutual passion—a very culinary passion!

In the summer of 2009, I met Xavier Tash again when I dined at his restaurant, Ranger Grill. I had told him that I would visit his place someday, but I never had an immediate opportunity because of my previous commitments to other plans. Now, I finally had a chance to fulfill Xavier's request. Aside from the cuisine, I was also eager to see how Mr. Tash was faring in his life.

I seriously wondered about the progress of his spiritual growth. Was he still following in his Christian faith? Did he need any more guidance? Could I be of some additional assistance? I figured that I would talk to him about it since I was going to dine at the restaurant anyway. Then again, there was a possibility that Xavier wouldn't even be there on that day. The chances were somewhat minute considering the schedule of an established actor in Hollywood.

Before visiting Ranger Grill on a casual Saturday night, I called in a few days before to make a precautionary reservation. The restaurant was a noticeable hit in the community, so I figured I shouldn't take a chance with the seating situation.

The phone rang for a few beats. Someone picked up and proclaimed, "Thank you for calling Ranger Grill. May I help you?"

I replied, "Yes, I was wondering if Xavier Tash is there?"

"Who is this?"

"My name is Steve. Steve Cha."

"Hey, Steve! Yeah, this is Xavier!"

Whoa! Xavier actually answered the phone! I thought. This moment was delightful for three reasons: first, Xavier was actually there on a weekday. Second, I was actually talking to the man without PAs hounding me, and last, Xavier remembered me!

I quickly got over my surprise as I spent the next minute catching up with the actor. He seemed to be in good spirits, mentioning that his personal life was healthy and that he had been at the restaurant on most days. I wanted to have a longer conversation, but I informed Xavier that I would save it for Saturday night, since I would finally be dining at his restaurant. Fortunately, Xavier informed me he was going to be there too. He was happy to hear the news that I was finally going to eat at his restaurant. He noted my reservation and cordially invited my friends and me to join him.

I definitely looked forward to this occasion. I'd be glad if the food itself was great that night, but with Xavier around, I knew his presence could only add to the experience. I didn't know what to expect, but it turned out to be something definitely worth remembering.

Visit to Ranger

When Saturday came around, I made my way over to Ranger Grill as planned. I arrived at the restaurant at about 5 P.M., accompanied by my church pals, Paul, Chris, and James. Upon arriving at the door, I immediately saw Xavier Tash seated at the table by the front entrance, working on some business reports. He quickly gazed up when I walked in with my friend James.

I asked, "Hey, Xavier. Do you remember me? I worked with you on Smash World."

It took awhile for my face to register in his mind, but Xavier was able to piece it together. He replied, "Yes, Steve, right? Wow, what are you doing here?"

"I came here to eat. I called you a few days ago and made the reservation."

Xavier looked a bit puzzled. He asked, "You called me? I don't really remember that."

"Yeah, I said I was Steve. It seemed like you remembered me."

Xavier chuckled as he said, "Oh yeah. I remember. I thought that was a different Steve! I didn't think it was you. Oh man, I'm sorry."

I guess it turned out that Xavier didn't remember me on the phone after all. What a bummer. So much for reason number three.

In any case, Xavier met me for the second time and James for the first time. Although James and I arrived as scheduled for the dinner, Paul and Chris came late, due to the traffic on the 405 freeway. When my two buddies finally arrived thirty-minutes later, they also greeted Xavier and were seated with James and me at our table.

I didn't know how I was going to chat with Xavier, since he may have been busy with his administrative work, but it turned out that I didn't have to worry about that at all. Xavier was dutiful in attending to us personally when we needed help in ordering the entrees, and he didn't stop there. After he delivered our requests to the kitchen, Mr. Tash grabbed a chair from another table and pulled it up to ours so he could converse with us, and not just for a few minutes, but a few hours. What phenomenal service!

Xavier indeed took his time giving us his attention. It seemed as if he did most of the talking, while James and I responded occasionally with laughter and/or comments. His first subject regarded the Smash World gig a year before. Xavier mentioned how he was utterly amazed that I approached him with religious topics while at work, especially given that it was the entertainment industry.

As Xavier recounted, "When Steve came up to me with this stuff, I was shocked. I thought this man was crazy! Who would do something like that in Hollywood?"

This statement only solidifies the truth that Christianity is, in fact, forbidden in the business, which is what I'd been saying all along. I found it fascinating to hear this come from a fellow brother in Christ. I guess that now I know what was running through his mind when I gave him the tract on the set. Behind his placid expression, Xavier was stupefied! Yet Xavier didn't intend for his comments to appear negative. In fact, he commended my boldness and conviction. He hadn't met too many people in the business, or life in general, who stood up for Jesus as I did. I guess this fact was true unless he was to meet Jonathan Khan.

Xavier switched gears and started to recount his recent experience on a movie he filmed in Asia. For the next ten minutes, Xavier astounded the three of us by addressing the surprisingly bad impressions he got from working on location. He described the racism he experienced with some of the folks because of his ethnicity, as well as his inability to connect with the people because of their materialistic concerns. Apparently, it was so flagrant that he actually stayed in his hotel most of the time when he wasn't working.

Despite the cons of his filming experience, Xavier mentioned that the great thing about working on high-budget films was the availability of resources. He illustrated an example with catering. While working on independent films in his earlier days, Xavier didn't have privileges like heavy-duty catering, craft services, or even a honey wagon changing room. The production couldn't afford them. Whenever Xavier needed to change into a costume, he would do so either in a car or in a restroom. Even the meals were cheap, as they were ordered directly from a fast food joint or a low-class restaurant. This is a sample work environment for an independent feature production.

Of course, all this changed when Xavier broke into major studio productions. He suddenly had access to better equipment, real catering, trailer dressing rooms, and an entire arsenal of attire suited to his personal sizes. This is truly the miracle of breaking in big in Hollywood. Most actors and directors have undoubtedly felt this when they made the transition from backyard to arena stages, whether it was Christopher Nolan (*Memento* to *Batman Begins*) or Scarlett Johansson (*Lost in Translation* to *The Island*).

I very much enjoyed discussing such industry observations with Xavier, but I felt I needed to address the issue of his personal faith. It was more important that I make a stand for the glory of God than to be content in my own personal gratification of his earthly conducts. I figured that my actions would definitely serve as an inspiration to my three friends as well.

After Xavier completed his discussion on his movie experiences, I asked him to elaborate on his Christian life. Fortunately, Xavier was open to talking about it. He described to us (although he already recounted it on Smash World) that he was raised in a Christian home while growing up in the south. His father was a Baptist minister, so Xavier was quite familiar with the motions of church, the philosophy, and the community. Xavier was currently not attending a church because of his busy work schedule. On a more personal note, he hadn't been motivated to return because of privacy issues. He didn't enjoy being recognized and bothered in the church because of his celebrity status.

This appeared to be a reasonable concern, but I still encouraged Xavier to start attending services. I stated, "I know issues will always arise in life, but nothing should stop you from coming before God. You must always keep that fellowship going. That's God's will. If you want to belong to a church with some great people, you can always come to mine or to James'. We have cool people in our ministries."

Xavier nodded silently, absorbing the assuring information. He was fully aware of what he needed to do. James and I briefly elaborated on our respective churches in the event

Xavier would be interested in visiting in the near future. It seemed as if Xavier was more inclined to visit James' church (Church Everyday in Northridge, California) because a popular 1980s actor, Philip Rhee (*Best of the Best*), was part of that congregation. I didn't really care about Xavier's choice as long as he was plugged into a healthy church body. I had good faith that he would be well cared for even if he chose James' church over mine.

I tied up the theme of reconnecting with God by concisely delineating the Lord's mission for His children in this world. I explained to Xavier that money and fame do not give any meaning to life. They will ultimately vanish. People were dying every day and heading straight to hell, which brings up our mission as Christians. I told him that we needed to be more careful with our time and energy. God has commissioned us to be salt and light to the dying world and to reach out to those who are eternally lost. That was the purpose of our lives as Christians on earth.

I explained, "All those people you saw and met in Asia, they will go to hell if they don't have Jesus to save them. They'll be judged for their sins, which are all the times they lied, stolen, fornicated, lusted, and idolized. We sometimes tend to think too highly of people's goodness and believe they are good enough to enter heaven on their own, but God will reveal everything done in darkness on Judgment Day. The Bible says there is none righteous in this world. If these people die without Christ, they will be guilty in their sins and perish. That should give you concern to reach out to these people."

What I advocated was very heavy in mood, especially for the festive occasion we were all supposed to be in. I decided to level off with that final thought and allow Xavier to absorb the instruction. He reflected solemnly for a moment.

Before we officially concluded the topic, Xavier requested a favor. He asked, "Do you think we can meet again so we can talk about this more in depth? I have some questions about Christianity that have always bothered me."

This was the first time anyone had requested such a service from me, let alone a celebrity. I was ready to accept the task. I was glad enough to have met Xavier in his establishment, outside of the boundaries of the entertainment industry. Now it appeared that I was going to have a second, more personal discussion with the actor. This time it was not going to be about the vanity life of Hollywood. It was going to be about God alone. It was going to be about spiritual life and death.

I just hoped my apologetics armor would be as sturdy as ever.

Visit to Ranger—Part 2

I met up with Xavier again one month later. Although it took awhile for me to get back to him, I was faithful in keeping my obligation. No matter how occupied I was, I vowed to always find time to help a brother, especially if it involved the matter of salvation and faith. This time, I brought my Bible with me.

When I arrived at the restaurant, the first thing I saw was Xavier in the kitchen, wearing an apron and dicing up some vegetables. It appeared that he was going beyond his role as owner/manager and playing the part of Iron Chef. I admired the fact that he was willing to perform the gritty, hands-on work, even when there were staff members available to do the job. It truly showed his down-to-earth approach to life.

After I greeted him at my arrival, Xavier motioned me to sit at a table toward the back of the restaurant. I complied and settled into the area with my Bible and additional apologetics resources. In a few minutes, Xavier joined me at the table, bringing along his plate of supper. He had apparently been preparing his meal in the kitchen when I arrived.

We began our conversation in the appetizer mode, which is another way of saying that it started out light. I casually recounted my week as Xavier followed suit with his own life, which involved mostly personal health and business. This moment was awkward only because Xavier was eating and I was not. In other words, I was watching him eat the entire time, which made the interaction feel somewhat incomplete.

When Xavier finally finished his meal, I initiated the question that took us directly to the real main course. I asked, "So, Xavier, you wanted to talk to me about something regarding Christianity? You had questions?"

Xavier wasted no time diving into the meal along with me. He candidly asked, "Well, my first concern is this. I know that Christians will go to heaven when they die, but they say that the only way to be saved is through Christianity. What about all those people of other religions? Are you telling me that the millions of Buddhists, Muslims, and people who have tried to live good lives will go to hell because they didn't follow the path of Christianity and believe in Jesus? Some of them have never even heard of such a thing."

As I illuminated using various prospects in Chapter 9, the theme of Christ's exclusivity has become one of the pressing concerns in all of Christian history. It reveals the frightening, and most times frustrating, exclusivity of the religion that only through faith in Christ can someone be saved. Every other path and philosophy automatically takes a soul into hell, regardless of whether people have heard about the Son of God or not.

It's tough even for followers of Christ to fathom, which is why believers sometimes make tragic compromises in the name of sentimentalism or ecumenical peace. They cave in to pressure to imply that Jesus is not the only way to heaven because of fear of persecution or being labeled condemning and narrow-minded. Sometimes they even declare so because that is what they truly believe! Though the Bible states clearly that Jesus is the way, the truth, and the life (see John 14:6), these believers, whether they are truly saved or not, simply cannot fathom a loving God sending good and uninformed people to hell for all eternity.

This is a trap that Jesus orders us not to fall into, regardless of the outcome of the prospect's reaction. We are to preach Christ faithfully as the way, the truth, and the life.[28] That is the essence of the gospel message. To preach otherwise would be heresy and may even reveal a professing believer to be a worker of Satan!

Although it may seem complex, there is a sound theological explanation for this question. First, I explained to Xavier that God doesn't give people free tickets to heaven simply because they failed to hear the gospel. If God really did give such free passes, then the best solution to evangelism would be total silence. Even murderers, rapists, and cannibals who've never heard the gospel would get into heaven. People would therefore be guilty of sin once they have heard the gospel but rejected it. However, this theology makes Romans 3:23 incorrect because the verse states that "all have sinned and fall short of the glory of God." The Bible says that all men are guilty of sin. So what is sin? And what is God punishing the ungodly for if they have never rejected a gospel message they have never heard of in their lives?

We get a clue to the real answer with regard to God's wrath against humanity by observing 1 John 3:4[29] which verifies that "sin is lawlessness" or "sin is the transgression of the law" (KJV). This law is eminently known to the world as God's Ten Commandments. First John 3:4 grouped with Romans 3:20[30] and 7:7[31] shows that the primary reason people suffer in hell for all eternity is because of the times they have contributed to the pains and evils of this world. They do so by their incessant lying, stealing, hatred, coveting, adultery, fornication, rape, murder, pride, deceitfulness, jealousy, greed, slander, and so on. As the Bible states, there is no such thing as the good people whom Xavier is talking about.

I explained to Xavier that people who have not heard of Christ will not get a free pass to eternal life, but will be justly punished for their transgression of God's Law. This is why Christian missionaries are striving diligently to spread the gospel message throughout the world. It is only through Jesus that a person can escape God's judgment, because He died for the sins of humanity. The blood of Christ is the only remedy for washing away sin. However, those who have the opportunity to hear the gospel message but reject it commit the unpardonable sin of blasphemy against the Holy Spirit. They will suffer greater eternal punishment than those who have been ignorant of the Way.

Xavier listened with a ready ear as I expounded on this grand concept. Although he probed the dilemma by asking a few additional questions, Xavier was impressed by what he heard. He claimed that the solution made more sense to him and that I had explained it in a manner no one had ever done before. This issue is an often-misunderstood one that raises many concerns, but needs to be understood completely by Christians. It is so utterly important that it will often determine whether a person comes to faith or not.

Xavier followed the salvation issue by raising a concern about ethical Christian practices. He asked how legitimate it was for him to appreciate teachings from other religious figures. For example, Xavier claimed to admire the philosophy and words of the Dalai Lama. In Xavier's own words, the Dalai Lama "teaches great things about life that sound very nice."

He used this topic as a link to also address a different theme altogether: the prevalence of Christian hypocrisy. It's no secret that there are some Buddhists who exude a more disciplined life of morality and spiritual fruits than certain Christians. This is a disheartening blow to the integrity of Christianity, yet this does not mean that the Bible is wrong. It simply means that the believer is either a false convert or one who is weak in certain areas, but striving to improve.

I informed Xavier that the main priority was for him to keep his eye on the truth of God's Word. Although the Dalai Lama's teaching may be of some wisdom and contain certain known truths about life, it is not the ultimate truth. It leads to eternal death. Erudition of Buddhist methods or any other philosophies should be exercised in apologetics to help unbelievers come to faith in Jesus Christ. They should not use them to drive others away from the cross. That should be the main extent of a Christian's involvement with other religions and beliefs. Everything a Christian needs is already in the Word of God. I did not refer just to the wisdom, but also the fulfillment that a soul gains through prayer, praise, and communion with the Lord Jesus.

Xavier shared and elaborated on his personal relationship with God through his prayer life. It was encouraging to hear that he made prayer a regular practice. He mentioned the various times he prayed during the day and the emotional impact it had on him. Xavier was further able be keep accountable to the Lord because of his connection with a Los Angeles Bible study group called the Greatest Bible

Study. He described it as a Bible study composed mainly of entertainment industry members.

Knowing that I was in the business, Xavier asked if I wanted my personal information to be relayed to the group so I could receive information about their meetings. I didn't really expect to come across such an offer, but I casually accepted. I didn't know anything about the GBS group, but I figured I had nothing to lose with such constructive networking. It may even become helpful if I needed to plug my prospects into a Christian body. I could even infiltrate the group and influence those people as well.

As I started to elaborate on the theme of being a witness for Christ in our modern society, Xavier abruptly stepped in and asked, "What do you think about the separation of church and state?"

I had no idea where that question came from, especially in the context of what I was previously discussing. This was the first time anyone had ever asked me to give an opinion on the government and religion issue. Although I was not an expert, I proceeded in a manner I felt was always fitting. I expounded on what the Word of God had to say regarding the matter.

I explained it this way, "I believe that the church should be separate from the state, yet that doesn't mean Christians should not continue to be salt and light in the political realm or be disconnected from them. The Bible says that Christians are to be obedient to the will of the government because God has providentially instituted them to reward good, restrain evil, and maintain order in the society. Believers are to obey the law, which includes paying taxes, giving to Caesar what is his, and venturing into combat against invading countries. The only instance when Christians can neglect civil order is if the government imposes laws that contradict the requirements they are suppose to fulfill toward God. Examples include blasphemy, ceasing evangelism, and so on. Other than that, the Lord God would not hold Christians accountable for such things as killing if done in the context of faithful, righteous service to the nation, such as defending against an enemy country if national peace and justice were at stake."

Xavier was in full agreement. He was actually astounded, exclaiming, "Wow, I like that answer!"

Xavier affirmed once again that my explanations were helping him to connect more dots. Things were making more sense to him in matters that he had never understood with other teachers or leaders. He was surprised that I wasn't actually a pastor or seminary student. This just shows how seriously I take my craft as a missionary for God. I'm willing to go to great lengths in my education so I can help skeptics come to faith.

Xavier thanked me for taking the time to visit him and talk about such things. He said that he hardly ever discussed religion with people in public and wished to engage in it more often. In fact, as we had nearly closed our discourse, one of the customers came to our table when he finished eating and commended us for discussing Christianity so boldly in public view! The customer himself couldn't believe his ears. He undoubtedly learned much from eavesdropping on our discourse.

My meeting with Xavier lasted for an incredible five hours. I didn't notice that the time zoomed by quickly, but in the realm of God, there is no time. That's why it seemed to go by in only a few minutes. Before I left, I gave Xavier a complementary *The Way of the Master* book by Ray Comfort. I told him to read the message carefully, since it was instrumental in changing my own life. I had confidence it would do the same for Xavier as well. Xavier thanked me and vowed to read the book immediately.

As I drove home that night, I reflected on my conversation with the actor. I wondered how the Lord would work in the man's life. *How much change will God produce?* I thought.

I imagined Xavier becoming so convicted after reading *The Way of the Master* book that he turned out to be a soul-winning machine in Hollywood. It would be the greatest observable miracle that God produced through my influence. It may even be groundbreaking, especially if that evangelistic zeal spread to other actors as well.

Although the possibilities were endless in God's will, it may be wise not to think too far in advance. One step at a time was already a solid model.

PRESTO!

I didn't talk to Xavier again for about six months. Because of my work schedule, church commitments, and other preoccupations, I never had an open window to follow up with him. Yet, I desired to see how my friend was doing. If nothing was going on in his spiritual life, I could always take pleasure in hearing about his professional and culinary activities, so I decided to contact Xavier out of the blue.

On a casual Saturday in the month of December, I called Ranger Grill. Xavier was in the house once again, so I had the privilege of speaking with him over the phone. He seemed to be doing very well in his life, and was glad to hear from me.

He asked, "How's everything been, Steve?"

I replied, "Everything is good. I've just been doing different things with church, evangelizing, and all that good stuff. It's been kind of slow on the work side, so I'm trying to hang in there."

"Aren't we all in this economy? But I'm glad you're doing well, Steve."

Xavier sounded upbeat. He filled me in on the positive trends that had been happening in his life. Even though business life was moderate, Xavier took pleasure in describing the optimism of his personal, family, and spiritual life. When I asked him how his walk with Christ was going, he responded with some surprising information.

Xavier exclaimed, "You've been such a big help and influence to me during the last year, Steve. You and other people have helped to bring changes in my spiritual life. I'm actually attending a church now. And I really like it!"

Words couldn't describe how happy I was for him. With Xavier's proclamation, I only thought of three words: Praise the Lord.

Chapter 17

BROTHER TO BROTHER

THE OUTCOME WITH Xavier Tash happened to be one of the most inspirational boosters for me to continue in God's kingdom work. Especially in the midst of opposition and discouragement in Hollywood, a physical manifestation of success was just what I needed. Either way, a Christian would be a bona fide success in God's eyes as long as he faithfully carries out the will of the Father, no matter the result of the prospect's choice. Effort is what ultimately counts.

In Xavier's case, it wasn't much of an evangelizing/ proselytizing process. It was more like edification/disciple-ship since he was already a fellow brother. Yet, even this process in and of itself can be very rewarding. It can lead a struggling believer to get back on his feet and start to walk healthy for the first time. And if it is in God's will, your influence may even inspire the brother to become a disciple-maker himself.

Whenever I'm not evangelizing the lost, I edify my brothers and sisters to be soul-winners for the kingdom of God. During my past Hollywood gigs, I met quite a few Christians from time to time, which saved me on my evangelism efforts, but that didn't mean I took a break and started reveling in secular topics. I still took the time to promote God's glory by seeing how I could help my brethren in their spiritual growth.

If everything in the area of salvation appears to be in optimal shape, I discuss with Christians the importance of the Great Commission[32] and being a diligent disciple-maker for Jesus Christ. Then I give them some resources: tracts, books, DVDs, sermon CDs, website references, so they can begin their education in that area. The amount of fruits they bear can only come about through the influence of the Spirit's working in the heart (Matt. 13:8),[33] which is why I plant seeds and pray fervently afterwards.

The Word of God also declares the significance, mandate, and eternal blessings of denying oneself in promoting the welfare of a fellow believer. Paul sums it up concisely with these words, "Therefore encourage one another and build up one another, just as you also are doing" (1 Thess. 5:11). It is interesting to note that this verse falls in the context of the end-times prophecies, describing the return of Christ to take His bride home before spilling judgment onto the earth during the Tribulation. Paul commands the church to be on guard with their faith as well as their discipleship.

The love and the fear of the Lord caused me to be fully aware of His command that I should not take chances in negating my responsibilities. Situations as with Xavier Tash gave me hope that my desire for saving souls was possible through a domino effect. If I could theoretically inspire another Christian to be an evangelist, then he could go out and start saving lives—lives that otherwise may not have been saved had it not been for my influence. Not only would my cause bear more fruit, but it would also bring more glory to God and allow more tongues to worship His name for eternity.

God is great in His sovereign plan, and He led me to assist a couple more of His actors in Hollywood, who also happened to be His children. Yes, the actors whom I met were actually Christians. Their eternal lives were most likely set, yet that didn't mean they didn't need less help in the area of understanding God's will. As always, this is where I came in.

A TEENYBOPPER'S DREAM

In one of my past gigs, I worked alongside the Jonas Brothers in their Disney channel television series, *Jonas Los Angeles*. Children and teens know this group very well, but older generations may not be familiar with them. The story is simple. The Jonas Brothers is one of America's most popular musical bands. They are dubbed as a teenybopper phenomenon because of their mass audience of young women and teen girls. What Backstreet Boys, N Sync, and 98 Degrees were to my generation of women, Jonas Brothers is somewhat to the generation of the 2010s.

Sadly, I had been out of touch with the trends and names of the musical artists in the industry for the last decade. I actually didn't know who the Jonas Brothers were until I was hired for one of their gigs a year before. I served as one of their back-up dancers for the 2008 MTV Music Awards. It was there that I learned of their unfathomable popularity. The hundreds of screaming girls during their live performance said it all. These teenagers literally worshipped the Jonas Brothers as if they were gods! It seemed as if the fans would even kill in order to get solitary time with the band members.

I worked with the Jonas Brothers again a year later, and this time on a much more intimate scale. I was so close to them on this occasion that I had the opportunity to meet each individual band member. I found it funny that I didn't care all that much about being in the presence of the Jonas Brothers, considering how many young teens would. However, this does not mean that I let the opportunity go to waste. Though the Jonas Brothers were never originally on my radar for desired prospects, I determined to make an impact in their lives nonetheless.

I was happy to see that on this day a great topic manifest itself as an icebreaker. It was groundbreaking in some ways. During one of the scenes, the show's guest star, Debi Mazar, uttered the blasphemous word, "Oh God!" when the Kevin Jonas character took her by surprise. This was typical Hollywood language, which I fully anticipated but wasn't fond of.

What happened next took me by force. Immediately after improvising that blasphemous line, Debi broke out of character and asked the director in the near distance, "I'm not supposed to say 'God' on the shoot, right?"

The director nodded. I soon learned that the Jonas Brothers forbade the crew to use the Lord's name profanely on the set! I couldn't believe what I saw and heard! Never did I think I was going to see the Lord's name defended and honored on a Hollywood set. This truly was earth shattering! Suddenly, I was given hope for the reality of this cause.

I remembered how Paul Kwak informed me in the past that the Jonas Brothers promoted a no-blasphemy policy in their work environments. I didn't know it was true until I witnessed it with my own two eyes. I was glad to see that the brothers were Christian, but to see them also take their faith a step further than the average Hollywood believer was inspirational. I was surely going to tell this to one of the Jonas Brothers!

After I clocked out that afternoon, I was quick to run up to Kevin Jonas, the eldest of the siblings. He was the only Jonas Brother who was readily available. He may have even been the best choice, considering he was the strongest evangelical Christian of the three brothers. Fortunately for me, I caught Kevin at a time when he was walking back to his honey wagon, which was out of the sight of most crewmembers.

I said to him, "I saw what you did earlier today. I just wanted to say that I like how you advocate not using the Lord's name in vain on set. It's truly inspirational."

Kevin looked a bit speechless, but responded in an upbeat manner, "Oh, why thank you! You know, it's nothing."

"Yeah, but it means a lot to me personally. I've been fighting for that same cause as well. But keep it up."

"Thank you once again. I sure will."

After that, I quickly held up one of *The Way of the Master* DVDs in front of Kevin and asked, "I'm curious, do you know the actor Kirk Cameron?"

Kevin replied, "Of course I do."

"Okay. Well, I wanted to give this DVD to you. Have you ever heard of a show called *The Way of the Master*?"

Kevin shook his head as he took the DVD from my hands. I elaborated by explaining, "It's a reality Christian television show that Kirk Cameron hosts. It's a program that teaches Christians how to share their faith in an effective manner. Check it out. It's awesome stuff!"

Kevin looked a bit intrigued. He replied, "Alright. I sure will."

The musician walked away with my DVD in hand, reading the content on the cover as he journeyed back to his trailer. My work with Kevin was one of the rare times, if not the first, that I gave a celebrity prospect a resource for edification rather than evangelism. I hardly ever connect with a Christian celebrity because I don't come across many to begin with. It just shows how many actors and actresses in Hollywood are not walking in faith. Even if they initially appear to be, they turn out to be on either the thorny ground or shallow soil camp, which represents the two categories of false spiritual conversion that Jesus spoke of in the parable of the soils in Matthew 13:1-23. This is why more mature believers must intervene in such situations—to provide help for the unbelievers, the false converts, and the strong believers who could use a little extra guidance.

Hollywood Comes to the Pews

In the last chapter, I reported how Xavier Tash connected me to a Bible study group called the Greatest Bible Study (GBS). In the winter of 2009, they invited me to one of their praise nights called *Kingdom Come*. Even though I had received countless invitations to attend GBS Bible studies and events in the past, I never had time to attend. I decided to show up at *Kingdom Come*, which was their largest gathering yet. Coincidently, some of my church comrades decided to venture there with me as well. Although they had no real association with the entertainment industry, they just loved to be anywhere where God's name was corporately worshipped.

When I arrived, I observed a few interesting things. There was a large body of worshippers—easily over a hundred. The interior space was very compact, much to my disinclination. Finally, many churches were represented on this Sunday night. Although some of these insights were intriguing to me, none compared to the sight of seeing a celebrity in the house. With us on this night was James Kyson Lee—best known for his character Ando on *Heroes*.

Never in my life did I expect to see a mainstream actor or actress in a church with me. I always envisioned it, yet I didn't know how often it happened or how I would feel if I were to experience it. I had worked with James Kyson Lee on *Heroes* nearly ten times as a background artist in the past. Believe it or not, I even had a personal conversation with the actor the first time I met him. This didn't take place on the set of *Heroes*, but rather at a Korean festival parade in Los Angeles.

During the parade, James rode on a carriage amidst the other attractions that paraded down the streets of Olympic Boulevard. The carriage bore a placard that read, "Star of *Heroes*." I didn't know who this actor was at the time and was curious to find out, so I boldly jumped onto the ledge of his carriage and began a conversation with him. Mr. Lee was hospitable enough to chat with me, given that he could have easily called security to restrain me from his presence.

It was here that I first learned about his role on *Heroes*. I told James that I was somewhat of an actor myself and had worked on *Heroes* a few weeks before (which was my very first extra's gig as the Japanese villager). He wasn't on my particular unit that day, but I told him that we could work together in the future. Interestingly, I worked with James exactly two days later on an episode of *Heroes* and he actually remembered me when I approached him!

I didn't know if James would still recognize me on this *Kingdom Come* night (since it had been over two years), but I figured that I would give it a try. I approached him after he finished chatting with one of his friends. James extended his hand out to me in a curious but accommodating, fashion.

I shook the actor's hand as I asked, "Hey, James, do you remember me?"

He replied, "You look very familiar. Remind me."

"I actually have a Facebook picture with you. I met you at the Korea Town festival two years ago and then worked with you on *Heroes* a few times."

"Oh, yes. I think I remember now. How are you doing?"

"Good. I didn't expect to see you here. I didn't even know you were Christian. I actually thought about approaching you on the set to evangelize you."

James chuckled, delighted to hear such news. Before that day, I honestly didn't know if James was a Christian or not. There were a couple of occasions when I wanted to share the gospel with him on the set of *Heroes* just to discover his spiritual status, but I never had the opportunity. Now I didn't need to worry about that. GBS apparently reached out to him, and here he was, worshipping with the rest of us. All I needed to do for my part was to make sure the man was being useful in Hollywood for the kingdom of God.

After James and I talked a bit more, I pulled out a copy of the "Hell's Best Kept Secret" DVD and asked, "Have you ever heard about a TV show called *The Way of the Master*?"

James replied, "No, I haven't."

"Do you know the actor, Kirk Cameron?"

"Oh yes. I know Kirk Cameron."

"This is his current television show. It's a reality television program that shows Christians how to share their faith. "Hell's Best Kept Secret" is one of their most important episodes. It literally changed my life two years ago. Check it out."

James looked impressed. Then he exclaimed, "Wow. Is this your only copy? If there are other people who need it, then you should make sure they get it."

I assuredly responded, "Oh, no. It's okay. Take it."

"You sure? I'll definitely take it and watch it, but I just want to make sure that there is enough for everybody. You can always mail one to me."

I was pleased to observe James' humility and consideration for others. Though I could have technically given my only available DVD to another person, I had no intention of passing up this opportunity to influence James' life. He may possibly ignore the material once I mailed it to him or consider it fan junk mail. That's how it is with most celebrities.

In response to his concern, I replied, "No, really. Take it. I want you to have it. I hope you learn a lot from it."

James nodded and said, "Thank you very much, Steve. I will definitely take a look at it. Have a great rest of the night."

I replied, "Okay. I'll see you around then."

James smiled and left to attend to the other guests, while glancing down occasionally at my DVD. I could only imagine how these celebrities would react after they watch the DVD. Some would probably find it intriguing, yet others would probably be irate. They might even end up harboring a bitter impression of Mr. Cameron.

I may be defaming Kirk's reputation in the industry, but I guess it's expected if I am heavily promoting his material in Hollywood. I suppose he would rejoice if such service was done for the sake of the gospel. In this case, celebrity identification with the Christian faith could possibly be advantageous. It may even give more credibility to the gospel message, since at one least one actor actually digs Christianity. I surely hope it gave inspiration to James Kyson Lee as well.

THE CHRIST EMPIRE STRIKES BACK

After my short meeting with James, the *Kingdom Come* service started. We began with musical worship, which lasted for well over thirty minutes. After the praise session came a sermon delivered by GBS founder, Jaeson Ma. Before I arrived, I had no clue who the pastor was and what he was going to address. Whatever it was, I knew it was definitely going to be aimed at stirring the hearts of the attendees, since the program had somewhat of a charismatic appeal to it.

Coincidently, the topic centered on the practice of carrying out a similar philosophy I had been conducting in Hollywood for the past three years. The subject matter was about being salt and light to the entertainment industry. Jaeson preached passionately about the significance of bringing the gospel into Hollywood and influencing the media content for the better.

The preacher summoned us to change film, television, and music with the life-changing truths of Christianity. It needed to be done because Hollywood was a dark place and its impact on the world was too great to ignore. Hollywood continued to promote immoral behavior every day. Without our will to take a stance, Satan would continue to brainwash the minds of people around the globe toward godless conduct and eternal damnation. Transforming Hollywood seemed like an ambitious undertaking, yet Jaeson had faith it could be done with God's power, but it would take prayer, purpose, and application.

This one-hour sermon left a noticeable impression on me as it probably did with others in attendance. I left that night feeling that my deepest concerns had finally been addressed. The only other person I can remember who emphasized such exclusive concerns about the entertainment field was Ray Comfort. In his book titled *Hollywood*

Be Thy Name (which also became a namesake episode for *The Way of the Master,* Season 3), Ray addresses the moral plight of Hollywood and how those ethical grounds are influencing the content being portrayed on a habitual basis. This in turn is shaping the lives of our modern-day culture for the worst. It is causing people to sin in ways that were unknown to previous generations. Most importantly, it is causing them to turn away from God.

In response to such a dilemma, Ray exhorts readers to infiltrate Hollywood in order to preach the gospel. Christian actors, directors, and producers must stand tall in entering Hollywood with a clear agenda to influence the lost and to produce quality projects that reflect timeless biblical virtues. Since media has a dominant influence on the world, the content produced by Christians can be efficacious in changing the trends of our times. These trends can mold society for the better, but ultimately they will allow the world's mind to be more receptive to the gospel of Jesus Christ.

This is my dream for Hollywood as well. At one point in my life, such an issue was not a concern for me. All I desired was to make extravagant, self-expressive films that would glorify my name, even if I had to incorporate excessive violence, language, sex, blasphemy, and godless philosophies into my work. God would only be a secondary influence in my life. Three years later, the tables have turned. The Lord Jesus Christ has now become the first priority of my life, and He requires my aid in transforming Hollywood to suit His holy purposes. What a glorious calling it is!

Whether it is Ray Comfort, Kirk Cameron, or Jaeson Ma, this revolutionary movement requires more aware-ness within the Christian body, and if it does receive the recognition it deserves, it will take off with full force.

Fortunately, the word has already gone out to some. The platform is set.

The only question remains: How many people are willing to step up to the challenge and preach that gospel truth to the unsaved in Hollywood?

Chapter 18

YEARS GONE, YEARS AHEAD

MY JOURNEY IN the entertainment industry has been inundated with joy, but also with much heartache. I endured financial difficulties in various seasons. I experienced numerous oppositions to my divine purpose. My body suffered fatigue from rising early every morning and spending an abnormal amount of hours on the set. I have been insulted, ridiculed, and slandered by every person in every department of the industry. Yet, if I could inspire just one person to become the next star for Christ with my life story, then those three years of patience and enduring will have all been worth it. Leading to this ultimate end was the purpose of my mission in Hollywood.

I thank you for taking the time to read this accounting of my life in Hollywood. I hope you enjoyed the tour into my memorable experiences on set, and I hope that much of it has been delightful for you to read. Some aspects you may have found comical. Others you may have found tragic. Some you may even find senseless, while others you may have found quite surreal. Regardless of your thoughts and opinions, the fact is they are my stories, unadulterated and told in all honesty.

You may be asking if these accounts really are true—if I actually met these extras and celebrities and if they truly responded in the manner in which I described. I firmly testify with all my heart that these stories are true. The events that I outlined, whether they involve Jonathan Khan or me, really occurred as I portrayed them. They are the truest, most down-to-earth insights into Christianity's influence in Hollywood. Whether it was with a celebrity, a background artist, or a production assistant, I made every effort to represent the influence of the gospel message in the lives of each person accurately regardless how they responded to my charity.

Although my stories undoubtedly serve as entertainment, my greater goal is to instill passion in your hearts for the Lord Jesus Christ. This book's purpose is to lift God's name on high, to expand His kingdom here on earth, and to allow you to become a part of that in whatever way necessary for you to arrive there.

If you are a non-Christian and my stories moved you to know more about Jesus Christ, I hope you will come to salvation as soon as possible. There's nothing more important you can learn than learning where and how you will spend eternity. Please do not take a risk with the afterlife. If you die and end up being wrong about the non-existence of hell, then there is no turning back from your eternal destiny.

To receive your salvation, you must first measure yourself by the holy standard of God, the Ten Commandments, to see how short you fall of His glory and why you need a Savior. Once you are fully convinced that you cannot save yourself because of your criminal record before God Almighty, you are then ready to receive the grace of God. Jesus Christ died on the cross to satisfy God's holy wrath, taking your original punishment unto Himself so you can be set free and be saved from hell. He lived a perfect, sinless life in order to give His righteousness to you in exchange for your sins, so you would have no capital punishment when you die. It will be as if you have never sinned at all!

This is Christ's amazing gift to you. This is how much God loves you. "For God so loved the world, that He gave His only begotten Son, that whoever believes in Him shall not perish, but have eternal life" (John 3:16). He loves us enough that He gave us a second chance to live with Him forever.

To receive this gift and be born again of the Spirit, you must repent of all your sins before God (confessing and turning from your love of sin). You must put your faith in Christ Jesus as your Lord and Savior. When you call upon God's mercy, He will grant it to you. He will forgive you of all sin, instill His Holy Spirit into your soul to give you righteousness, and you will pass from death (hell) into life (heaven) instantly. You will know of God's existence and His work in your life because of your new desires—the spiritual fruit you will eventually bear for His kingdom. This is the peace and joy found in living a Christ-centered life.

If you are already a soundly saved Christian reading this piece, then I ask for your prayers. Please pray that God will send more missionaries into Hollywood in the sector of film, television, commercial, and music. Pray that He will faithfully produce more prophets who will boldly preach the truth in such a sin-loving environment. Hollywood is destroying so many people by its wicked ways. Their mindset extends to the billions of people around the globe, causing them to stumble and steer farther away from the will of God.

My heart pleads as I ask for your help in this matter. You may not have a passion or an interest to work in Hollywood and make a spiritual impact, but your prayers can still make a difference. Please pray that God will be generous enough to send more laborers into Hollywood to preach the gospel faithfully and influence the media content for the betterment of the world.

To those who feel a special summoning to be one of the Hollywood laborers for God, I exhort you to be faithful to your calling. Take up your God-given duties and start reaching out to the lost all around you. Whether you desire to enter acting, directing, film editing, sound, cinematography, or even background acting like me, please become inspired and equipped to share your faith, and start evangelizing the lost. It is a frightful thing to do, but as I have learned, we can do all things through Christ Jesus who strengthens us. If you need help in learning how to evangelize, you can simply do as I did: go to www.wayofthemaster.com and watch the tutorial videos. You can also research through the abundant resources available at the Living Waters Ministry store at www.livingwaters.com.

If you cooperate with the power and the will of the Holy Spirit, He will take you to heights that you will have never dreamt. The pains and anxieties will all be worth it. This is the miracle and the blessing of kingdom work. Even if your career is at risk (regardless of the field you are in), just remember that the Lord works in the lives of those who trust in Him. By the end of the day, it is all about God's glory.

The question we must always ask ourselves is what is more important, our earthly career or our heavenly blessings? The temporal or the eternal? The seen or the unseen? No situation is more tempting than the fame and glory that Hollywood offers, yet this can be a very positive test to our devotion to God's lordship. It may even reveal what god we truly serve in this life.

We must be dutiful always to advance the way of life and not that of death.

A Date with Destiny

I end this chapter by sharing a shocking incident that happened when I worked on the 2008 MTV Music Awards. The day before the actual televised ceremony, the background talents and I were called to Paramount Studios for a whole day of laborious rehearsal. Early in the day, I met a colleague actor named Cru Ennis (lead star of the independent film, *The Frankenstein Brothers*) in the background holding set.

Since I had a few minutes on hand, I took the opportunity to give Cru a *Good Person Test* and evangelize him. He read through the booklet, surprisingly convicted by the Ten Commandments and how it personalized his past transgressions. I took the time to explain to Cru about God's holiness exemplified through the Law and how its purpose was to lead him to the saving grace of Jesus Christ so he wouldn't have to answer to God for his sins in the future. Cru was impressed by my witnessing to him and admitted that he was a believer. I didn't know if this meant that he was saved or not, but I took his word for it since he informed me that he was actively involved in sharing about Christ's second coming through his Christian T-shirt business.

During the lunch break a few hours later, the background artists and I sat outside of the Paramount Commissary. Cru sat at a table that was close to mine, eating with a husky African-American gentleman who was one of the security guards for the Jonas Brothers act. As I looked down on my meal, ready to scoop up a bite, I suddenly heard the security guard scream, "Officer! Help! Officer!"

I glanced up and saw the security guard holding Cru's head upright as he sat motionless in his seat. Cru's eyes were wide open and his expression was dead still. The police officers and paramedics, who happened to have been nearby when the guard called for them, rushed over to Cru. They examined him and checked his pulse.

I sat motionless with dozens of other people surrounding the area. As I gaped at Cru's immobile body, I asked myself, *Is he dead?*

As I anticipated the worst, Cru slowly moved his head around. He blinked as the paramedics asked repeatedly if he was all right. Cru had apparently regained consciousness and was able to affirm his well-being to the staff helping him. He claimed he didn't know what happened in the moment of his collapse, but he was alright nonetheless. Cru managed to continue with the rest of his day in good shape, although many of us around him remained disturbed for quite a while.

Nobody ever knew what caused Cru's mysterious blackout. Although I was glad that Cru was alive, I could only imagine my sense of horror had he actually died at that moment. The irony would have been evident, considering I had shared the message of salvation with Cru just a few hours before!

In all my gospel presentations, I always warn my prospects not to put off accepting God's grace because they don't know when they're going to die. It could literally happen at any moment. Hypothetically, if Cru was an unbeliever and he rejected the message outright, then his death would have rightly proven my point and even bolstered the power of my warning! How incredibly scary is this thought?

Moments like these tell us not to take time for granted, especially when it comes to evangelizing unbelievers. We never know when death will come knocking at our door.

Some of us may be fortunate enough to survive instances like this, while others may be taken immediately. Regardless, we will all face death someday, and after that, eternal punishment awaits. There is only one answer to the dilemma of sin, death, and hell, and that is Jesus Christ. We must be attentive to hear His cry in our hearts, whether it is for our own salvation or for the salvation of others. There is nothing more pressing than this call.

I pray for God's richest blessings upon your life. Keep the vertical connection strong by obeying God's greatest command, which is to love Him with all your heart, mind, soul, and strength. Perfect this and allow it to lead you to establishing the horizontal connection—loving your neighbor as yourself. There is no better way to love your neighbor than to look out for his or her eternal welfare, especially those who are distant strangers or enemies. There is nothing more satisfying and fulfilling than bringing an unsaved person to the saving knowledge of Jesus Christ. Only then will you understand the truth of your mission on earth. Only then will you see how much you have to live for and that your presence can truly make a difference in this world.

Scripture ends with Jesus proclaiming, "Yes, I am coming quickly" (Rev. 22:20). Indeed the King is soon approaching. The Lord can come back at any time, so tell one person how to be saved today. Unleash your love and be a hero for the world.

Chapter 19

A BEAUTIFUL DAY

BRIGHT SUNSHINE AND cool winds exemplify another typical day in the life of Southern Californians. Life is rampant but perfunctory. Citizens bustle to get to school and work in order to serve their mechanical roles for society—a great cycle of life that characterizes much of the modern world. One particular day, however, was anything but typical, at least for a certain group of people in Culver City.

As the heat brims down on the Sony Studios lot, an adrenaline-filled preparation is underway on Stage 29. A locker room full of passionate minor league baseball players prep for the big game as the Oakland A's general manager, Billy Beane, marches through the locker room, giving some much-needed inspiration to every athlete he approaches. The players are pumped, as is Billy. However much they are at odds at accomplishing their goals, these athletes are going to go out into the world and make their impact.

The situation involving Billy Beane (played by Brad Pitt) and the rest of the baseball players in the changing room is a physical enactment of a scene from the feature film *Moneyball*, in which I observed the action firsthand on set. Yes, my work life in Hollywood had officially resumed once again! They lifted my suspension and I was back in business.

I was actually back in town long before this *Moneyball* gig on August 23, 2010, but this time frame of work shows how God has been faithful in keeping me alive in this particular mission. This mission that I have highlighted throughout this book is the unprecedented, privileged, and dangerous task of bringing the gospel message to a popular but much overlooked tribe in the world. This tribe, as you may have guessed, is Hollywood.

I didn't know how much longer my background career would last, but I trusted God to utilize me in whatever way He chose for my benefit. He may want me to continue working as an actor for the next week, the next month, or the next year. He may even want me in the business for the rest of my life! Whatever the case, I will faithfully serve Him to the end, especially if it will lead major league players to the salvation of Jesus Christ.

Moments like these show I must always be ready to swing my bat when stepping up to the plate. In the case of *Moneyball*, I planned to end with a home run.

MONEY SHOT

After thirteen hours of labor, the *Moneyball* crew finally called for a wrap. The people were no doubt excited for such a declaration since it was time to go home. I was probably the most anxious because I was now going to carry out my evangelistic agenda. This was always the time of the day when I went full blast with my actions for Christ. Yet, today

I had a set plan for one special person. I was going to carry it out no matter what!

As everyone was busy gathering their belongings together to leave the set, I looked across the locker room and saw Brad Pitt jog out. Apparently, the actor wasted no time in high-tailing it out before everyone else did.

Oh no! I can't lose him! I thought. Earlier in the day, I was actually able to converse with Brad on two separate occasions. These conversations were quite short and informal, but it nonetheless built a bridge that established me as a friendly colleague in his eyes. Now that everything was in place, I couldn't let this moment go to waste. There was too much at stake!

I was quick to follow behind Brad's footsteps by chasing him from behind. I sprinted out of the locker room, through the dark corners of the sound stage, and out the stage doors. As I burst through that door, I saw Brad seated on the production's golf cart, ready to ride away to his trailer about three blocks away.

A split second before Mr. Pitt started the vehicle, I ran up to him and exclaimed, "Oh Brad! Before you go, I just wanted to say it was good working with you today."

Brad responded cordially. He shook my hand and replied, "It was a pleasure."

In my left hand was a special *Million Dollar Bill* (the celebrity edition with Brad Pitt's cartoon caricature on the front) that I had ready for this moment. I presented it to the actor and said, "Oh, yeah, here's a little tip for you."

Brad took the tract and looked down at it. With an excited smile, he asked me with straightforward curiosity, "What is this?" as he continued to examine the bill on both sides. Although it was a funny moment in some ways, it was also a bit awkward and scary. Not only did Brad expect an answer, but he asked it in the presence of the PAs and staff members standing around his golf cart. They gazed at me, probably ready to tear me apart if I gave the wrong explanation.

Brad asked again, "What is this?"

I responded, "It's you on the cover! Your face is on the bill."

Brad scrutinized the tract a bit more, unable to see the full details because of the late-night darkness. Then he said, "Cool, I'll check it out later."

The actor revved up the golf cart and immediately drove away, back to the trailers. It was the last opportunity I had to speak with him that night. It's scary to think that if I had arrived at his golf cart just two seconds later, I would have completely missed my chance to relay the gospel message to him. Although it wasn't the most ideal scenario for my presentation of the gospel message to the actor, I did what I had to do. This was definitely better than doing nothing. It was by God's divine providence that I was able to get to Brad at all.

This circumstance was peculiar in that no PA barged in to stop or lecture me. I initially expected something to happen, considering Brad Pitt was only one of the biggest movie stars in the world! Whatever the reason for my easy access to the actor, I didn't dwell much on it. Peace was definitely good, and I gladly went along with it.

I walked with the flock of background artists back to the holding area to sign out. Before the night ended, I was able to give "The Greatest Gamble" DVD to my last prospect, the Director of Photography, Wally Pfister (Academy Award winner for *Inception*).

I don't know how Brad responded to the message on the back of the tract; whether he casually smirked at it or gave it some thought. Even though he seemed friendly to me during the day, I had no idea how he felt about my post-work actions. If it wasn't a concern for him, had it been one for the production staff? Based on how the night ended, I thought I was safe—until two weeks later.

On September 14, 2010, the course of my status as a background artist changed forever. I received a letter from Central Casting Agency that read:

Dear Steven,

After careful consideration, we have decided to terminate your employment.

Pursuant to California Labor Code, employment with Central Casting is at will and completely consensual. The employment relationship may be terminated at any time, for any reason or no reason, without cause and without notice, by either the employee or Central Casting.

Your termination is effective immediately. **This decision is final.**

We wish you well in your future endeavors.

Sincerely,

Central Casting

The unthinkable had finally happened. I was officially fired from Central Casting, the agency that first started my background career and provided seventy-five percent of my work opportunities for three solid years. It was not a mere suspension, but a total termination from the company.

After many occasions of violating company policies regarding communication (and proselytizing) with principle actors, I had finally worn out the agency's patience. The Brad Pitt incident proved to be the last straw in their decision to release me. In the past, whether it was with *Heroes* or *Better Off Ted*, I had suffered only wounds in the course of battle. This time, however, I had actually been killed off.

With no further access to the largest casting company in Los Angeles, there were really no further options. My background career was pretty much over. It may have even been the nail in the coffin to my Hollywood dreams in general. In any case, the glorious death of my Hollywood career was in faithful service to my Lord Jesus Christ.

I didn't know where my life would take me from this point or what my next great mission would be, but I had faith in God's agenda. Questions of what I would do for the rest of my life and how to make the wisest decisions for the future were real issues to consider, yet I took joy in knowing that the Lord God was the ultimate author of my life, now and forever.

My time on earth is merely a work in progress until the final day when I stand in God's presence to observe the full collage. Only then can I look back on my life and truly see the meaning and beauty behind everything. When I do, I wish to see it heavily painted with the touch of God's hands and not my own. Only God Himself can paint a masterpiece, thus I need to be in constant association with Him in everything I do so as not to paint my own world, which would only be filled with smears of despair and destruction.

I may have good reason to be angry and fearful for tomorrow, yet in those moments when I start to entertain hopelessness, I feel my Savior's approaching presence. I hear His soothing words to me, saying, "Do not be afraid, my child. I am with you now, every day, and always. Do not be afraid. Do not be afraid…"

At the sound of this assurance, I can only smile back at my God and proceed in bright optimism. The memoirs of my Hollywood moments may end here, yet my life story is only beginning. It will go on for as long as I am here and continue throughout eternity.

Every day is truly a beautiful day for God's beloved servants.

DISCUSSION GUIDE

Chapter 2: The Wonder Years

1. Have you ever been curious about the state of your existence? Has such a thought caused you to consider the meaning of life?

2. Is the existence of God reasonable? How can we know who He is and what He requires of us? Reflect on the simple truths revealed in Romans 1:18-20, Romans 2:14-16, and Psalm 8:3-9.

3. Describe the following concepts:

   Spiritual amnesia

   The vertical connection

   The horizontal connection

   Do you currently have the vertical and horizontal connections intact, or are you suffering from spiritual amnesia? If the latter is so, what is the solution to your dilemma?

4. At what time in your life did you first learn about Jesus Christ? What convinced you that He is the truth? How has your perception of Him changed from the time you were first exposed to Him to the present moment?

5. Have there been times when you've failed to obey God because you loved something in the world much more? Has this totally altered the direction of your life? What did this person, job, or possession seemingly promise that the Lord God couldn't give to you?

Chapter 3: Road to Fame

1. Do you have an interest or passion in the media world? If so, what field are you most interested in? Film, television, commercials, theater, or music?

2. Has there been a time when you thought the Lord was guiding your life toward a desired profession or goal, only to have it backfire and fail? Have you been severely disappointed by such an outcome or have you grown more in optimistic faith?

3. Does your work or social environment pose any challenges to your faith? How can you stand firm amidst these temptations and struggles?

4. Has God ever used burdens, trials, and loneliness to bring you back to Him after a period of separation? What has this taught you about self-sufficiency and the importance of dependence on Christ?

5. Though you may have salvation, you may feel you still lack passion or purpose in your life. List two or three practices you want the Lord to stir in your heart (ex. prayer, evangelism, financial generosity) and pray for the Holy Spirit to transform you through such desires and

deeds. Make it a goal to perform each of the practices at least once every day.

Chapter 4: Enlightenment

1. Have you ever witnessed someone sharing his spiritual faith in the workplace? What was your reaction to such a stunning feat?

2. How often do you evangelize people in the professional, social, or public world? If not, what is holding you back? Is it fear? Or could it be a lack of love for your fellow neighbor?

3. Have you ever been enlightened by a teaching or event so powerful that it changed your whole Christian life overnight? Have you experienced it outside of church? If so, what does this say about how God operates in life?

4. Does your gratitude for your salvation make you want to share it with others on a daily basis? What will inspire you to be a practical evangelist?

5. If you do not know how to share your faith, make a vow to learn today, since effective evangelism is not as easy as it appears. Living Waters Ministry is a good place to begin your education. Visit their website, livingwaters. com, and learn evangelism from such teachings as "Hell's Best Kept Secret" and WDJD. Set a time where you can practice your evangelism with church friends and/or unbelievers at least five times total.

Chapter 5: Master and Apprentice

1. As a beginning evangelist, you may find it difficult to interact with your prospects. Do you know of any knowledgeable Christians whom you can team with

to evangelize unbelievers? What do you think you can learn from this partnership instead of going solo in the early stages?

2. What is the importance of verbally communicating the gospel truth to a prospect instead of performing "silent evangelism" through your ethical behavior? What does the prospect gain or miss out on if you don't speak out openly? Reflect on Romans 10:17 and Matthew 16:15.

3. Have you ever been in witnessing encounters with atheists or agnostics? What are the differences in and challenges of both views? How can you effectively defend your faith, and even speak the gospel message to these people, in a manner that is productive?

4. Why is it important that a person be humbled before he or she can receive the good news of the gospel? Is it wise to cast pearls before swine? What hindrances do pride and self-righteousness pose to saving faith?

5. Describe your feelings regarding the first time you evangelized a stranger. What kind of excitement did this stir in you? Did it cause you to want to engage in evangelism more often? Ask God to open up more doors for you to share your faith with the lost.

Chapter 6: The Fire Burns

1. Read Luke 5:1-11 and Matthew 9:9-13. Have you listened to your Master's call to leave your treasured possessions and priorities behind to follow Him? Make a commitment today to take your Christian life to the next level and start living for the Lord in a radically new way.

2. How much do you value a single soul (no matter how close or distant they are)? Would you be willing to give up your job or any positions of security to help a single person find salvation if necessary?

3. Have you ever been so influenced by the lifestyle and philosophy of a Christian that it caused a revolution in your own Christian walk? Does this give you a desire to model an excellent Christian life for others as well?

4. Why is it important to develop an evangelist mentality early on in the Christian life? How can this philosophy inspire you to undertake other Christian services, such as serving in church or living a morally righteous lifestyle?

5. Sometimes there is no positive response from your prospects after you proselytize them. What do you do as a final step in getting unbelievers to think more seriously about their eternity?

Chapter 7: The Insider's Scoop

1. Every day, God puts different people in your path to influence. How can you make the most of such evangelistic opportunities? Does this cause you to be more alert in your outreach and self-sacrificing ways?

2. Describe a time when the Lord gave you a prime opportunity to converse with someone about the things of God, especially when you originally thought such a moment was not possible. What do occasions like these say about the sovereignty of God and your importance in making a difference in life?

3. Why is it that when we first engage with people, we talk about anything other than how they can get saved? Do you have the urgency in your soul to warn people

about their eternal predicament, considering it may be their last day on earth or the last chance you ever see them?

4. Do you find it a joy to verbally strengthen a Christian brother or sister, even if the environment seems totally unfitting for a spiritual dialogue? How can your friend benefit from such edification?

5. There may have been times when you've edified a fellow Christian, but you felt that it had no impact. Do you trust in the Lord to bring about changes in the life of the person you dealt with? Be in fervent prayer for the Lord to work wonders.

Chapter 8: Facing the Giants

1. Have your fears ever cost you a chance to evangelize someone you really wanted to reach out to? What has this taught you about the sensitivity of time, opportunities, and your own love for the lost? How can you overcome your fears?

2. When we finish a grueling day of work or school, we hardly think of staying behind an extra few minutes to evangelize a desired prospect. List two or three colleagues/friends you want to reach out to, and ask the Lord to give you wisdom and heart when dealing with these prospects at the appropriate time.

3. Do you ever feel that cold-turkey evangelism is too bold a way to reach out to prospects (especially celebrities) in certain situations? Is it better to witness in such a way or to not evangelize at all? Why?

4. When you see Christians who are unskilled in evangelism, do you take it upon yourself to model evangelism

for them to learn? Or do you simply refrain from the act altogether for the sake of keeping them in their comfort zone? Be mindful that your ways can make lasting impressions.

5. Read Matthew 19:23-24. Does such a verse cause you to work harder on and pray for the rich and famous people of this world? Why is it more difficult for the wealthy to enter the kingdom of God than the poor?

Chapter 9: Dazed and Confused

1. Do you feel uncomfortable questioning the salvation of professing Christians, knowing that they can get angry and your analysis may end up being wrong? Is it better to give such people the benefit of the doubt or evangelize them and risk being wrong?

2. Describe your thoughts on people who believe in "God" but who aren't Christian. Does such a "relationship" produce saving faith? Why is it important that people come not to a universal notion of god, but to the God of Jesus Christ?

3. How do you deal with apostates who abandoned faith because they suffered pains and troubles in their lives? Do such pain and suffering indicate that God does not exist or that He is not good? Be committed to bring comfort and healing to these people, but at the same time stress the importance of true saving faith.

4. Have you ever met a professing Christian who didn't believe that Jesus was the only way to heaven? How do you respond to unbiblical notions such as these? Reflect on Acts 4:12 and John 14:6 for a firm conviction on the gospel truth.

5. When you see people being improperly converted to Christ (false conversion), do you come to question the content of your gospel presentation? How can you know if your evangelism is deficient and needs improvement? In everything, examine the Bible to see what Jesus did, whether it's agreeable or confrontational.

Chapter 10: To Law or Not to Law

1. Why is it important to use God's Law in your gospel presentation? What would happen if you fail to incorporate it into your evangelism? Read Mark 10:17-31 and ask yourself why Jesus didn't simply tell the rich young ruler to merely believe in Him after the ruler asked about the way of eternal life.

2. What is the problem of guaranteeing a wonderful or happy plan during a gospel presentation? What do you think this particular plan conjures up in many unbelievers' mind? Do they represent the trials, tribulation, and persecution that Christ talked about in Scripture?

3. Do you believe the gospel message should meet the unbeliever's need for happiness or righteousness? Is the gospel truth about people's life on earth or life in eternity? About self-fulfillment or self-denial?

4. One effect of the Law of God is that it breaks people's hope of gaining salvation based on their own merits, and shows them why they need a Savior. Can this realization be achieved any other way? Can God's grace truly come to someone who doesn't know of God's justice first?

5. Familiarize yourself with God's Law, God's justice, God's mercy, God's grace, Christ's sinless life, Christ's atoning death, God's imputed righteousness to sinners, the Great White Throne Judgment, heaven, and hell. Do you feel

you understand the gospel message enough to explain it to a prospect step-by-step? Practice it with a fellow Christian or pastor.

Chapter 11: Teacher Above Pupil

1. Do you feel there is a gospel presentation or evangelism method that can sell to everyone it comes across? If not, why?

2. Have you ever watered down or distorted the gospel message just to make it more agreeable to your prospects? What is the danger of continuing on in such pragmatic approaches?

3. How important is it to study apologetics, knowing of other religions and philosophies in the world? Will such research shake your faith or strengthen it? How will this make you a better evangelist?

4. Does the fact that God alone elects and draws people to salvation deter you from participating in outreach? Why is it important that we carry on with evangelism no matter what? What does this reveal about human responsibility and divine sovereignty?

5. Does the Bema Seat Judgment give you any inspiration to be more obedient to Christ? What do you need to do now in order to make that future day a grand blessing and not a bitter disappointment?

Chapter 12: The Lone Ranger

1. As a believer, are you offended by any of Jesus' words in the Bible? Do you find any of Christ's teachings or actions to be too harsh, demanding, or counterproductive? If so, what could this possibly say about your

maturity, personality, or maybe even the state of your salvation?

2. Do you get discouraged when people mock your evangelism methods, though you conduct them with the best attitude and biblical accuracy? Should such unpopularity be a sign that you must change your message?

3. Do you pass out gospel tracts or have done so at some time in your life? What is the benefit of tracts? How does it make your evangelism more effective and far reaching? Consider having a stock on hand to pass out to people you meet on a daily basis, especially those who don't have time to dialogue with you.

4. Has there been a time when a professing Christian persecuted you for sharing the gospel biblically? What does such a distressing event tell you about the state of mainstream evangelism approaches today?

5. Does bad reputation and religious persecution frighten you? Does it make you want to quit being a messenger for God? Remember 1 Peter 4:12-19 and take comfort in knowing that your works are being blessed.

Chapter 13: Top Dogs

1. If you were to meet an important person, whether celebrity, businessman, or politician, would you use such an opportunity to advance your own agenda for earthly success or would you advance God's agenda by evangelizing him/her?

2. Have you ever had difficulty deciding when to evangelize your prospect, especially when you have an identifiable time frame on how long you will be with this particular

person? Ask the Lord to give you discernment, but be faithful to get the job done by the time the day is over.

3. Do you believe it is necessary at times to present gospel resources in attractive, non-religious form, so hardened unbelievers would be willing to invest their time in it? Be wise to not put unnecessary stumbling blocks before unbelievers, but at the same time do not compromise the absolute claims of the gospel message.

4. Do you find that real-life heroes (cops, fireman, humanitarians, etc.) are more open when you evangelize them? If yes, why? If not, what does this tell you about the depth of man's depravity and the futility of good works?

5. Have you ever bent professional or other secular expectations in order to advance the cause of the gospel? When professional/government rules conflict with Christ's agenda, which should you choose?

Chapter 14: The Days of Noah

1. Do you see current world events as indicative that the rapture and the tribulation are coming? In light of such haunting times, how will you live better knowing that Christ's return for His church is around the corner? Does this make you want to evangelize lost sinners with more urgency?

2. Do you see the world's normalized practice of lawlessness (ex. fornication, blasphemy, abortion, etc.) as something to be concerned about? How can you honor the Lord in the way you live and stand up for ethical issues amidst conflicting opinions and agendas?

3. Postmodernism has allowed most every religion to be accepted as truth in the name of tolerance. Why is

such a trend ultimately dangerous? Do you support the practice of other religions and philosophies or do you take a stand to promote the gospel in the midst of such challenges?

4. Do you ever find that when you mention religious leaders like Buddha, Muhammad, and Krishna, it doesn't strike a nerve, but when you mention Jesus, it causes controversy? If so, what does this tell you about Satan's work and the truth of Christ's claim?

5. Do blasphemy, sex, foul language, and excessive violence in film/television worry you? If so, how can you take a stand against what's on television or in the theatres? Make a list of four or five television shows/movies that contain blasphemy or immoral conducts and send letters to the show's producers voicing your concern.

Chapter 15: One Hard Blow

1. Has there been a time when your negligence in a matter caused a dent in your Christian reputation, especially in front of non-Christians? How do you recover from such mishaps and set your reputation right once again?

2. Would an employer's demand that you not share your faith in the workplace cause you to cease evangelism? Are there times when you need to disobey your boss' orders in order to save someone's soul?

3. In the workplace or social sphere, you may not be privileged to share God's name positively, but others may use His name profanely. Is such a practice fair? How can you stand up to religious discrimination in your workplace, using it not as a means to express vengeance, but as a constructive opportunity to allow God's glory to manifest through your influence?

4. Has your career ever been in serious jeopardy because of your faith and evangelistic lifestyle? Can your workplace standards and your spiritual obligations ever come to a compromise?

5. Despite hardships, trials, tribulation, and persecution, where does your faith stand? Do you believe God works everything out for your good? Or do you have reason to abandon Him and wallow in self-pity and anger? Reflect on Jeremiah 29:11, John 14:14, and Isaiah 41:10.

Chapter 16: Blast from the Past

1. Sometimes you evangelize people and you never see them again. Has there been a time when your influence was so great that your prospect sought for your presence once again? Describe this experience and the outcome.

2. Are there times when you need to bring up serious spiritual topics during a festive occasion? What can be at stake if you don't bring up such concerns during such a moment?

3. If a struggling believer wanted to engage with you about tough objections to Christianity, would you feel ready to address the person's concerns? If not, could this be a wake-up call for you to deepen your understanding of the Bible?

4. Though a Christian follows in the teachings of Jesus, is it wise for him to also take interest in the wisdom of other religious teachers, such as the Dalai Lama or Buddha? What are the dangers of this practice? What can you do to help others trust in God's Word alone and not in the words of false teachers and prophets?

5. Has there been a time when you saw your patience and spiritual labor pay after a lengthy period of wait? What does this tell you about God's faithfulness and promises? Be committed to continually help the lost see spiritual truths despite disappointing results.

Chapter 17: Brother to Brother

1. You may not need to evangelize fellow believers, but do you still work to edify them by teaching them to be soul winners for God? Remember that this is also one of the key components of the Great Commission.

2. Make a list of friends, relatives, and acquaintances you want to teach and/or inspire on how to evangelize. Pray that the Lord will work a marvelous domino effect through your actions.

3. Blasphemy and profane use of the Lord's holy name is commonplace in Hollywood. How can you honor the Lord's name or cause it to be respected in the workplace? Do you know of any Christian who unknowingly uses the Lord's name in vain as well?

4. Do you believe that the ethical philosophy advocated in most Hollywood films (ex. no-clause divorce, fornication, blasphemy, narcissism) influence society's trends and behaviors? To what degree? Does such a Hollywood agenda make it more difficult for the gospel to penetrate the heart of the public?

5. If you are considering Hollywood as a part-time or full-time commitment, what are some of the things you can contribute to make it a godlier environment? Do you plan to change the content of media for God's glory?

Hollywood Outreach List

Make a list of ten Hollywood names (ex. actors, actresses, directors) that you want to see come to saving faith in Jesus Christ. Write them below:

1. _____

2. _____

3. _____

4. _____

5. _____

6. _____

7. _____

8. _____

9. _____

10. _____

Pray for the names on this list at least once a month, giving special attention to each individual name. Share two or three names with friends or people in your fellowship group and have a prayer time for all the names in the prayer pot. Be courageous to evangelize these celebrities if they ever come across your path. God is a worker of miracles, so always be ready to do your duty!

"How then will they call on Him in whom they have not believed? How will they believe in Him whom they have not heard? And how will they hear without a preacher? How will they preach unless they are sent? Just as it is written, 'How beautiful are the feet of those who bring good news of good things'"—Romans 10:14-15.

ENDNOTES

1. *The Good Person Test* is a tract from the Living Waters Ministry, founded by evangelist Ray Comfort. *The Good Person Test* presents the Ten Commandments in an interactive, trivia-like form to reveal the sinful nature of the participant and thus lead him or her to the need of the gospel message provided in the latter half of the presentation. www.livingwaters.com.
2. But I tell you that every careless word that people speak, they shall give an accounting for it in the day of judgment. (Matt. 12:36)
3. The Almighty – we cannot find Him; He is exalted in power and He will not do violence to justice and abundant righteousness. (Job 37:23)
4. O let the evil of the wicked come to an end, but establish the righteous; for the righteous God tries the hearts and minds. (Ps. 7:9)
5. The Rock! His work is perfect, for all His ways are just; a God of faithfulness and without injustice, righteous and upright is He. (Deut. 32:4)

6. Or do you not know that the unrighteous will not inherit the kingdom of God? Do not be deceived; neither fornicators, nor idolaters, nor adulterers, nor effeminate, nor homosexuals, nor thieves, nor the covetous, nor drunkards, nor revilers, nor swindlers, will inherit the kingdom of God. (1 Cor. 6:9-10)

7. Yet He will by no means leave the guilty unpunished. (Ex. 34:7)

8. But the cowardly and unbelieving and abominable and murderers and immoral persons and sorcerers and idolaters and all liars, their part will be in the lake that burns with fire and brimstone, which is the second death. (Rev. 21:8)

9. For when Gentiles who do not have the Law do instinctively the things of the Law, these, not having the Law, are a law to themselves, in that they show the work of the Law written in their hearts, their conscience bearing witness and their thoughts alternately accusing or else defending them, on the day when, according to my gospel, God will judge the secrets of men through Christ Jesus. (Rom. 2:14-16)

10. The Living Waters website is www.livingwaters.com.

11. The Eternal Productions website is www.eternal-productions.org

12. I will pour out on the house of David and on the inhabitants of Jerusalem, the Spirit of grace and of supplication, so that they will look on Me whom they have pierced; and they will mourn for Him, as one mourns for an only son, and they will weep bitterly over Him like the bitter weeping over a firstborn. (Zech. 12:10)

13. For where your treasure is, there your heart will be also. (Matt. 6:21)

14. The rich young ruler is found in Mark 10:17-30.

15. Many a man proclaims his own loyalty, but who can find a trustworthy man? (Prov. 20:6)
16. Jesus said to him, "I am the way, and the truth, and the life; no one comes to the Father but through Me. (John 14:6)
17. And there is salvation in no one else; for there is no other name under heaven that has been given among men by which we must be saved. (Acts 4:12)
18. Now the deeds of the flesh are evident, which are: immorality, impurity, sensuality, idolatry…just as I forewarned you, that those who practice such things will not inherit the kingdom of God. (Gal. 5:19-21)
19. Or do you not know that the unrighteous will not inherit the kingdom of God? Do not be deceived; neither fornicators, nor idolaters…will inherit the kingdom of God. (1 Cor. 6:9-10)
20. Or do you not know that the unrighteous will not inherit the kingdom of God? Do not be deceived; neither fornicators, nor idolaters…will inherit the kingdom of God. (1 Corinthians 6:9-10)
21. For not knowing about God's righteousness and seeking to establish their own, they did not subject themselves to the righteousness of God. (Romans 10:3)
22. For God so loved the world, that He gave His only begotten Son, that whoever believes in Him shall not perish, but have eternal life. (John 3:16)
23. And He was saying to them all, "If anyone wishes to come after Me, he must deny himself, and take up his cross daily and follow Me." (Luke 9:23)
24. For by grace you have been saved through faith; and that not of yourselves, it is the gift of God; not as a result of works, so that no one may boast. (Ephesians 2:8-9)

25. Jesus answered and said to him, "Truly, truly, I say to you, unless one is born again he cannot see the kingdom of God." (John 3:3)

26. "For I know the plans that I have for you," declares the LORD, "plans for welfare and not for calamity to give you a future and a hope." (Jeremiah 29:11)

27. If you ask Me anything in My name, I will do it. (John 14:14)

28. Jesus said to him, "I am the way, and the truth, and the life; no one comes to the Father but through Me." (John 14:6)

29. Everyone who practices sin also practices lawlessness; and sin is lawlessness. (1 John 3:4)

30. Because by the works of the Law no flesh will be justified in His sight; for through the Law comes the knowledge of sin. (Romans 3:20)

31. What shall we say then? Is the Law sin? May it never be! On the contrary, I would not have come to know sin except through the Law; for I would not have known about coveting if the Law had not said, "You shall not covet." (Romans 7:7)

32. "Go therefore and make disciple of all the nations, baptizing them in the name of the Father and the Son and the Holy Spirit, teaching them to observe all that I commanded you; and lo, I am with you always, even to the end of the age." (Matt. 28:19-20)

33. And others fell on the good soil and yielded a crop, some a hundredfold, some sixty, and some thirty. (Matt. 13:8)

ABOUT THE AUTHOR

Steve Cha was born and raised in Los Angeles. He graduated with a B.A. in Asian American Studies from the University of Los Angeles California. He currently attends Fuller Theological Seminary in Pasadena, California, where he is working towards a M.A. in Theology. Steve is a member of Screen Actors Guild of America and American Federation of Television and Radio Artists. As a professional actor and voiceover artist, Steve has worked on over a hundred film, television show, and commercial productions in Hollywood. Steve is also founder and director of the Los Angeles-based Bible fellowship called Uncensored, and speaks at churches to promote the Great Commission.

MEDIA ZONE

For additional resources, updates, and events
regarding Steve Cha and *Hollywood
Mission: Possible,* please visit Steve's official website: www.hollywoodmp.blogspot.com
or his Facebook page.

For speaking engagements at your church or
Christian event, book signings, and media-related
appearances (television, magazine, and radio),
please contact Steve at:
hollywoodmission@gmail.com